Modern Furniture Designs, 1950-1980s

Modern Furniture Designs 1950-1980s

An International Review of Modern Furniture

Klaus-Jürgen Sembach, editor

Schiffer Publishing Ltd
4880 Lower Valley Road, Atglen, PA 19310 USA

Library of Congress Catalog Card Number: 97-80086

ISBN: 0-7643-0382-1
Printed in the United States of America

Published by Schiffer Publishing Ltd.
4880 Lower Valley Road
Atglen, PA 19310
Phone: (610) 593-1777; Fax: (610) 593-2002
E-mail: Schifferbk@aol.com
Please write for a free catalog.
This book may be purchased from the publisher.
Please include $3.95 for shipping.

Please try your bookstore first.

We are interested in hearing from authors
with book ideas on related subjects.

Contents

Introduction

The series "New Furniture" has appeared eleven times at regular intervals. It began in 1951 and then it was customary for a volume to appear every two or, at the very least, every three years. The chain was broken in 1971 and this present edition contains, along with much that is new, above all a resumé of the contents of previous volumes.

A dispassionate conclusion might be that development in the past twenty-five years has stagnated and that it is apparent that there have not been enough examples to warrant further reports. Does this mean that good furniture has become unfashionable or has designers' imagination failed them?

The problem can probably not be regarded in such simple terms. The disruption we observe is more deep-seated. Our attitude towards the symbols of progress is not the same as it used to be; the social changes in the past twenty to twenty-five years have played their part in forming our attitude towards the materialization of objects in our environment. Our awareness of the way architecture and ambience function has become more acute and more critical. There has been a general spreading of skepticism of the "latest development." Even attempts to create radical changes renounced a new outward appearance. The different attitudes of different generations is indeed striking: whereas progressive ways of thinking after the First World War went hand-in-hand with an endorsement of the avant garde in architecture and design, the situation fifty years later was exactly the opposite. The direction was towards forms from the past, not from the future.

The younger generation's indifference and even contempt for modern furniture, expressed by its preference for cheap, old things, showed at the same time, however, that it took modern products seriously. Their value was appreciated so little that people thought they could be accepted straight away and without much thought. They represented too much for that. They were the representatives of an age that was mistrusted. After all, furniture does more than just carry out a function; it reflects convictions as well. The affinity of convictions and outward form has been stressed over and over again-both positively and negatively. Show me how you live and I will tell you what you are like. In this respect furniture acquires a psychological, and even a political meaning.

If one pursues the attitude described above into the present - and it is by no means a thing of the past - then today's catch-phrase should be: no future= no modern design. It is easy to come back with a reply to that. One only has to turn round the equation: no modern design = no future. If one accepts this premise, it is a reminder that if new technical-and that also means commercial-developments do not occur, the roots of our existence are thereby endangered.

To wish to deny this, or to alter it radically, would be like living in a topsy-turvy utopia. The most that can be achieved is a modification of the trend, directing it with more care and greater awareness. The furniture industry is perhaps a good example of this, cultivating as it does at the moment an increased sense of tradition instead of offering new trends at any price. This refers to the fact that it increasingly reissues "classics", that is to say furniture that was designed fifty or more years ago. The new trend in this is the production of old furniture that does not, however, seem so old as to be out of date. This policy does not ignore, as does the antiques trade, the production side; it merely uses it in another way.

But that is only one aspect of this ingenious process. What is so special about it is that traditional objects are produced which still have the aura of the avant garde. The past and the future are drawn together in a remarkable way. One is not operating somewhere in the distant past but in one's own still tangible short history, and one senses at the same time that these things will survive much that is younger than they are. It must come as a surprise to untrained observers to discover how old the ideas are that led to the creation of these objects. They will hesitate to decide in favor of them today and postpone the decision until they have got more used to them.

It could be argued that this represents the perfect solution, the happy mean in every respect. The demand for both the past and the present can be catered for simultaneously and with absolute conviction. And so we have reached a standstill; the demand for the future has been put off for the time being. One could cynically add the speculation that the young people who reject this furniture today are the best customers for these quasi-old things tomorrow, as this furniture enables them to take the unavoidable step forward without having to reject the conviction that progress is suspect. The necessary distance still remains.

If one refrains from regarding furniture principally as documenting certain attitudes, the fact that its further development has recently come to a standstill points to another phenomenon. Here it is less a matter of something generally encountered than of an individual problem. In connection with furniture, the purely functional aspects confront the emotional. We do not only live with furniture, we also live through it. In time it becomes part of ourselves and it continually expresses something of our expectations and wishes. It can break free of us easily through simple decay, for us to escape from it is less easy since we need it in more than one respect.

Our instinct for freedom has increased lately and it does not only include external conditions but also the objects that surround us. Any kind of harassment is troublesome, the material no less than the mental. Objects have the power to be a burden on one's existence merely by being there, not to mention their formal quality.

It is not necessary to go back to the nightmarish situation at the end of the 19th century to discover the reasons why individual people would like to avoid having too much furniture. More recent developments have, of course, taken this need increasingly into account but they were only partially successful. It was a hard road to the desired emptiness. Art Nouveau brought about the first change, both formal and in the number of objects filling a room. But the aesthetic demands they made increased considerably; they required that one's whole life should be turned into an art form. Rooms were not arranged so much according to their owners as vice versa. Very few people were willing or able to make such a sacrifice.

The picture began to become clearer in the 1920s but the purist stance assumed was hardly able to serve as a generally valid model with which people could identify. They were able to understand and appreciate its purported severity, but its absolute demands had a confusing effect that was not very inviting. What was displayed was more a purifying form for the moment than one that could be endured for a longer period of time. The balance between the formal intention to make a statement on the one hand and the expectation of a free, relaxed way of life on the other, which came about around 1930, came too late to be able to have an effect in the highly charged political and economic climate at the time. Now, however, half a century later, what came out of that period-as has already been noted-have become the main ingredients of our formal view of the world. The exemplary designs from the years 1925 to 1933 now hold sway in Olympus. The new gods on the highest pedestal are the furniture from that period. Zeus is the Barcelona armchair (ill. 36) by Mies van der Rohe, Aphrodite the chaise lounge (ill. 19) by Le Corbusier and Pallas Athene his small armchair (ill. 18). One could distribute the whole mythological cosmos in this way; there would be no lack of examples.

So now that lucid severity which had been longed for for such a long time has become reality after all. The ideal has materialized. If the matter is thus regarded, many of us live in paradise.

The furniture mentioned above had never completely disappeared from the market, but real acclamation for it has only come in the past few years when it became apparent how well it fitted into the general mood of the age. At the same time, people set about greatly increasing the numbers of the club. Today it is possible to choose among numerous examples from the late 1920s and early 1930s. However, before this situation was reached several intermediate phases had to be overcome. This book deals mainly with them.

It is impossible to overlook the fact that the results of the post-war years have turned out somewhat more profane that the heroic products of the early years would have led one to expect. Much was obviously created to challenge the gods; still some has the appeal of its mongrel origins. The furniture of Charles Eames and Arne Jacobsen, all of it from about 1950, is without doubt entirely legitimate and well-behaved progeny. It demonstrates the virtues of a second generation. Its appearance is lighter, more unhampered and somewhat less concerned with posture than that of its forbears. The positioning of the chair legs is characteristic of this: they are pushed nonchalantly forward at an angle and are not squared off so severely. The offspring behave confidently, just like someone does who knows he comes from a good family.

This new beginning was truly auspicious. Around 1950 it was possible to believe that development could be continued after a grey interval and not be disturbed a second time. If one leafs again through the first volume of "New Furniture" today, one is surprised how much of what one remembers as being good already existed then, in 1951. Apart from the above-mentioned objects, that is also true for the chairs by Max Bill, Egon Eiermann, and Hans J. Wegner.

The ability of these things to please while at the same time being demanding was new, and reduced their elitist character. They do not have the same effect as the high schools of interior design. But this agreeable quality was obviously misunderstood to mean that it could be unhesitatingly imitated. The consequence of this slight relaxation in style was that the dam broke and a flood of inferior products was washed ashore. The standard of furniture from the 1950s was terrible; the most favored form resembled mollusk, the kidney-shaped table, typical for that time, is still remembered today with foreboding. Characteristic of the 1950s is the steep plunge from the good model to the poor copy.

The second question posed at the beginning of this introduction has not yet been answered. Has designers' imagination failed them? This question is probably phrased wrongly as well. Here it not so much a matter of ability itself than of the necessity of having to prove this ability. This book is able to do just that, to show what has been tried out and produced in the past thirty years. Some designs were useful, others were not. This long process of elimination and evaluation naturally involved a certain amount of disillusionment. Everything that we really need is there already. This is something everyone has to accept these days. No future for modern design? Rather extreme objects are being produced whose affected style is able to suggest that kind of desperation.

The future probably lies in those half-designed objects developed so successfully in Sweden. Their form and price place them very cleverly between junk and solid bourgeois household effects, between somewhat gaudy casualness and rather solid order. Is this the adequate solution for reduced needs? Only a future volume can answer that question.

Classical Models Reproduced

The return of historical influences noticeable at the moment is a quite general phenomenon of our time. It is not a uniform orientation and displays at least two aspects. One is a move towards the historical as a result of a general love of the past, the other because it sees a better form for modern things in the past. The first attitude is ill-considered, opportunist and sentimental for the most part. It is usually described by the term "nostalgia", and it is basically against everything modern. The second is based on the conviction that using traditional ideas represents a more sensible kind of progress than creating new ones. It judges the historical according to its present value, and sees it relatively and not absolutely.

If one transfers this characterization of present trends onto the level of practical examples, the recreated furniture of Charles Rennie Mackintosh is a representative of the first aspect. The two high-backed chairs (ills. 5, 6) can really only be noted because of their ludicrousness, and not because they are decisive for us in any way. They were once an ingenious challenge and remind us of the time when vehement attacks on logic and functionality were still allowed. It is indicative of the attitude that led to their renaissance that it is these designs that have been reproduced and not those that really make sense and are useful-for example, the runged chairs Mackintosh designed for the Willow Tearoom in Glasgow.

A similar situation is to be found with the chairs and armchairs of Josef Hoffmann (ills. 7-9), whose period can be clearly seen in the same way, but which are nevertheless a great deal more practicable than the Scot's. They were designed from the outset with functionality in mind and not intentionally contrary to it. It could also be doubted whether it makes sense to reproduce the furniture of Gerrit Thomas Rietveld (ills. 11,12). At the time the red and blue chair was created it was more of an artistic demonstration using a chair as an example than a chair with exemplary artistic form. But its bulky appearance is deceptive: it is comfortable to sit in.

The zigzag chair by the same designer was the forerunner of a form that is more convincing now in plastic than in wood, which is unsuitable for such treatment. Rietveld's furniture gives the impression of being museum exhibits that have got into much too profane surroundings by mistake. Whereas one knows from the start that one cannot use Mackintosh's chairs, one feels with Rietveld's that one is not allowed to. One may admire them but not try them out.

1 **Werner M. Moser** 1929 Switzerland
Chair of wood with rattan seat

The furniture that can be included in the second category we mentioned is the kind that was designed in the 1920s and the early 1930s and which "is still as modern today as it was then" (ills. 13-49). There is a completely different justification for continuing to produce it than there is for the return of examples of Art Nouveau. It does not represent quotes from the past whose selection is more or less accidental. It demonstrates that a continuity of proven designs makes sense and is possible. This observation is not only supported by the furniture of Ludwig Mies van der Rohe (ills. 31- 34,36-38), Marcel Breuer (ills. 23,26-30) and Alvar Aalto (ills. 40-49); it becomes clearer when one looks at the examples from the Thonet production (ills. 2,3), for the most part anonymous and whose "timelessness" is a continued source of admiration.

Their presence provides a vital corrective for the present.

2 **Works Design** 1859 Austria
Chair "No. 14" of bentwood with rattan seat

3 **Works Design** 1870 Austria
Armchair "No. 209" of bentwood with rattan seat

4 **Charles Rennie Mackintosh** 1918 Great Britain
Table "D.S.2" and armchair "D.S.4" of ebonized ashwood with sea grass seat

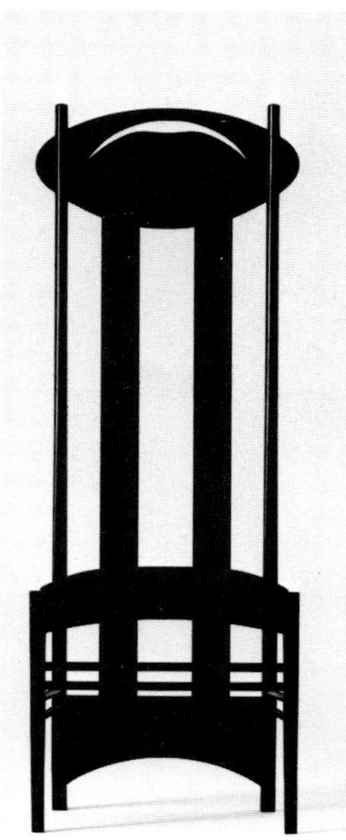

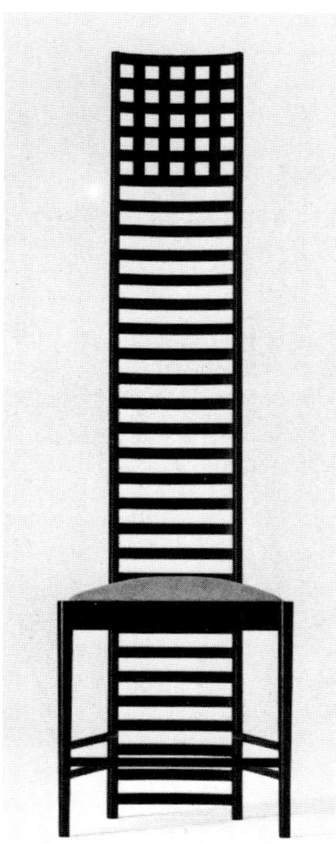

5 **Charles Rennie Mackintosh** 1897 Great Britain
Chair "Argyle" of ebonized ashwood with upholstered seat

6 **Charles Rennie Mackintosh** 1902 Great Britain
"Hill House 1" chair of ebonized ashwood with ladder back and upholstered seat

10 **Walter Gropius** 1910 Germany ▷
Bench "D51/2" and armchair "D51" of black stained ashwood with loose cushions

7 **Josef Hoffmann** 1903 Austria

Armchair "Purkersdorf" with frame of wooden laths in white high-gloss finish, spanned with black and white straps, loose seat cushion

8 **Josef Hoffmann** 1908 Austria

Armchair "Armlöffel" of chalked and ebonized ashwood with loose seat cushion

9 **Josef Hoffmann** 1909 Austria

Armchair "Fledermaus" of beech bentwood with upholstered seat and back

11 **Gerrit Thomas Rietveld** 1918 Netherlands

Lounge chair "Red and Blue" of beechwood, frame with black and yellow aniline finish, seat and back with blue and red lacquer finish

12 **Gerrit Thomas Rietveld** 1934 Netherlands

Chair "Zig-Zag" of elm and table "Crate 4" of solid unfinished beechwood

13 **Mogens Koch** 1932 Denmark

Folding table "MK" of ashwood and folding chair "MK" of beechwood, seat and back covered with canvas or leather, stitched armstraps in leather

14 **Kaare Klint** 1933 Denmark

"Safari chair" with detachable frame of ash, held together with leather straps; seat, back and loose cushion in oxhide or canvas; also stool available

15 **Le Corbusier, Charlotte Perriand, Pierre Jeanneret** 1928
France
Table "LC6" with steel base and top of ash or glass

16+17 **Le Corbusier, Charlotte Perriand, Pierre Jeanneret** 1928
France
"Fauteuil grand confort LC2, LC3" with chrome-plated, black or colored tubular steel frame; loose cushions with polyurethane and Dacron padding, fabric or leather upholstery

18 **Le Corbusier, Charlotte Perriand, Pierre Jeanneret** 1928
France
Revolving armchair "LC7" with tubular steel frame, back and seat cushion padded with polyurethane and fabric or leather upholstery

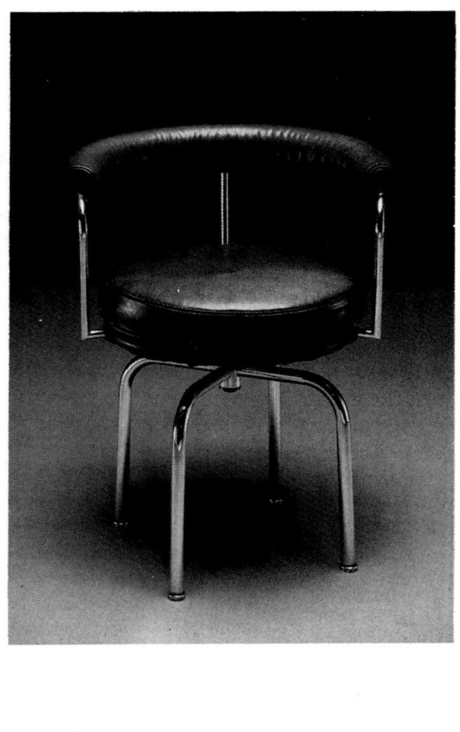

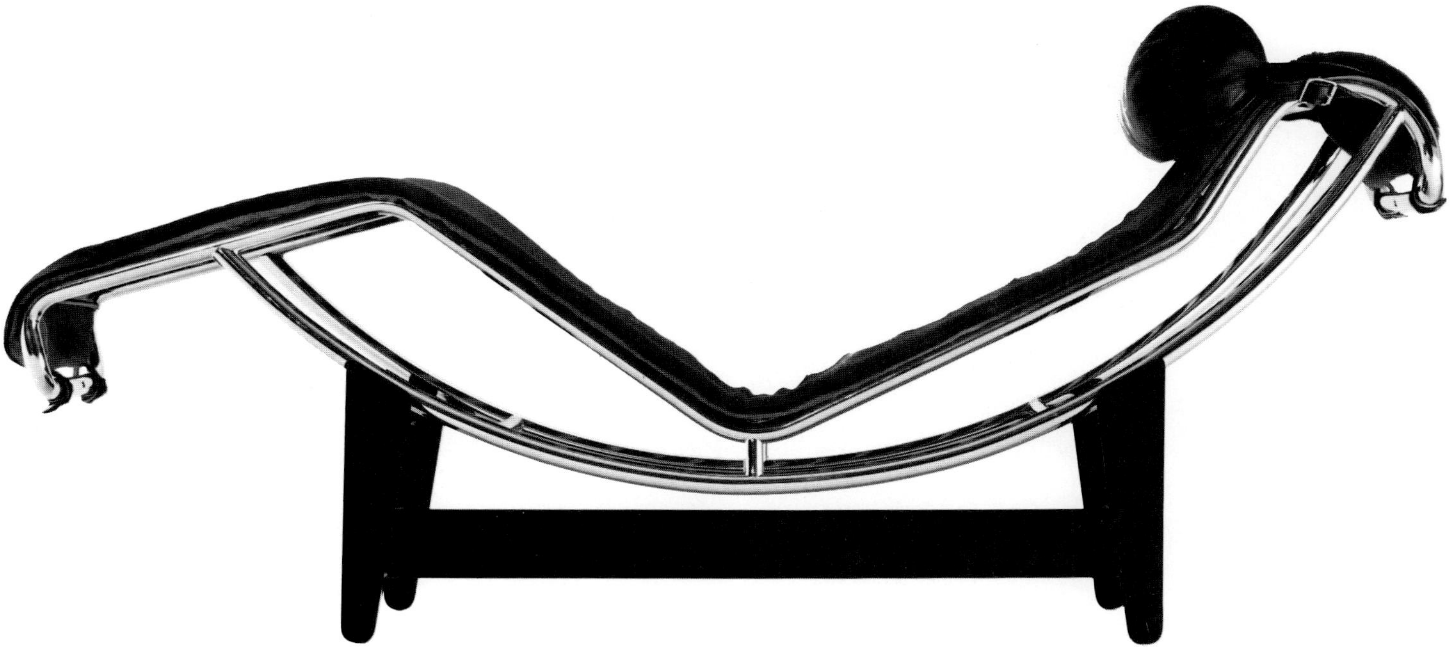

19 **Le Corbusier, Charlotte Perriand, Pierre Jeanneret** 1928
France

Lounge chair "LC4" with adjustable polished chrome-plated or matte black enamel steel frame and matte black or colored enamel steel base. Mat of skin, leather, or fabric; headrest padded with Dacron and leather cover

20+21 **Le Corbusier, Charlotte Perriand, Pierre Jeanneret** 1928
France

Easy chair "LC1" with adjustable back. Frame of chrome-plated or matte black enamel tubular steel, arm rests of leather straps, seat and back covered in skin, leather, or fabric

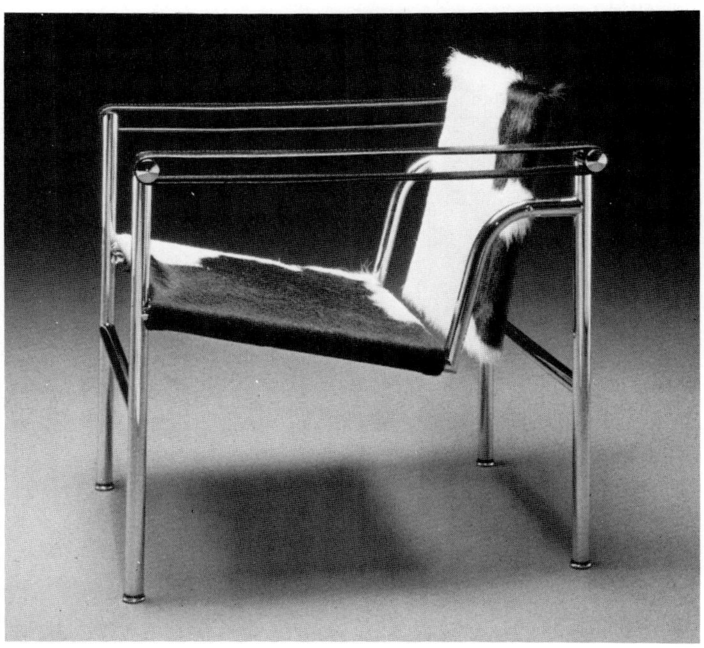

22 **Mart Stam** 1926 Netherlands
Chair "S33" with chrome-plated tubular steel frame, seat and back of leather

23 **Marcel Breuer** 1928 Germany
Cantilevered chair with or without armrests; base of chrome-plated tubular steel, seat and back with bentwood frame and cane

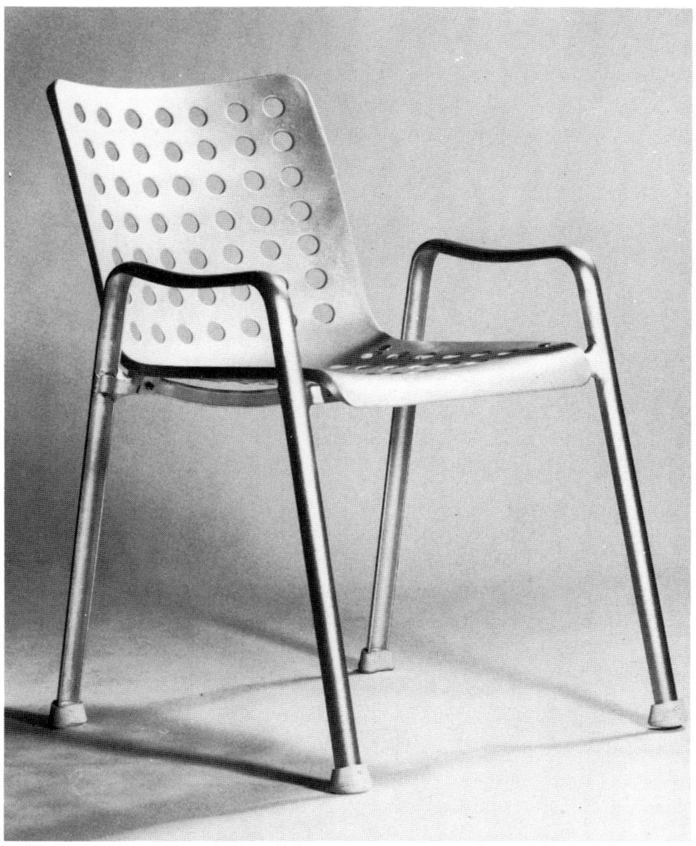

24+25 **Hans Corey, Hans Fischli** 1939 Switzerland
Stacking chair "Landi" of light metal alloy

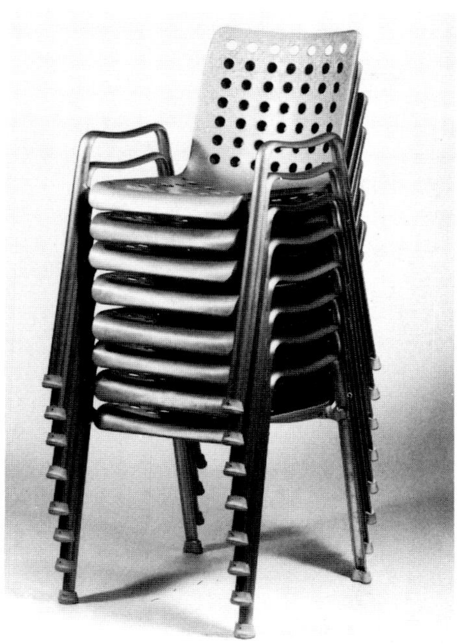

26 **Marcel Breuer** 1927 Germany

Easy chair "D4" with demountable frame of chrome-plated tubular steel; seat, back, and armrests of iron thread straps

27 **Marcel Breuer** 1925/26 Germany

Coffee table "Laccio" with chrome-plated tubular steel frame and top of wood or plastic laminate

28 **Marcel Breuer** 1925 Germany

Easy chair "Wassily" with demountable frame of chrome-plated tubular steel; seat, back, and armrests of leather slings

29 **Marcel Breuer** 1928 Germany

Easy chair "S35L" with chrome-plated tubular steel frame, seat and back of leather

30 **Marcel Breuer** c. 1928 Germany

Desk "S286" with chrome-plated tubular steel frame, top and drawers of wood

	26
27	28
29	30

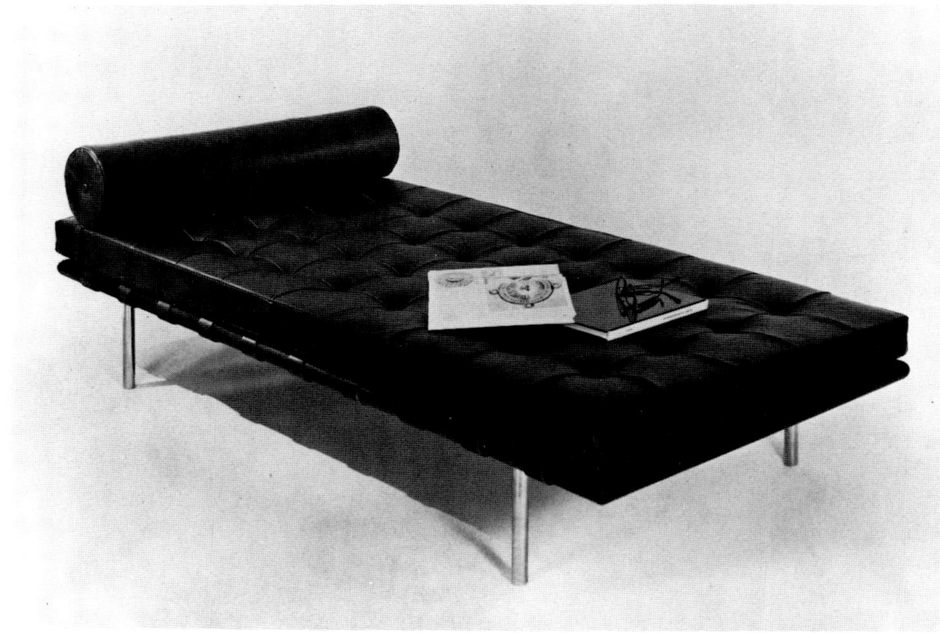

31 **Ludwig Mies van der Rohe** 1930
Germany
Day bed "258" with foam rubber upholstery and leather cover, frame of teak in oiled finish, chrome-plated metal legs

32 **Ludwig Mies van der Rohe** 1926
Germany
"MR" chair "S 533 LF" with chrome-plated tubular steel frame, seat and back of leather

33 **Ludwig Mies van der Rohe** 1929
Germany
"Barcelona" table "252" with frame of chrome-plated spring steel and glass top

34 **Ludwig Mies van der Rohe** 1927
Germany
Coffee table "259" with frame of chrome-plated tubular steel and top of smoked glass

35 **Eileen Gray** 1927 USA
Occasional table "E 1027" with chrome-plated tubular steel frame and glass top

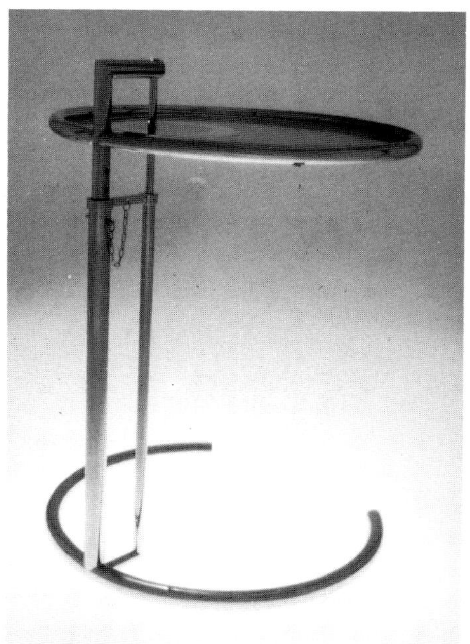

31	32
33	34
	35

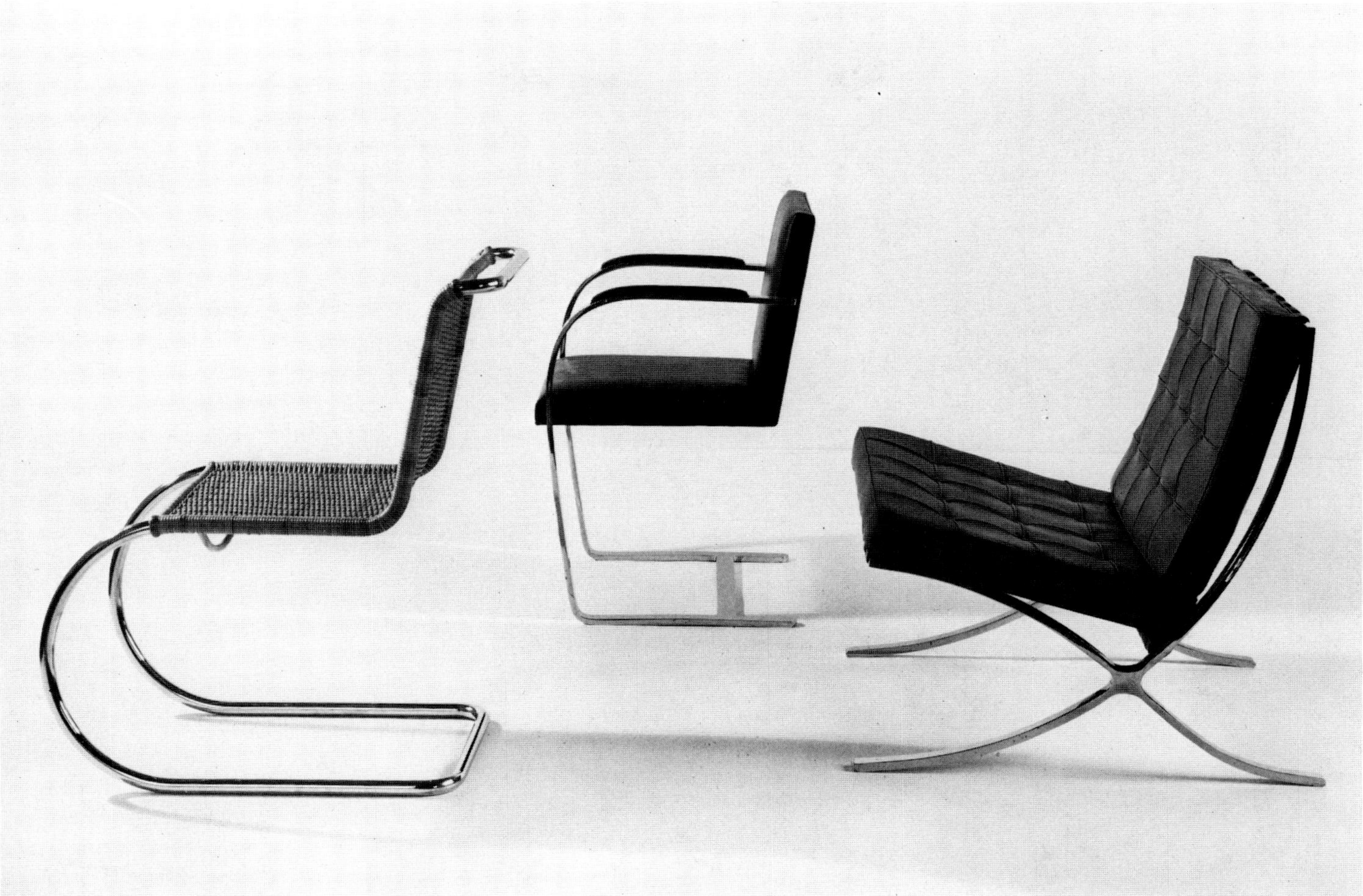

36 **Ludwig Mies van der Rohe** 1926, 1930, 1929 Germany
"MR" chair "S533" with tubular steel frame and canework seat and back; "Brno" chair "245" with frame of spring steel and fabric or leather-covered upholstery; "Barcelona" chair "250" with frame of special spring steel, loose seat and back cushions covered with leather (from left to right)

37 **Ludwig Mies van der Rohe** 1930 Germany
"Tugendhat" chair "254" with frame of chrome-plated special spring steel and loose cushions covered with leather

38 **Ludwig Mies van der Rohe** 1931 Germany
Chaise longue "241" with chrome-plated steel tube frame, continuous roll and pleat cushion with linen cover supported by rubber straps

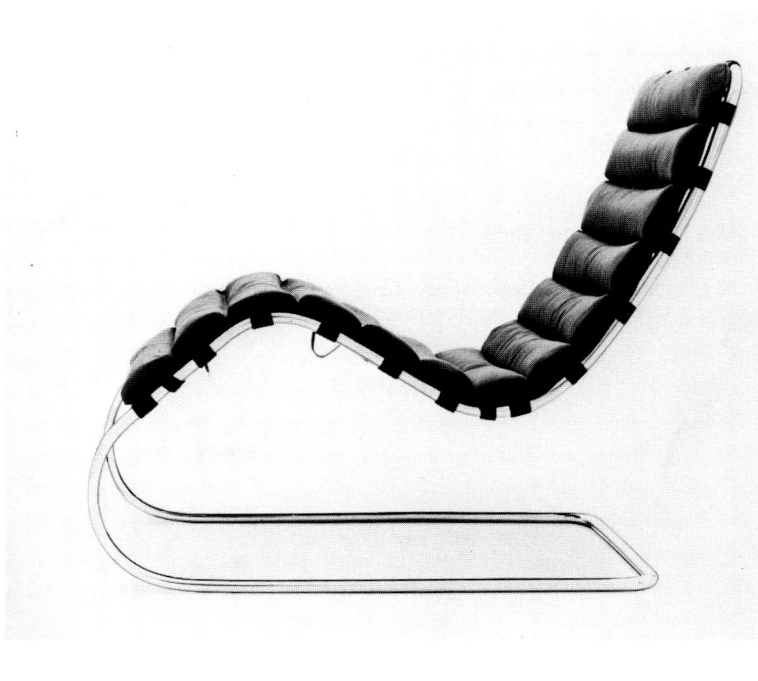

39 **Bruno Mathsson** 1933–35 Sweden

Lounge chair and ottoman "Pernilla" with laminated beech frame, seat and back of webbed straps or with canvas or leather upholstery

40+41 **Alvar Aalto** 1947 Finland

Coffee tables with bases of molded laminated wood and tops of plywood or glass

42 **Alvar Aalto** 1954 Finland

Coffee table with base of molded laminated wood and top of wooden slats or glass

43 **Alvar Aalto** c. 1947 Finland

Stools with frame of laminated birchwood and seat with webbed straps or canework

44 **Alvar Aalto** 1954 Finland

Stool of bent, solid wood, construction with fanned bends

40	41	42
43		44

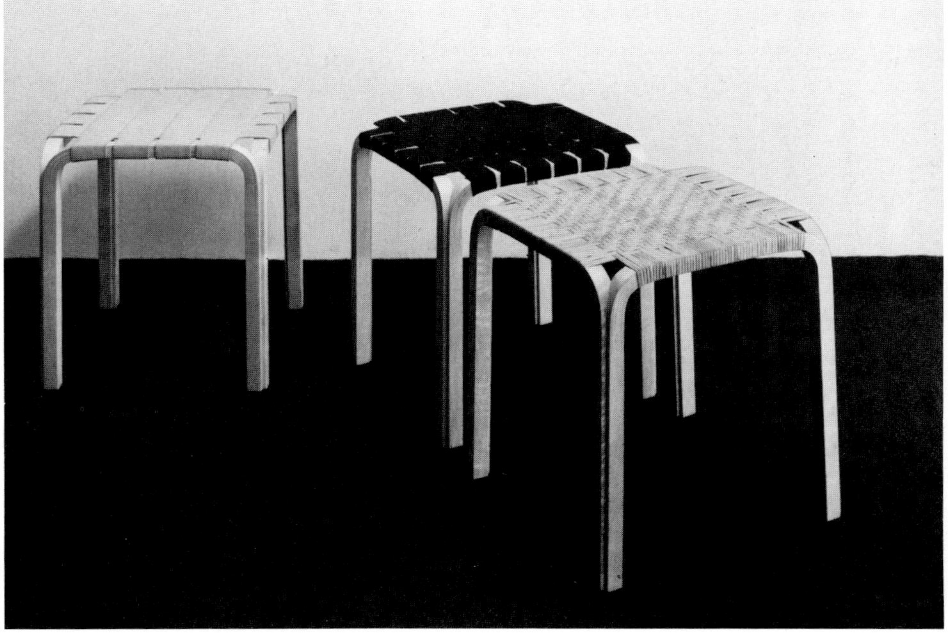

45 **Alvar Aalto** 1929–35 Finland

Stacking stools and chairs of birchwood

46 **Alvar Aalto** c. 1947 Finland

Armchair with frame of molded laminated wood, seat and back of cane

45
46 47 48
49

47 **Alvar Aalto** 1929–33 Finland

Armchair with frame of molded laminated wood and seat of molded plywood

48 **Alvar Aalto** 1935–39 Finland

Armchair with frame of molded laminated wood and seat of webbed straps

49 **Alvar Aalto** 1929–33 Finland

"Paimio" armchair with frame of molded laminated birchwood, seat and back of molded plywood

Chairs and Armchairs

When someone sits down in a chair, the way he sits allows conclusions to be drawn about his psyche and character. The choice of a chair is also to a large extent self-presentation; it can range from occupying a throne to meekly sitting around on a foot stool. Whether a person leans back in a chair or sits nervously on the edge, whether he relaxes across the whole seat or sits bolt upright, whether he stretches his legs out or winds them nervously round the chair legs, whether his hands are placed on the arms or in his lap-hardly any other piece of furniture permits such an array of gestures as the chair. Of all similar articles we probably

have our most intimate and revealing relationship with it.

The variety of different kinds of chairs has always greatly helped this behavioral phenomenon of course, but nowadays it occurs more than in the past. Because of the numerous examples in existence, the 20th century could be called the age of the chair-a fact that is probably connected with the growing trend towards individuality in this century. To each his own unmistakable chair, that he may be recognized.

The choice ranges from traditional wooden chairs to ones made of steel tubing combined with wood or plastic and ones made entirely of synthetic materials. The change in forms was also a change in materials, or rather, new materials produced forms different from previous ones. One must note, however, that the latest designs are not necessarily the best. The various kinds are about equal.

We like to remember the early wooden chairs by Max Bill (ill. 61), Georg Leowald (ills. 56,62), Egon Eiermann (ills. 69,109) and Finn Juhl (ill. 83) and do not feel they are old-fashioned compared with the grille or plastic shells by Harry Bertoia (ills. 209-211) and Charles Eames (ills. 263,264), and decidedly not so compared with the plastic and cushion designs by Verner Panton (ills. 394,395) and Olivier Morgue (ills. 410-412).

A "conventional" chair such as Gio Ponti's (ill. 50) is still valid today; in fact, despite its twenty-five years it appears almost avant garde today. After all the ups and downs we have had since then with modern chair design, some of which were very unfortunate, our appreciation of such an economical, disciplined, yet lively solution has been heightened. The traditional design of the Chiavari chair has been assimilated by Ponti with a logically modern interpretation. The original form has not been lost, but in rendering it more concise its earlier multiplicity of form has been replaced by a general spiritualisation. Here, a chair is still a chair and nothing but a chair, yet in an incomparable way. Ponti's design also shows us how severe a product was able to look, approaching the typical postures of the 1950s but not becoming their slave.

As convincing as the Italian chair is the Danish one by the designer Hans J. Wegener (ill. 80).

50 **Gio Ponti** 1957 Italy

Chair "Superleggera" with frame of ash-wood and rattan seat

It, too, is now over thirty years old. It is unmistakably "Scandinavian" in every detail, but so subtly so that it is capable of overcoming our exhaustion caused by a surfeit of teak furniture. So far as the use made of wood is concerned, this chair represents possibly the quintessence of the Scandinavian style, its most perfect product. When one sees this chair in a shop-it is still being produced completely unchanged-it is like meeting an old person whose wisdom quite naturally arouses our adoration.

It is quite amazing that almost at the same time, and "right next door" so to speak, such a completely different chair could be created as Arne Jacobsen's (ill. 170), probably the most successful combination of a shaped wooden seat and steel tube legs. The differences in the materials used make it hard for us to see the affinity of spirit and attitude the two Scandinavian chairs possess. Strictly speaking, they are not very far apart. Their high formal discipline is in both cases the result of a responsibility that still considered itself so close to the rudiments of modern development that it was not capable of being superficial or precipitous. Younger generations of designers became visibly bolder, but also presumptuous and effect-seeking. The American counterpart to the chair by Arne Jacobsen is the one Charles Eames designed in 1946 (ill. 166). Its use was, however, somewhat limited as it presented itself primarily as an office chair. This impression was caused by the back, which did not form a whole with the rest of the chair and was only joined to it in the middle. This is a detail that is also suitable for a chair for home use, but it was easy to see that the office chair had been used as a model. A successor to the lightness and perfection of this chair first appeared in David Rowland's metal stacking chair (ill. 202).

The principle of the skeletonized separation of supports and shell-shaped seats was continued by Charles Eames in the lounge chair (ill. 51), which is one of the most striking pieces of furniture of our time. This chair is both functionally and in its choice of form and material a product capable of presenting extremely frugally and precisely the spirit and ability of our time. This object bears unmistakable witness to technical design-it reminds one of a car or aeroplane seat, although neither exists in this form. It betrays such brilliant intelligence that it is impossible to observe this chair only as what it is designed to be. One has to see in it a fragment of a realized ideal. Here, industrial requirements and human designing capability have come together in an incomparable way.

The chair that Dieter Rams designed some years afterwards (ills. 378,379) could be regarded as the "younger brother" of the lounge chair. In this case the combination of individual shell-shapes and cushioned parts is almost conventional, except that the solid elements are now made of plastic and not molded wood. Nevertheless, despite the obvious details, the German example's more bourgeois attitude compared with the free thinking of the American cannot be overlooked.

51 **Charles Eames** 1957 USA
Lounge chair "670" and ottoman on cast aluminum swivel base, rosewood veneer molded plywood frame with leather-covered polyfoam and down upholstery (cf. ill. 343)

52 **Bengt Akerblom** c. 1950 Sweden
Chair in birch

53 **Karl Erik Ekselius** 1953 Sweden
Chair with beech frame and upholstered seat

54 **Works Design** 1952 Denmark
Stacking chair in beech

57 + 58 **Jørgen Høj** 1955 Denmark
Chair in fumed oak or teak, seat with fabric slings

◁◁ 55 **Nanna and Jørgen Ditzel** 1955 Denmark
Chair with teak frame, seat of wickerwork

◁ 56 **Georg Leowald** 1954 Germany
Chair with wooden frame and seat of wickerwork

59 **Paul M. Volther** c. 1953 Denmark
Stacking chair of wood

60 **Grete Jalk** 1957 Denmark
Collapsible chair "3-2" of fumed oak

63 **Ejner Larsen, A. Bender Madsen** 1955 Denmark

Chair with teak frame, seat and back of leather

64 **Ejner Larsen, A. Bender Madsen** 1957/58 Denmark

Chair "1652/1653" with teak frame, seat in cane or upholstered

65 **Børge Mogensen** 1947 Denmark

Chair with oak or beech frame, seat in cane

66 **Børge Mogensen** 1954 Denmark
Chair with oak frame, seat and back of teak

◁◁ 61 **Max Bill** c. 1950 Switzerland
Chair with wooden frame, seat and back of molded plywood

67 **Carl Auböck** 1960 Austria
Stacking chair "4906" of beech

◁ 62 **Georg Leowald** 1954 Germany
Chair with beech frame, seat and back of molded plywood, also with plastic-covered polyfoam upholstery

68 **Hans J. Wegner** 1952 Denmark
Stacking chair of wood

69 **Egon Eiermann** c. 1950 Germany
Chair of molded plywood

70 **Works Design** c. 1951 Sweden
Armchair of molded plywood

71 **Niko Kralj** 1954 Yugoslavia
Demountable chair with frame of molded laminated wood, seat and back of molded plywood

72 **Ilmari Tapiovaara** 1959 Finland
Stacking chair "Alak" with frame of molded laminated wood, seat and back of molded plywood

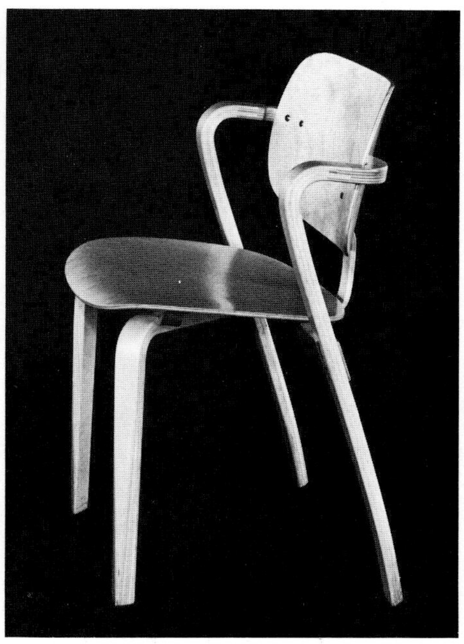

73 **Charles Eames** 1946 USA
Chair of molded and bent birch plywood

74 **Poul Kjaerholm** 1952 Denmark
Chair of molded laminated wood

75 **Sori Yanagi** 1956 Japan
Collapsible stool "Butterfly" of molded plywood

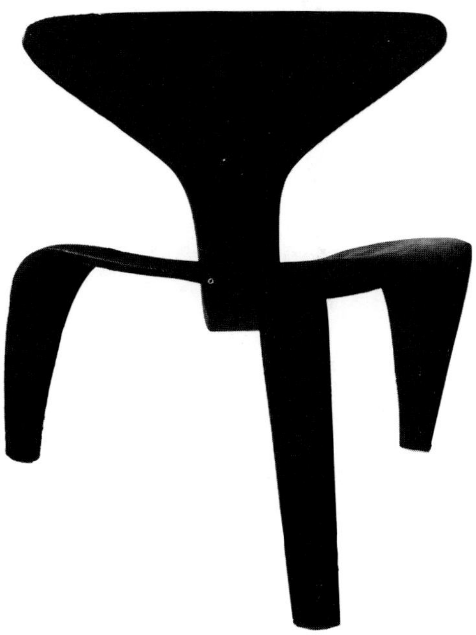

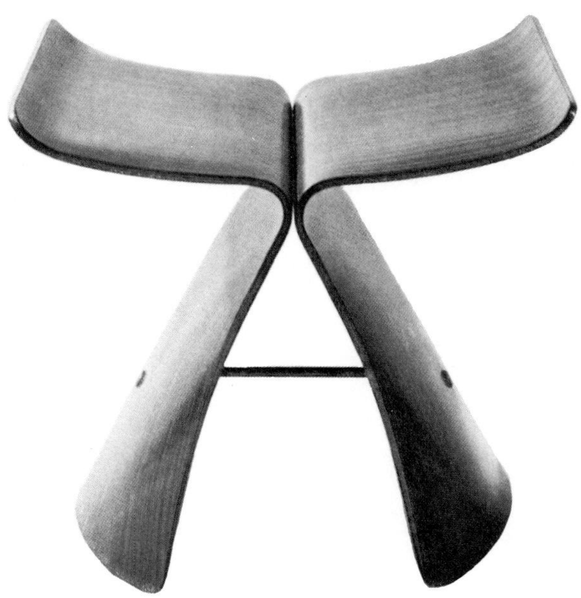

◁◁ 76 **Peter Hvidt, Orla Mølgaard Nielsen** c. 1951 Denmark
Stacking armchair of wood

◁ 77 **Ejner Larsen, A. Bender Madsen** 1949 Denmark
Armchair with wooden frame, seat and back of molded plywood

80 **Hans J. Wegner** 1949 Denmark
"The chair (JH501)" with teak frame and canework or upholstered seat

◁◁ 78 **Ejner Larsen, A. Bender Madsen** c. 1957 Denmark
Armchair "1656" in teak with upholstered seat

◁ 79 **Ejner Larsen, A. Bender Madsen** 1959 Denmark
Armchair "2842/L" with teak frame, seat and back of strong leather

81 **Ejner Larsen, A. Bender Madsen** 1957 Denmark
Armchair "1638/Tr" in teak with rattan seat

82 **Ib Kofod-Larsen** 1958 Denmark
Armchair with rosewood frame, upholstered seat and back

83 **Finn Juhl** 1955 Denmark
Armchair with teak frame, upholstered seat and back

84 **Georg Leowald** 1954 Germany
Armchair "352B" with frame of wood, seat and back of molded plywood

85 **Finn Juhl** 1964 Denmark
Stacking armchair "196" with teak frame, seat and back upholstered

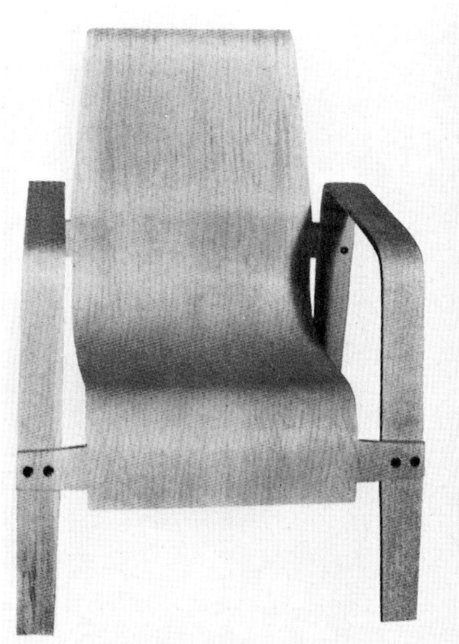

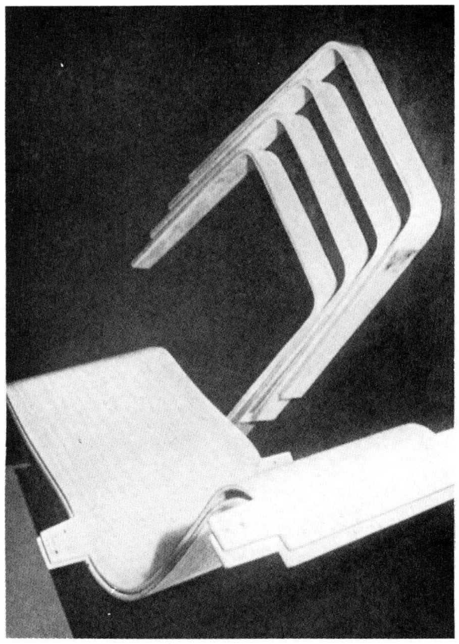

86+87 **Vittoriano Viganò** 1946 Italy

Collapsible stacking armchair "VV/46" of bent plywood, assembled with brass bolts

88 **Roberto Mango** 1954 Italy

Collapsible chair with frame of wood, seat and back of molded plywood

89 **Georg Leowald** 1954 Germany

Chair with wooden frame, seat and back of molded plywood

90 **Carlo Bartoli** 1968 Italy

Chair "Mito" of ash in natural or lacquer finish

91 **Gerd Lange** 1973/74 Germany
Chair "2200" of solid oak, side parts of plywood, seat and back of plastic

92+93 **Sören Nissen, Ebbe Gehl** 1979 Sweden
Stacking and linking chair "Jet" with frame of bent laminated oak, seat of molded oak, also upholstered

94 **Wilhelm Ritz** 1959 Germany
Chair "402" of laminated beech, seat and back upholstered

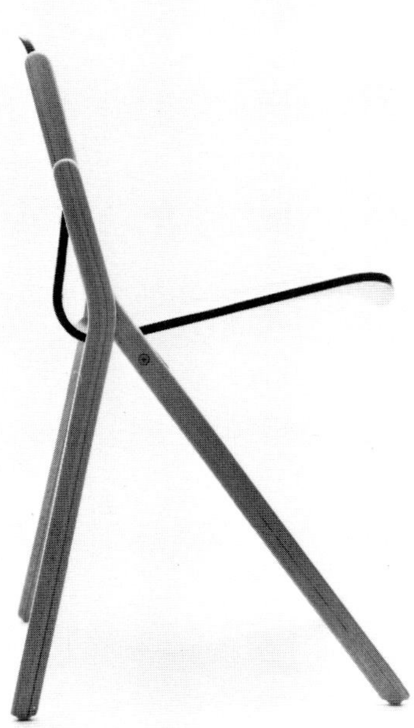

95–97 **Niko Kralj** Yugoslavia

Chairs and armchairs with wooden frames, seats and backs of perforated molded plywood

98+99 **Peter Hvidt, Orla Mølgaard Nielsen** 1950 Denmark

"AX" chair and armchair with laminated beech frames, teak seats and backs

100 **Alberto Rosselli** 1954 Italy

Chair with laminated bent wood frame, seat and back of molded plywood

101 **Franco Albini, Luigi Colombini, Ezio Sgrelli** c. 1950 Italy
Armchair with movable seat and back, foam-rubber padding

103 **Kai Kristiansen** 1960 Denmark ▷
Chair "4110" with teak frame, upholstered seat with leather or fabric cover

104 **Herbert Berry, Christopher Cattle** 1962 Great Britain ▷
Chair in ash or mahogany with polyfoam cushion on a base of molded plywood

105 **Terence Conran** 1962 Great Britain ▷
Dining chairs "Summa SU 22/23" in ash, pine, or teak, backs in wood with or without upholstery

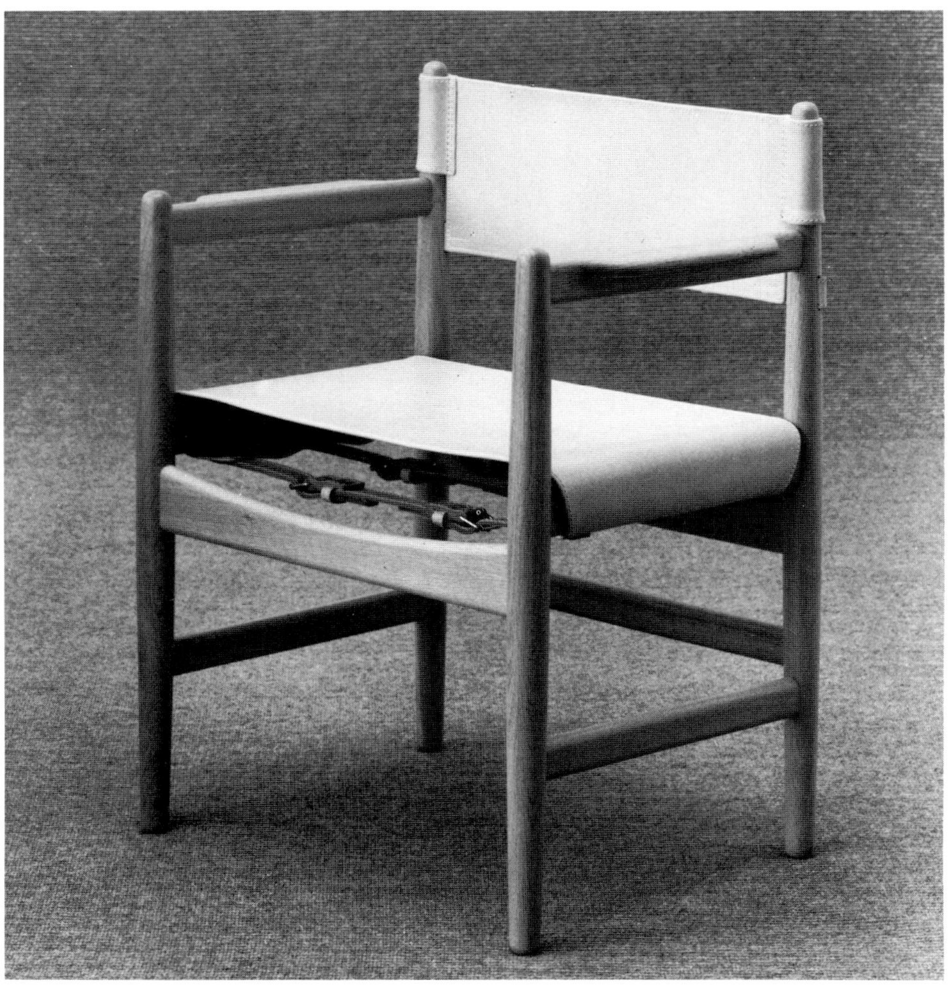

102 **Børge Mogensen** 1955 Denmark
Armchair "Øresund" in oak with removable leather slings

106 **Gio Ponti** 1964 Italy

Armchair "1215" in mat finished walnut with rattan seat

107 **Bruno Rey** 1972 Switzerland

Range of lacquer-finished stackable chairs "2100" with seats and backs of high-pressure-molded plywood, frames of solid beech and die-cast aluminum joints. Also with upholstery

103	106
104	
105	107

108 **Carlo De Carli** 1954 Italy
Collapsible chair "683" with ash frame, seat and back of molded plywood with chrome-plated metal fittings

109 **Egon Eiermann** 1952 Germany
Folding chair with beech frame, seat and back of molded plywood

110 **Jack Ränge** c. 1950 Sweden
Folding armchair with seat slings in canvas and leather straps

111 **Franco Albini** c. 1950 Italy
Folding armchair with wooden frame, seat and back of plywood

112 **Marco Zanuso** c. 1950 Italy
Folding armchair "Bridge" with wooden frame and polyfoam upholstery

113 **Frei Otto** 1967 Germany

Stackable knock-down chair with frame of beech, ash, or rosewood, canvas or leather slings

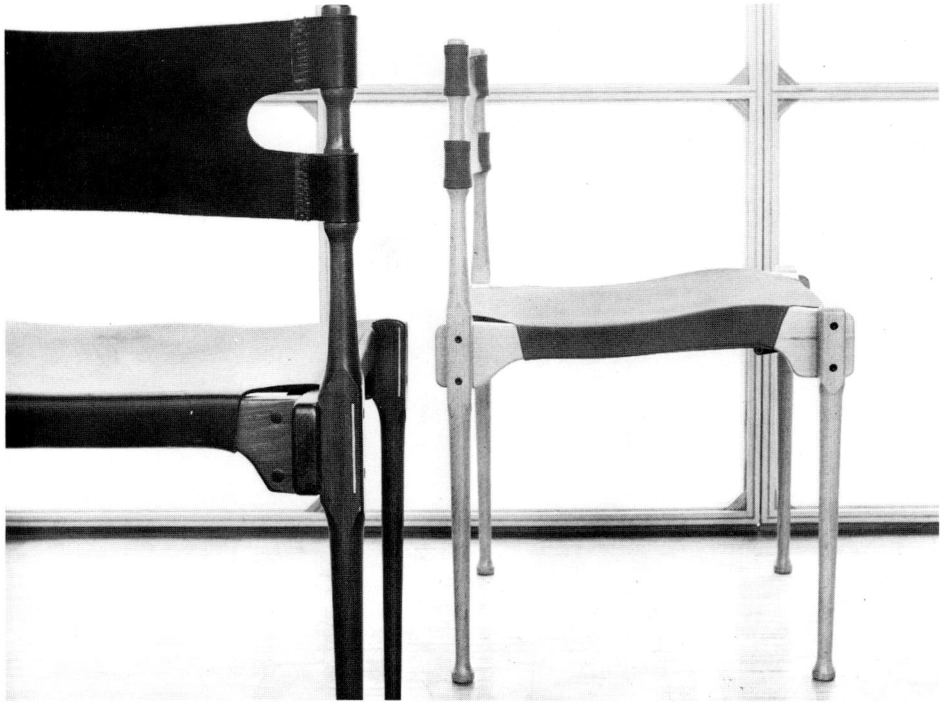

114+115 **Jonathan De Pas, Donato D'Urbino, Paolo Lomazzi** 1975 Italy

Demountable chair "Linda" and armchair "Lindapiù" with supple joints, frame of ash or beech, seat and back of canvas or cowhide

116 **Gerd Lange** 1966 Germany

Furniture series "Bofinger Farmerprogramm" in knock-down construction. Wooden parts of ash in natural finish or stained are joined and then connected by means of canvas slings

117 **Henrik Iversen, Harald Plum** 1964 Denmark

Lounge chair "PH76" and stool "PH77" with frames of beech and fabric or leather cover

118+119 **Ernest Race** 1953 Great Britain

Stackable folding deck chair "Orient Neptune" of molded laminated beech in clear lacquer finish, brass fittings, nylon belting

120 **Lauge Vestergaard** 1970 Denmark

Folding chair and stool "139" of beech with canvas slings. Adjustable headrest

121 **Don Knorr** c. 1950 USA

Stool in birch with leather seat

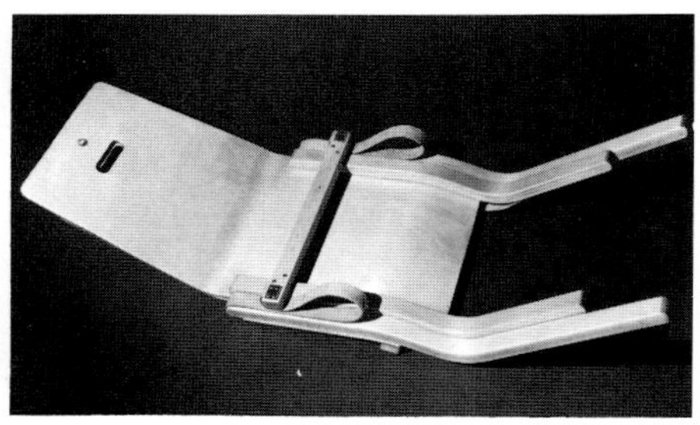

117	
118	119
120	121

122 + 123 **Jonathan De Pas, Donato D'Urbino, Paolo Lomazzi** 1975 Italy
Folding chair "Sanremo" with frame of ash, seat and back with canvas slings

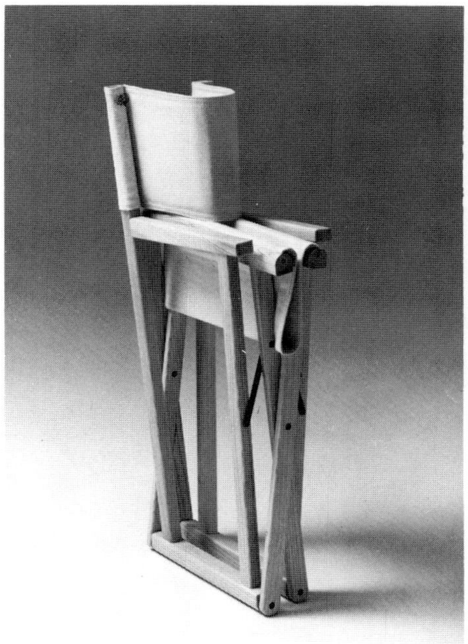

124 **Esko Pajamies** 1962 Finland
Folding chair "Finnsafari" with frame of molded beech veneer, seat, back, and side straps of leather

125 + 126 **Günter Sulz** 1971 Germany
"London Chair" with folding frame of beech, stained or lacquered, canvas slings. Matching table with plastic top

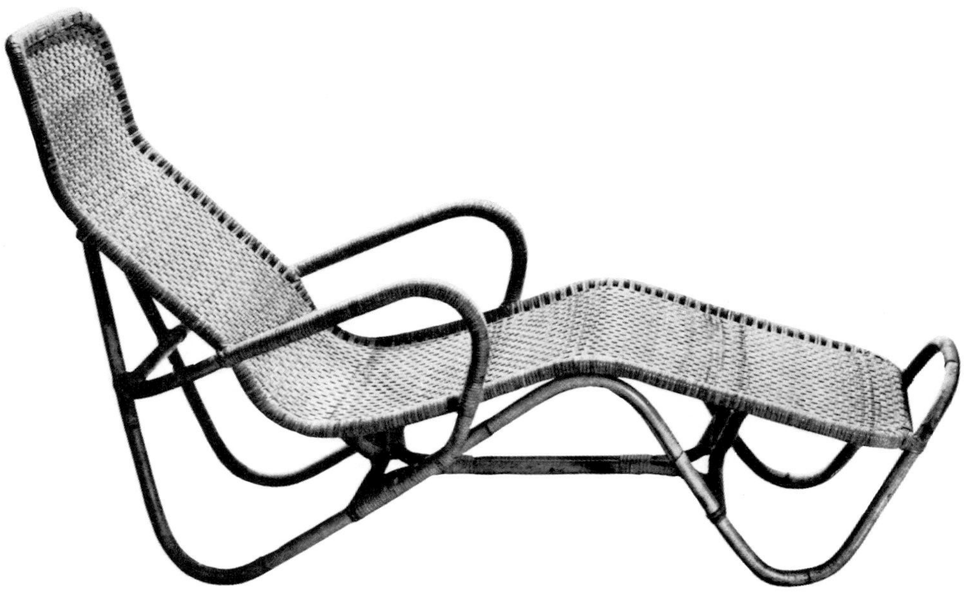

127 **Kolling Andersen** 1950 Denmark
Rattan lounge chair with seat of wickerwork

128 + 129 **Nanna and Jørgen Ditzel** 1950 Denmark
Chair with wooden base and rattan seat

130 **Franco Albini** 1951 Italy
Easy chair of rattan

131 **Egon Eiermann** 1952 Germany
Easy chair of rattan

132 **Egon Eiermann** 1957 Germany
Easy chair of rattan

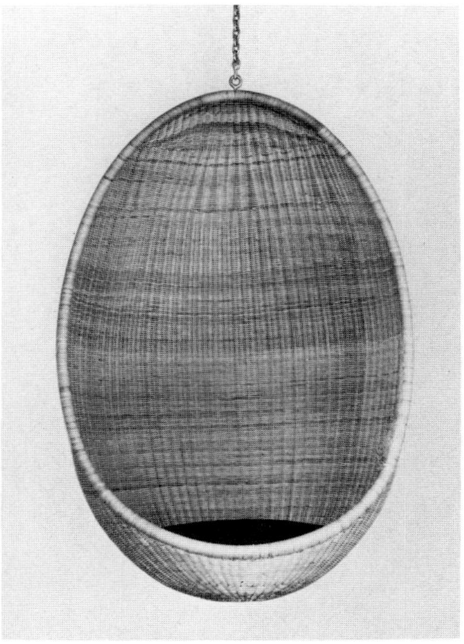

133 **Nanna and Jørgen Ditzel** 1959 Denmark
Rattan hammock hanging on a chain

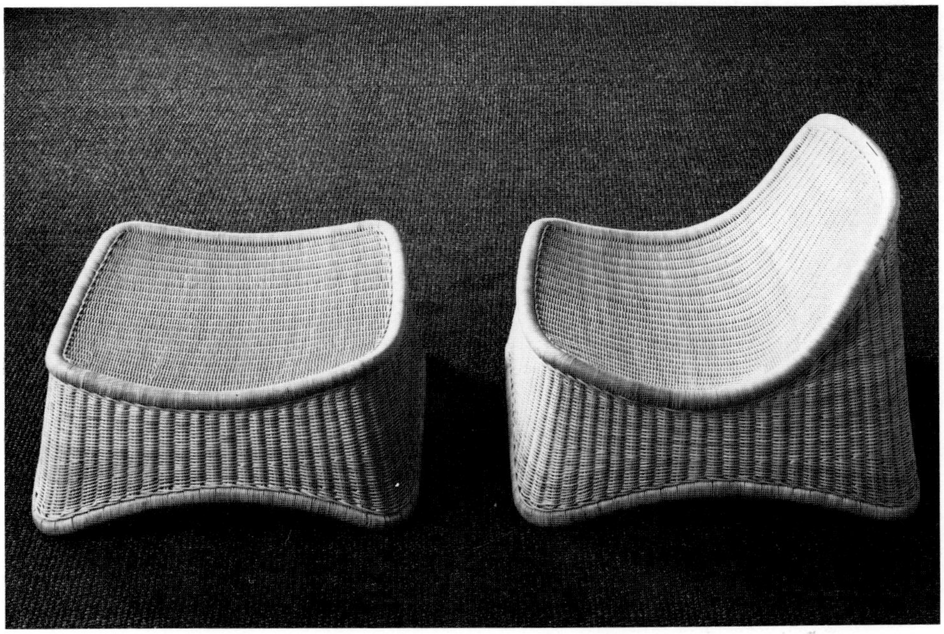

134 **Nanna Ditzel** 1961 Denmark
Easy chair and footstool of rattan

135 **Isamu Kenmochi** 1961 Japan
Easy chair of rattan with loose cushion

136 **Albrecht Lange, Hans Mitzlaff** c. 1951 Germany
Easy chair with laminated wood frame, rubber straps and loose cushions

137 **Pierre Jeanneret** c. 1951 France
Easy chair with wooden frame and polyfoam cushions on rubber straps

138 **Alf Svensson** c. 1953 Sweden
Easy chair with wooden frame and loose cushions

139 **Sonna Rosen** c. 1951 Sweden
Armchair in birch

142 **Folke Ohlsson** c. 1953 Sweden ▷
Upholstered easy chair with wooden frame

143 **Florence Knoll** 1955 USA ▷▷
Lounge chair with teak frame and polyfoam upholstery

◁ 140 **Works Design** c. 1951 USA
Chairs and armchairs with wooden frames and seats with straps or upholstery

▷ 141 **Otto Haupt** 1951 Germany
Easy chair with bentwood frame and fabric straps

144 **Eero Saarinen** c. 1950 USA

Upholstered armchair "61" with laminated birch frame and innerspring construction

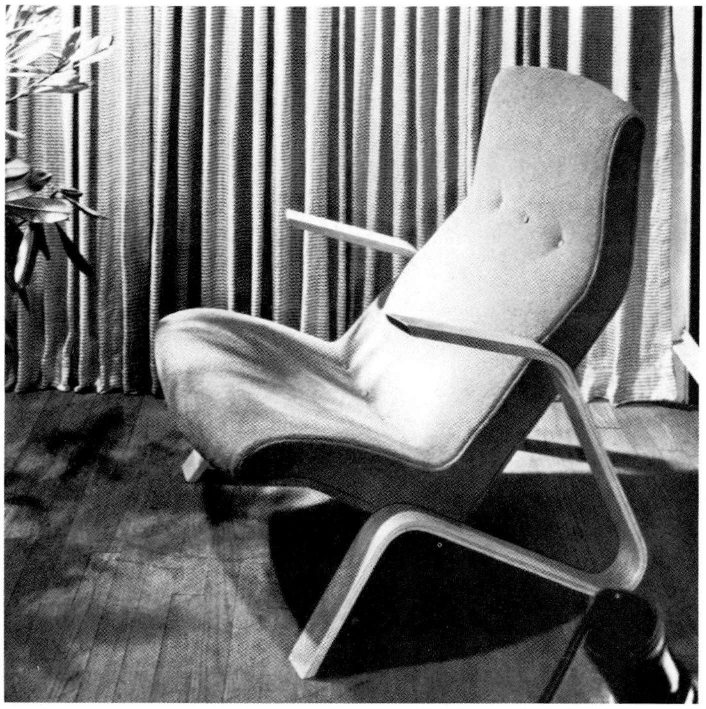

145 **Arne Jacobsen** 1962 Denmark

Easy chair "4335" and ottoman "4533" in natural finished oak with fabric-covered polyfoam upholstery; stool may also be used as side table when cushion is removed

146 **Joe Colombo** 1966 Italy

Easy chair "Supercomfort 1000" with frame of bent plywood in natural or white lacquer finish. Removable cushions covered with leather. Inserted tension springs of plastic may be relaxed or tightened

147 **Marco Zanuso, Richard Sapper** 1964 Italy/Germany

Easy chair "Woodline" with frame of molded laminated wood. Seat of wood with loose leather cushions

148 **Poul Kjaerholm** 1971 Denmark

Lounge chair with frame of laminated wood and leather upholstery

149 **Kembo Team** 1978 Netherlands

Armchair "Eutektos" with frame of solid beechwood laminate, seat and back of plastic or upholstered and with leather or fabric covering

150 **Finn Juhl** 1945 Denmark

Armchair with frame of oiled teak, upholstered seat and back, loose seat cushion

151 **Finn Juhl** 1958 Denmark

Armchair "136" in teak with polyfoam upholstery

150	152
151	153
	154

152 **Works Design** c. 1955 Denmark

Armchair "116" in teak with polyfoam upholstery

153 **Ole Wanscher** c. 1955 Denmark

Armchair "119" in teak with polyfoam upholstery

154 **Folke Ohlsson** 1953 Sweden

Armchair with wooden frame and polyfoam upholstery

155+156 **Edvard Kindt-Larsen** 1954 Denmark

Armchair with beech or teak frame, seat support of rubber straps, and loose cushions

157 **Karl Erik Ekselius** 1953 Sweden

Armchair with wooden frame and polyfoam upholstery

158 **Folke Ohlsson, Alf Svensson** c. 1953 Sweden

Upholstered settee and armchair with wooden frames

162 **Franco Albini** 1954/55 Italy ▷

Armchair with wooden frame, seat and back of plywood, polyfoam upholstery

163 **Herbert Hirche** 1957 Germany ▷▷

Upholstered armchair with cherrywood or teak frame

159 **S.H. Vakassian** c. 1950 USA

Armchair with wooden frame and polyfoam upholstery

160 **Marco Zanuso** 1951 Italy

Armchair "Senior" with metal frame and foam rubber upholstery

161 **Marco Zanuso** 1951 Italy

Armchair "Baby" with wooden frame and foam rubber upholstery

164 **Lewis Butler** c. 1956 USA

Armchair with beech frame, walnut back, loose polyfoam cushions

165 **Roland Gibbard** 1963 Great Britain

Easy Chair "Q" with frame of beech, back of beech veneered plywood, seat supported on rubber webbing. Loose polyfoam cushions with detachable fabric covers

169 **Arne Jacobsen** 1952 Denmark ▷

Three-legged stacking chair of molded beech plywood and steel tube base

170 **Arne Jacobsen** 1955 Denmark ▷▷

Four-legged stacking chair of molded beech plywood and steel tube base

166–168 **Charles Eames** 1946 USA

Dining chair and low side chair of molded walnut plywood, steel rods, rubber shock-mounts

171 **Søren Hansen** 1953 Denmark
Stacking stool with steel tube frame and wooden seat

172 **Arne Jacobsen** 1955 Denmark
Chair of molded plywood with steel tube base

173 **Arne Jacobsen** 1957 Denmark
Chair of molded plywood with metal base

174 **Egon Eiermann** 1952 Germany
Chairs with steel tube frames and molded plywood seats and backs

175 **Gastone Rinaldi** 1955 Italy
Chair "DU66" with metal base, seat and back of molded plywood

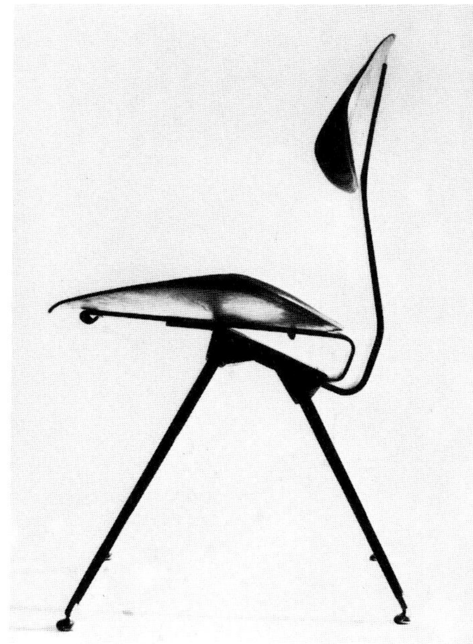

176 **Friso Kramer** 1954 Netherlands
Chair with metal frame, seat and back of molded plywood

177 **Friso Kramer** 1955 Netherlands
"Revolt" chair with steel frame, seat and back of molded plywood

178 + 179 **Osvaldo Borsani** 1958 Italy

Folding chair "S 88" with lacquered tubular steel frame, seat and back of molded plywood

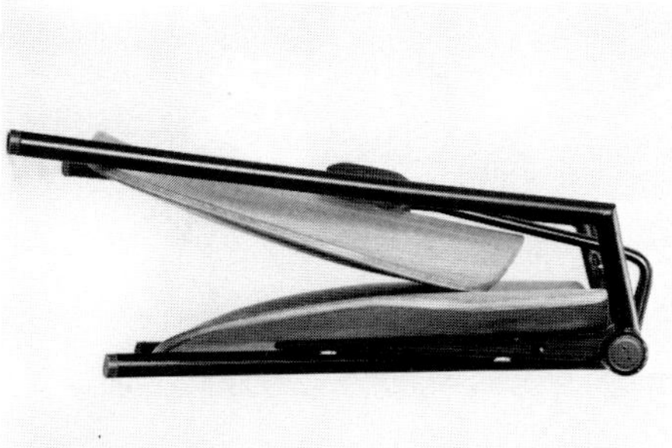

180 **Kurt Nordström** c. 1957 Sweden

Chair "145" with black lacquered tubular steel frame, seat and back of molded plywood

181 **Theo Tempelman** 1960 Netherlands

Chair "41" with tubular steel frame, seat and back of teak or upholstered

182 **Gastone Rinaldi** 1960 Italy

Chair "S 7" with tubular steel frame, seat ànd back of molded plywood veneered in various woods or upholstered

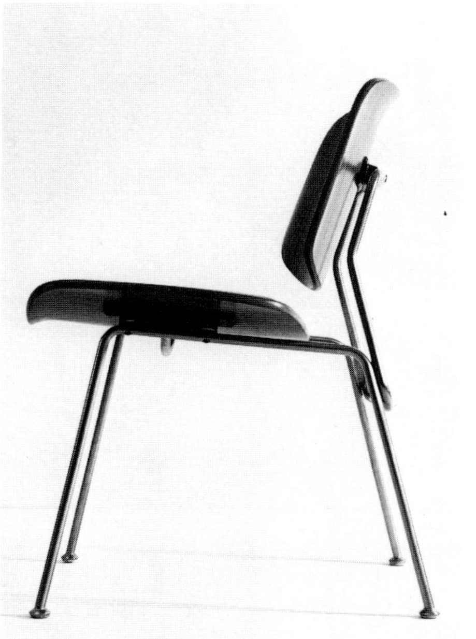

183 **Robin Day** c. 1953 Great Britain

Stacking chair with tubular steel frame, seat and back in molded plywood with plastic laminate

184 **Eva and Nils Koppel** 1949 Denmark

Stacking chair with steel tube frame and plastic-laminated molded plywood seat and back

185 **Hans Bellmann** c. 1952 Switzerland

Chair with chrome-plated steel tube base and birch seat

186 **Ray Komai** c. 1950 USA

Chair with metal frame and seat of molded plywood

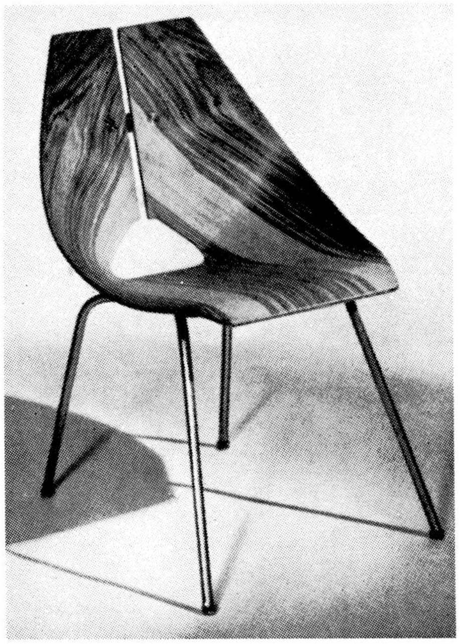

187 **Hans Coray** c. 1952 Switzerland
Chair with steel tube frame and molded plywood seat and back

188 **W. Rietveld** c. 1952 Netherlands
Chair with steel tube frame and molded plywood seat and back

189 **Albert Rauch** c. 1953 Switzerland
Chair with chrome-plated steel tube frame, seat and back of molded laminated wood

187	188	189
	190	
	191	192

190 **Peter Hjorth** 1956 Denmark
Chair with tubular steel frame, seat and back in one piece of molded and perforated veneer wood

191 **Friso Kramer, Jaap Penraat** c. 1953 Netherlands
Upholstered armchair with steel tube frame

192 **Ilmari Tapiovaara** 1952 Finland
Stacking armchair "Lukki" with steel tube frame and molded plywood seat and back

193 **Works Design** c. 1953 Sweden
Swivel chair with metal frame and adjustable back, seat in molded laminated wood with or without upholstery

194 **Hillevi Sepponen** c. 1952 Finland
Swivel chair with metal frame, seat and adjustable back in molded wood

195 **Armin Wirth** c. 1953 Switzerland
Folding chair with aluminum frame, seat and back of molded plywood

196 **Tokujiro Kaneko** c. 1952 Japan
Height-adjustable office chair with steel frame and upholstered seat and back

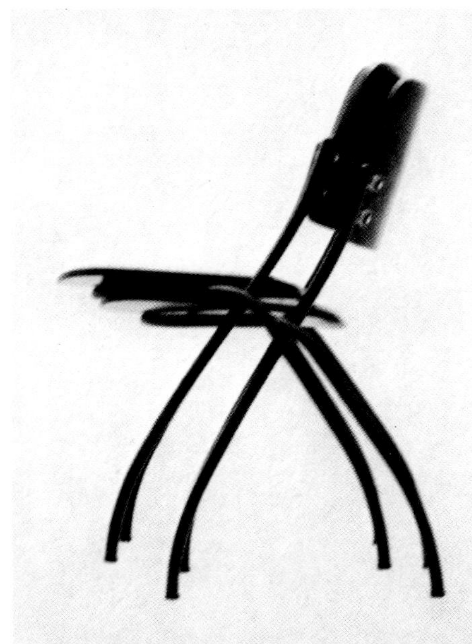

197 + 198 **Nanna and Jørgen Ditzel** 1958 Denmark

Stacking chair "150" with nickel-plated tubular steel frame with inlaid steel rod in all bendings. Seat and back of plastic-laminated beech with edge and rail profiles of solid wood. The chairs are linked by a steel bar which goes through the rails and is fastened with a rubber ring

199 + 200 **Ilmari Tapiovaara** 1958 Finland

Stacking chair "Nana" with lacquered tubular steel frame, seat and back of molded plywood lacquered or covered with fabric. Linking chair with armrests

201 **H.Th. Baumann** 1956 Germany

Folding chair with chrome-plated tubular steel frame, seat and back of molded plywood

204 **Achille and Pier Giacomo Castiglioni** ▷
1957 Italy

Stool "Mezzadro" with stem of chrome-plated steel, seat lacquered in various colors or chrome-plated, foot-rest of beech

205 **Rodney Kinsman** 1974 Italy ▷▷

Chair "omkstack" with chrome-plated or lacquered steel tube frame, seat and back of sheet metal

202 **David Rowland** 1964 USA

Stacking and linking chair "GF 40/4" of chrome-plated or plastic-laminated steel-rod. Seat and back panels of contoured sheet steel in plastic laminate. Clear plastic linking devices and gliders

203 **Ernest Race** 1950 Great Britain

Chair "Antelope" with painted steel-rod frame and seat of molded plywood

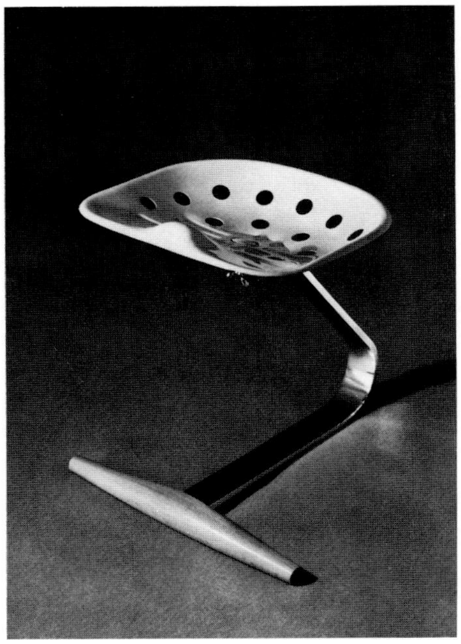

206 **James C. Witty** c. 1952 USA
Folding chair with metal frame and perforated metal seat and back

207 **A.J. Milne** c. 1951 Great Britain
Garden chair with steel tube frame and perforated metal seat and back

208 **Charles Eames** 1951 USA

Chair with formed wire seat, removable cushion, wire rod frame

209–211 **Harry Bertoia** 1952 USA

Lounge chair "423", stool "424", chairs "420" and "421" with steel rod bases, formed wire seats and removable polyfoam upholstery

208 | 209
210 | 211

212 **Warren Platner** 1964/66 USA

Lounge chair "1705" and ottoman "1709" with electronically welded steel wire bases, copper- or nickel-plated. Polyfoam upholstery on plastic seat shells with loose cushions

213 **Verner Panton** 1960 Denmark

Deck chair "T-2" with base and seating shell of steel wire with loose polyfoam cushions

214+215 **Verner Panton** 1958/59 Denmark

Series of chairs in different heights and shapes. Cone of wire, exterior in fabric, interior upholstered in polyfoam with fabric cover, legs of stainless steel

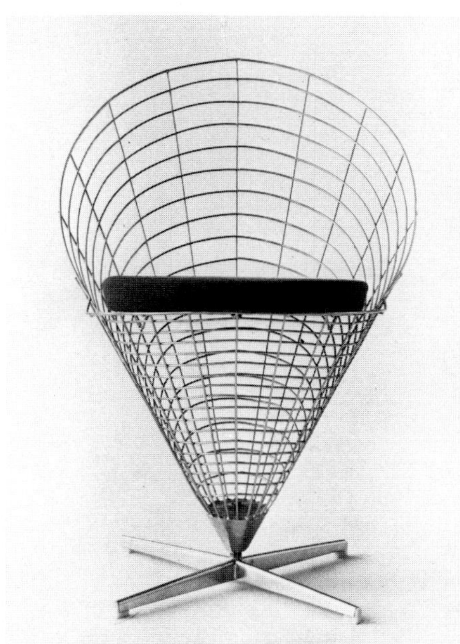

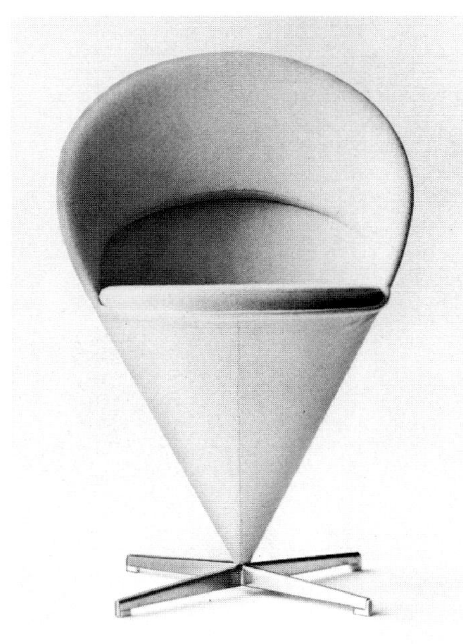

216 **Robin Day** 1963 Great Britain

Range of chairs with seat shells of injection-molded plastic and a great variety of additions: bases for multiple seating, for stacking and linking chairs, for swivel chairs, high bar stool frames, legs of beech, armrests, writing arm. Also with upholstery

217 **Ib Kofod-Larsen** 1955 Denmark

Chair with chrome-plated tubular steel base, seat of fiberglass with loose polyfoam cushion

218 **Esko Pajamies** 1961 Finland

Stacking chair "TU-520" with base of spring steel and seat shell of fiberglass-reinforced polyester, also with armrests and upholstery

219 **Don Albinson** 1965 USA
Stacking and linking chair "1601" with cast-aluminum frame, seat and back of injection-molded plastic. Also with armrests, writing arm, chrome-plated book rack, and tabletops

220 **Works Design** 1969 Germany
Linking and stacking chair "Multi" with frame of chrome-plated or mat black epoxy-finished tubular steel and plastic seat and back

221 **Giancarlo Piretti** 1967 Italy
Stacking and linking chair "106" with cast-metal frame and plastic-laminated legs of tubular steel. Seat and back of molded plywood in beech, walnut, rosewood, or upholstered

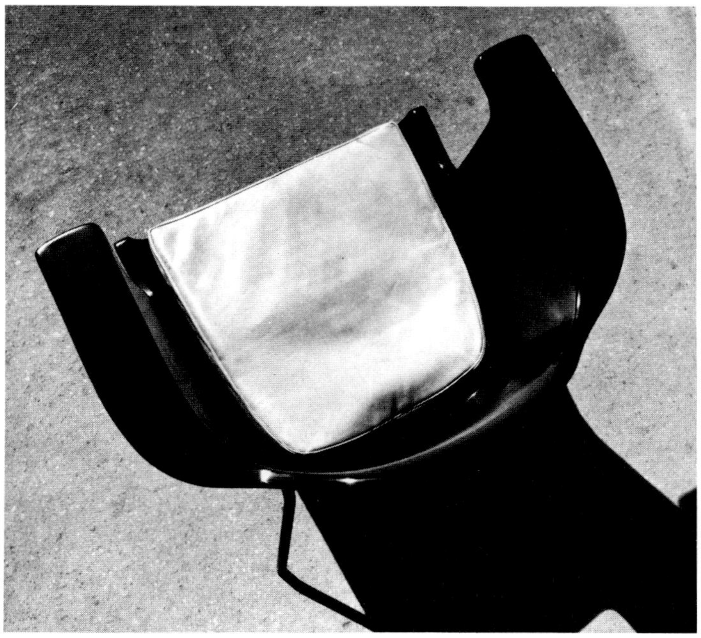

222 **Angelo Mangiarotti** 1949 Italy
Armchair of molded plastic with metal tube frame and loose cushion

223 **W. and E. Guhl** c. 1950 Switzerland
Chair with plastic seat shell and metal legs

224 **Vermund Larsen** 1956 Denmark
Stacking chair with chrome-plated tubular steel base and fiberglass seat

225 **Harry Bertoia** 1955 USA
Chair "427 P" with black lacquered metal base and plastic seat shell

226 **Kai Lyngfeldt Larsen, Steen Eiler Rasmussen** 1960 Denmark
Chair "333" with tubular steel frame, seating shell of fiberglass

222	223
	224
225	226

227–229 **Charles Eames** 1949–53 USA
Chairs of molded plastic with underframes of cast aluminum, metal tube or wire rods

230+231 **George Nelson** 1958 USA
Chairs with seat shells of molded reinforced plastic with fixed or flexible back, curved tubular steel legs

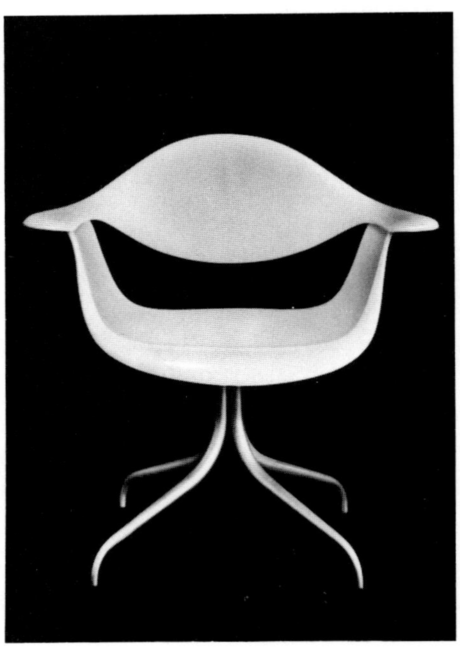

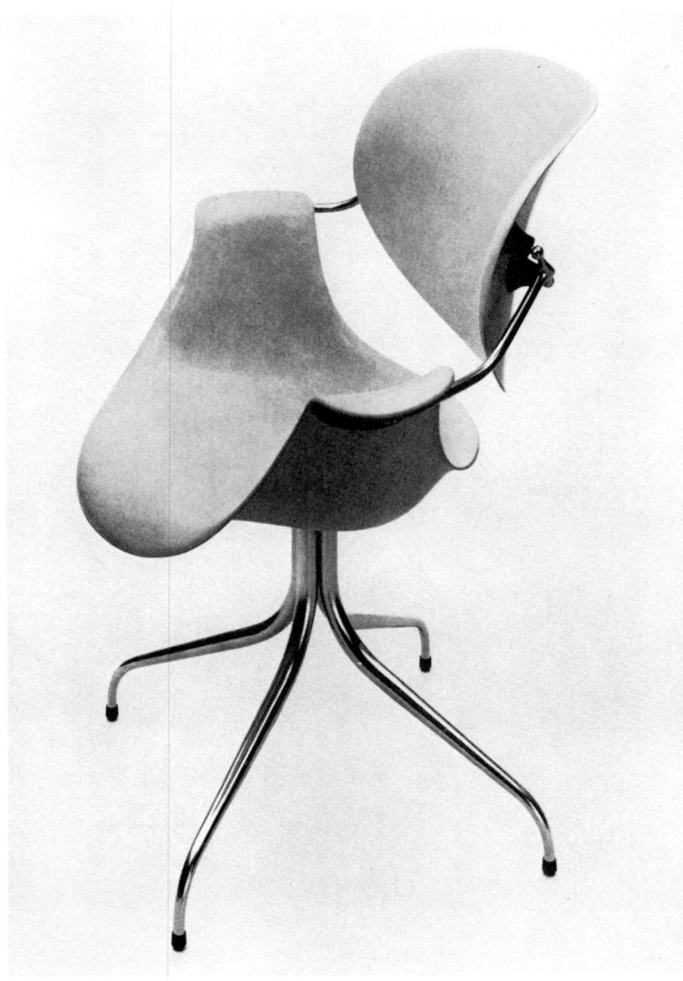

232 **Antti Nurmesniemi** 1959 Finland

Chair with steel frame, seat upholstered in polyfoam with leather cover

233 **Hans Ell** 1966 Germany

Stacking and linking chair "1000" with frame of chrome-plated or stove-enamelled steel tubing, seat and back of injection-molded plastic

234 **Gerd Lange** 1971 Germany

Stacking and linking chair "SM 400 K Nova" with frame of chrome-plated tubular steel and seating shell of polyamid, also seat and back pads

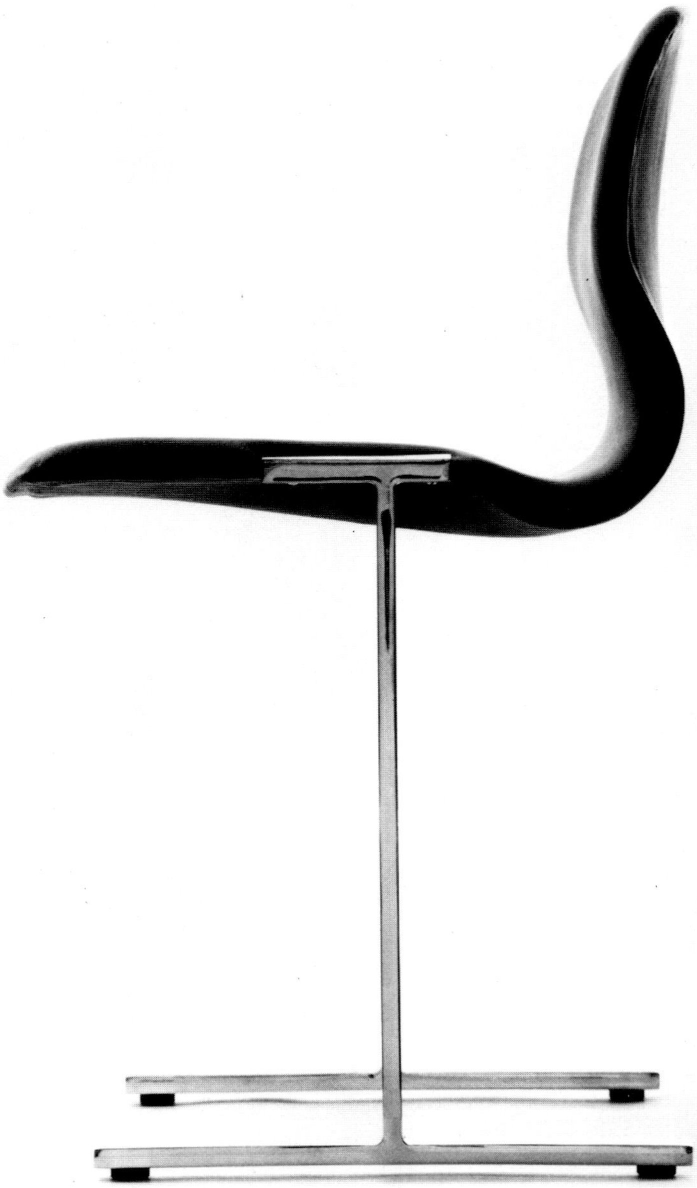

235 **Marco Zanuso** 1970 Italy

Stacking and linking chair "Miniseat" with seat shell of fiberglass-reinforced polyester and chrome-plated steel tube base

236 **Ferdinando Buzzi** 1971 Italy

Chair "102" with frame of chrome-plated tubular steel; seat and back of molded plywood with polyfoam upholstery

237 **Jørgen Kastholm** 1976 Denmark

Stacking chair "Serie 1500" with base of chrome-plated tubular steel and seating shell of plastic, also with removable upholstery

238 **Reiner Moll** 1978 Germany

Chair "Binar" with chrome-plated steel tube frame and hollow body seating shell of plastic

239 **Klaus Franck, Peter Beck** 1974 Germany
Chair "614/1" with chrome-plated tubular steel frame, seat and back of molded beech plywood

242 **Arne Jacobsen** 1962 Denmark ▷
Armchair "3200" with chrome-plated metal frame, upholstered seat, back in teak

243 **Roland Rainer** 1960 Austria ▷
Chair "702" with nickel-plated steel frame and upholstered seat; back upholstered or veneered in various woods

244 **Dieter Waeckerlin** 1960 Switzerland ▷
Armchair "W55" with chrome-plated metal frame, polyfoam upholstery covered in leather or fabric

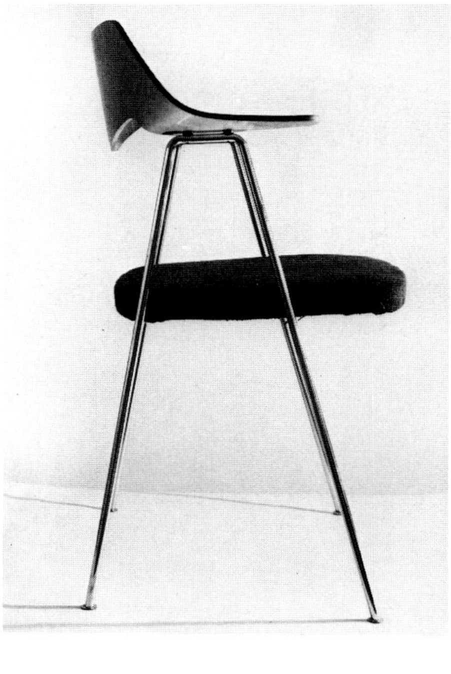

240 **Robin Day** c. 1952 Great Britain
Armchair with chrome-plated steel tube frame, seat of plywood with polyfoam upholstery, back and armrests in one piece of molded plywood veneered in walnut

241 **Carlo Santi** 1972 Italy
Chair "Santana" with frame of chrome-plated tubular steel, upholstered seat

245 **Poul Kjaerholm** 1956 Denmark
Chair with chrome-plated tubular steel frame, seat and back of cane

246 **Verner Panton** 1956 Denmark
Stacking chair with tubular steel frame, seat and back of plastic strings

247 **Albrecht Lange, Hans Mitzlaff** 1954 Germany
Armchair with tubular steel frame, innerspring seat and back upholstered in polyfoam, armrests in saran

248 **Gastone Rinaldi** c. 1950 Italy
Armchair with chrome-plated steel tube frame, seat and back with polyfoam upholstery

249 **Dirk van Sliedregt** 1953 Netherlands
Stacking chair with lacquered tubular steel frame, seat and back of rattan

250 **Hans Eichenberger** 1955/56 Switzerland
Armchair with chrome-plated tubular steel frame, cane-wrapped back and polyfoam seat covered in leather

251+252 **Poul Kjaerholm** 1959 Denmark
Stool "33" with mat finished chrome-plated steel frame, cushion covered with oxhide

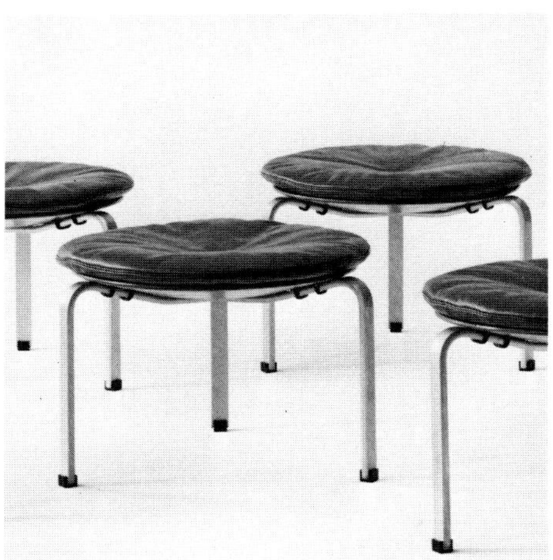

253 **Achille and Pier Giacomo Castiglioni** 1969 Italy
Chair "Castiglia" with frame of chrome-plated or white lacquered steel tube and leather or canvas slings

254 **Marcello Minale, Brian Tattersfield** 1969 Great Britain
Stackable armchair "MTP 1" with chrome-plated tubular steel frame, seat and back in rattan or with black leather slings

255 **Poul Kjaerholm** 1961 Denmark
Folding stool "91" with mat finished chrome-plated steel frame and oxhide or canvas seat

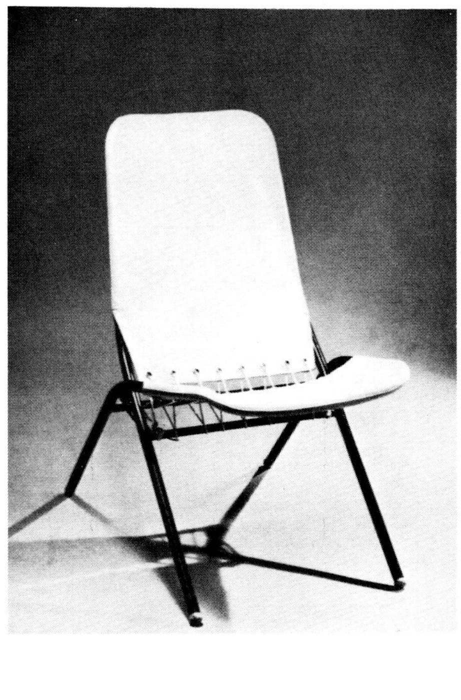

259 **Giancarlo Piretti** 1969 Italy
Folding chair "Plia" with frame of chrome-plated steel, seat and back of transparent plastic

◁ ◁ 256 **Gae Aulenti** 1971 Italy
Folding chair "April" with frame of stainless steel, seat and back with canvas or leather slings

◁ 257 **Fred Tydor** c. 1950 USA
Folding armchair with aluminum tube frame and canvas slings

◁ 258 **Olof Pira** c. 1952 Sweden
Folding chair with steel tube frame and canvas slings

260 **Renato Zevi** 1970 Italy
Folding chair "Z-15" with frame of chrome-plated tubular steel. Seat of wood and back of metal, plastic-covered

261 + 262 **Eero Saarinen** 1951 USA
Chairs "71" and "72" with polyfoam upholstered seat shells of plastic, various steel frames

263 + 264 **Charles Eames** 1960 USA
"La Fonda" chairs with shells of fiberglass and polyfoam upholstery, frames of chrome-plated cast aluminum

265 **Poul Kjaerholm** 1960 Denmark ▷
Chair "9" with mat finished chrome-plated steel frame, seating shell covered in ox-hide

▽ 266 **Gastone Rinaldi** 1953 Italy
Chair "DU 30" with lacquered tubular steel base, polyfoam upholstery

▽ 267 **Giotto Stoppino** 1969 Italy
Stacking chair "Maya" with molded plastic seat, without cover or covered in fabric or leather; frame of chrome-plated tubular steel

268 **Pierre Paulin** 1961 France
Lounge chair "549" with chrome-plated steel frame, seating shell of molded laminated wood upholstered in polyfoam

269 **Pierre Paulin** 1964 France
Easy chair "121" with chrome-plated metal base; seat shell of molded laminated wood with polyfoam upholstery covered in fabric, loose seat cushion

270 + 271 **Georg Leowald, Friso Kramer** 1959/67 Germany/Netherlands

Range of height-adjustable swivel chairs on aluminum pedestals with gliders or casters; seat shells of fiberglass-reinforced polyester with upholstered seat and back

272 **Jørgen Rasmussen** 1967 Denmark

Swivel chairs "1904" and armchair "1908" with height-adjustable base of die-cast aluminum and plastic casters or gliders; seat and back of injection-molded plastic, polyfoam upholstery

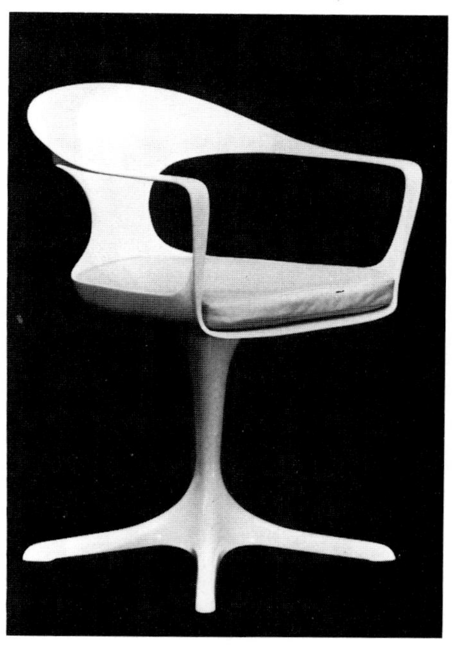

273 **Arne Jacobsen** 1968 Denmark

Swivel office chair of plastic

274 **Konrad Schäfer** 1969 Germany

Office swivel chair of fiberglass-reinforced plastic with polyfoam upholstery covered in leather or fabric

275 **Works Design** 1971 Italy

Seating shell "Modus" of injection-molded nylon with various frames of aluminum, also with armrests of black ABS and writing arm

276 **Andrew Ivar Morrison, Bruce R. Hannah** 1970 USA

Swivel chair "2328" with height-adjustable steel base, armrests and legs on casters of die-cast aluminum; detachable polyfoam upholstery, fixed at the frame with plastic hoods

277 **Ettore Sottsass jr.** 1970/71 Italy

Office swivel chair of plastic, part of "Synthesis 45" office furniture system (see ills. 776–8). Polyfoam upholstery with covers of fabric. Back and seat height-adjustable

278 **Wilhelm Ritz** 1971 Germany

Office swivel chair "232" with upholstered seating shell in two parts of fiberglass reinforced polyester, height-adjustable, infinitely tilting back, casters, with or without armrests

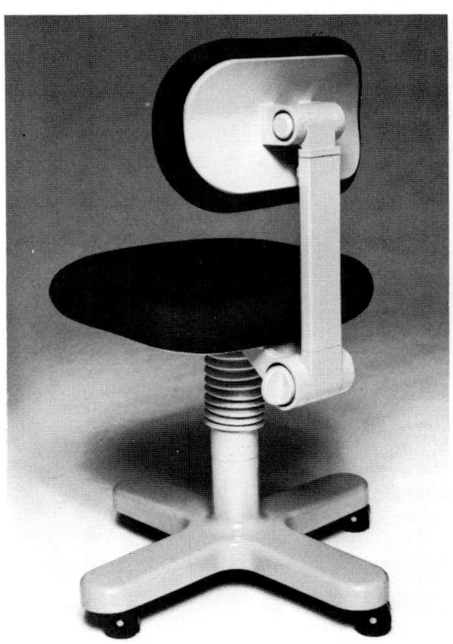

279 **Jorge Ferrari-Hardoy, Antonio Bonet, Juan Kurchan** 1938 USA

"Hardoy" lounge chair "198" with frame of steel rods and canvas or leather covering

280 **Germano Facetti, John Ollis** 1956 Great Britain

Lounge chair with spring steel frame and canvas slings, collapsible for transport

281 **Works Design** c. 1952 Sweden

Stool with metal frame and seat slings in canvas or leather

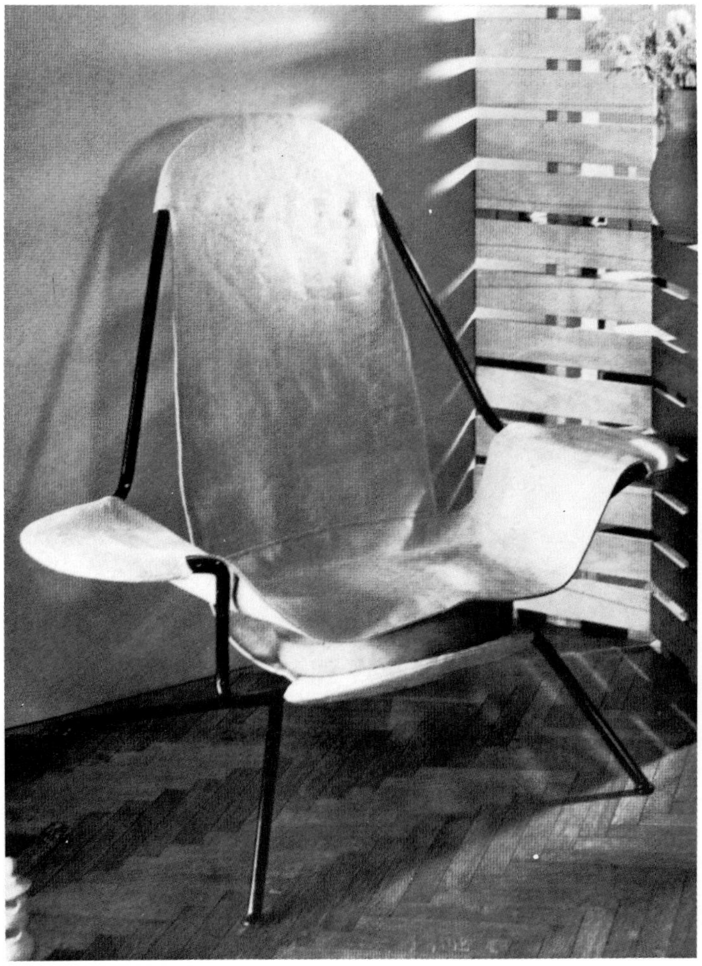

282 **Paolo A. Chessa** c. 1950 Italy
Armchair with metal frame, canvas slings and polyfoam cushion

283 **DAM (Designers Associati Milano)** 1969 Italy
Chair "Baffo" with frame of chrome-plated tubular steel and suspended leather seat

284+285 **Esko Pajamies** 1965 Finland
Knock-down chair with frame of chrome-plated steel and seat slings of canvas

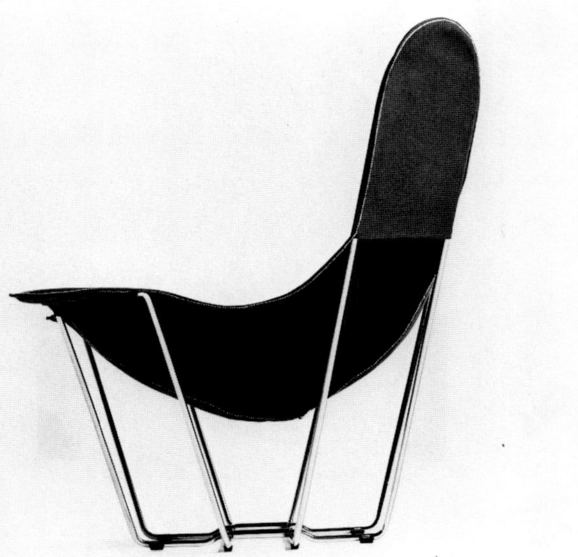

286 **C. de Vries** c. 1950 Netherlands
Armchair with steel tube frame and seat slings in canvas

287 **Norman Cherner** c. 1953 USA
Lounge chair "120" with black steel frame and upholstery

288 **Otto and Ridi Kolb** c. 1953 USA
Armchair with steel tube frame and leather slings

289 **Pierre Paulin** 1955 France
Easy chair with tubular steel frame of two components, seat slings of canvas or leather

290 **Pierre Paulin** 1964 France

Folding chair "675" with frame of chrome-plated metal and leather slings

291 **Verner Panton** 1956 Denmark

Lounge chair and foot stool with tubular steel frame and canvas slings

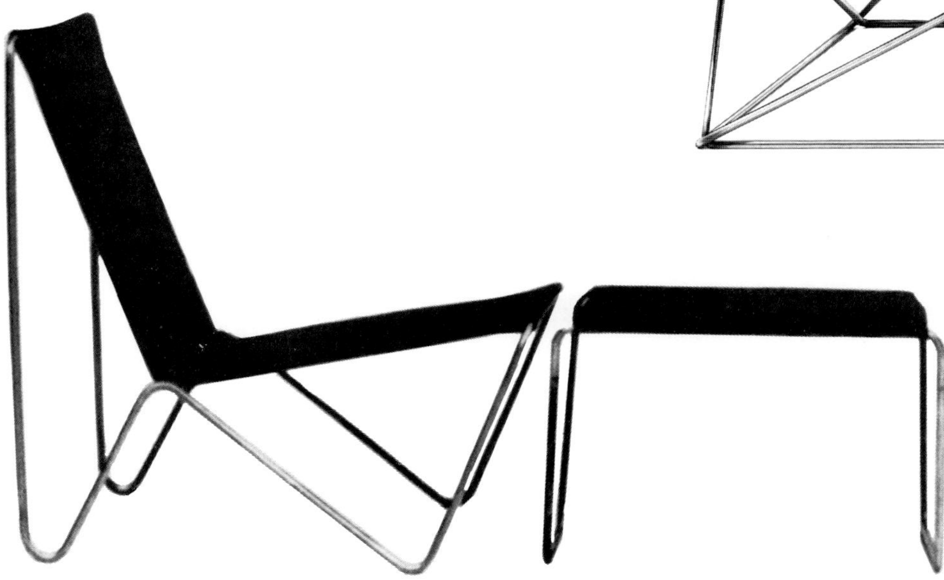

292 **Paulo Mendes da Rocha** 1956 Brazil

Armchair with lacquered tubular steel frame and leather slings

293 **Rolf Gutmann** 1954 Switzerland

Folding lounge chair with tubular steel frame and canvas slings

294 **Poul Kjaerholm** 1952 Denmark
Easy chair with steel frame, corded seat and back

295 **Hendrick van Keppel, Taylor Green** c. 1950 USA
Lounge chair and footstool with tubular steel frame and corded seat

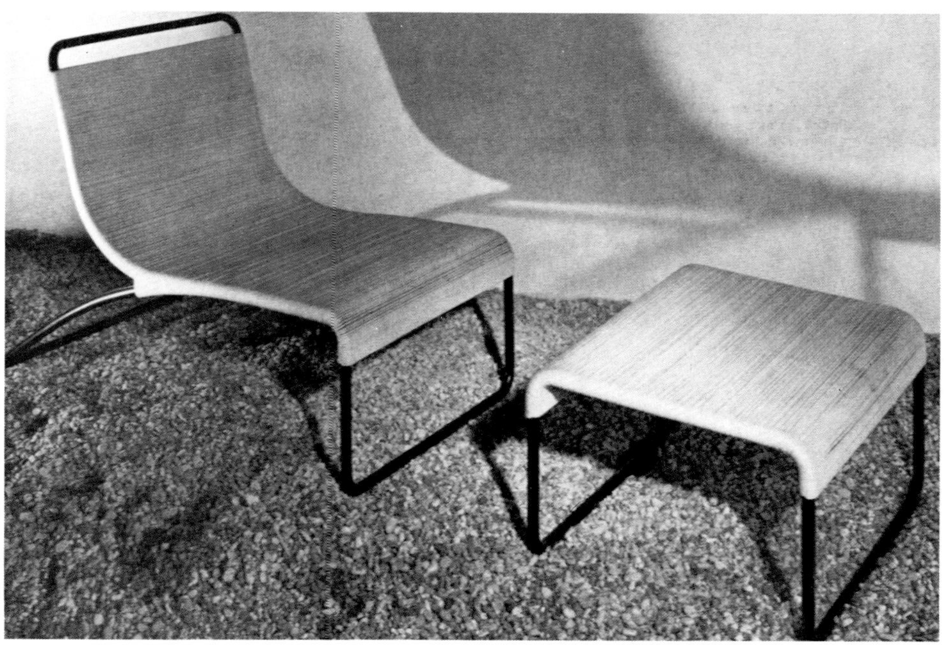

296 **Hans Eichenberger** 1957 Switzerland
Lounge chair with chrome-plated tubular steel frame and rubber webbing

297 **Maija-Liisa Komulainen** 1952 Finland
Easy chair with tubular steel frame and fabric slings

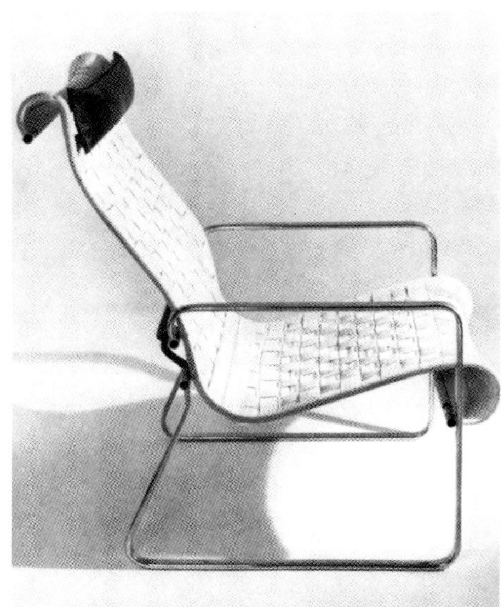

298 **Marco Zanuso, Richard Sapper** 1964 Italy/Germany

Easy chair "Fourline" with metal frame, seat and back of fabric or leather joined by hinges and equipped with sewed-in metal springs. Seat is adjustable, allowing four different body positions

299 **Osvaldo Borsani** 1961 Italy

Armchair with spring metal frame, foam-rubber padding covered with fabric, plastic, or leather

302 **Court Noxon** 1957 Canada

Easy chair "7957" with sectional steel frame, seat and back with rubber webbing and reversible cushions

303 **Florence Knoll** c. 1954 USA

Easy chair "51" with metal base, seat and back with polyfoam upholstery

304 **Alf Svensson** c. 1951 Sweden

Easy chair with steel tube frame and loose cushions

300	301
302	303
304	

◁ 300 **William Armbruster** c. 1950 USA
Easy chair with frame of square steel tubing, fabric straps and loose leather-covered polyfoam cushions

◁◁ 301 **William Armbruster** 1958 USA
Easy chair "MS-951 B" with polished bronze frame and loose cushions

305+306 **William Katavolos, Ross Littell, Douglas Kelley** 1952/53 USA
Chairs with chrome-plated and black enameled steel frames and leather seats

307 **William Katavolos, Ross Littell, Douglas Kelley** c. 1952 USA
Easy chair with chrome-plated steel frame and leather-covered polyfoam upholstery on fabric straps

308 **Herbert Hirche** 1961 Germany
Easy chair "562", armchair "561", and stool "563" with square tubular steel frames in lacquer finish, polyfoam upholstery

309 **Herbert Hirche** c. 1950 Germany
Chair with frame of chrome-plated steel, fabric straps and loose cushions

310 **Robert Haussmann** 1955 Switzerland
Collapsible easy chair with flat steel spring frame, leather straps and loose cushions covered in leather

311 **Cees Braakman** c. 1952 Netherlands
Easy chair with frame of lacquered steel tube

312 **Herbert Hirche** 1953 Germany
Easy chair with steel tube frame and polyfoam upholstery

313+314 **George Nelson** c. 1953 USA
Lounge chairs with chrome-plated steel frames and polyfoam upholstery

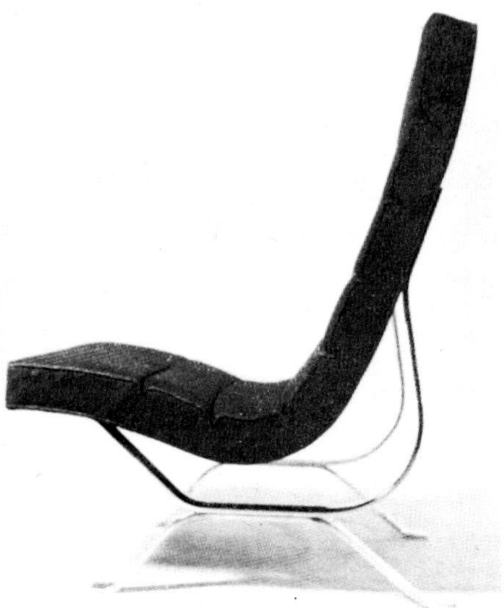

315 **Nicos Zographos** 1959 USA
Chair "301" with stainless steel frame, seat and back of plywood with polyfoam upholstery and leather cover

316 **Poul Kjaerholm** 1956 Denmark
Easy chair "22" with chrome-plated flat steel frame, seat and back of wickerwork or with leather slings

317+318 **Poul Kjaerholm** 1953 Denmark
Chair with steel spring frame and molded plywood seat

319 **Poul Kjaerholm** 1968 Denmark
Easy chair "20" with base of chrome-plated steel and oxhide cover

320 **Jan Dranger, Johan Huldt** 1972 Sweden
Easy chair "Stuns" with frame of lacquer-finished tubular steel. Slings and covers of the polyfoam upholstery in canvas or corduroy

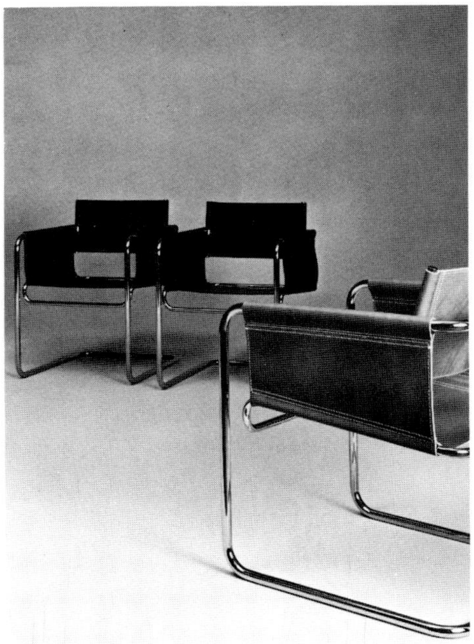

321 **Studio Tipi of Toffoloni-Palange** 1971 Italy
Armchair "Z-22" with frame and seating support of chrome-plated tubular steel. Slings in leather

322 **Esko Pajamies** 1971 Finland
Easy chair "Juju" with frame of chrome-plated or lacquer-finished tubular steel, removable fabric slings and loose cushions

323 **Giorgio Decursu** 1971 Italy
Easy chair "Cetra" with frame of tubular steel in mat or chrome-plated finish. Detachable upholstery with leather or fabric covers

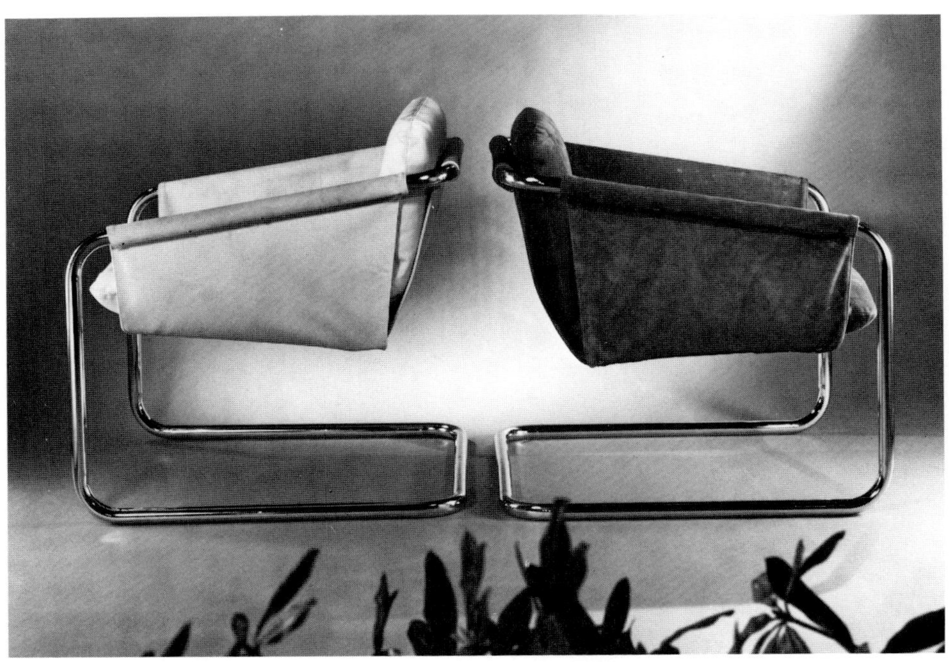

324 **Frank Mingis** 1972 USA
Easy chair "Premier" with frame of chrome-plated tubular steel. Covers of polyfoam cushions and slings in canvas or suede

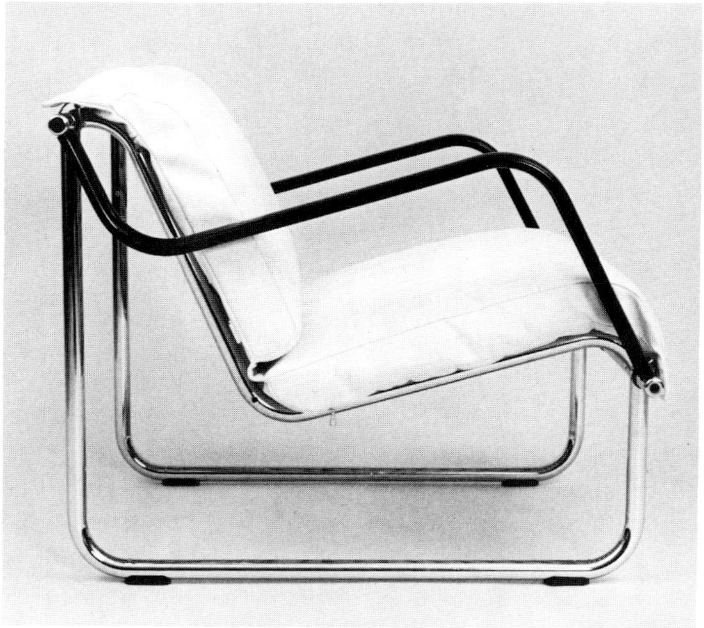

325 **Ueli Berger** 1960 Switzerland

Collapsible chair "BE 60" with chrome-plated steel tube frame and leather or canvas slings

326 **Yrjö Kukkapuro** 1971 Finland

Collapsible easy chair "Remmi" with frame of chrome-plated or stove-enamelled tubular steel. Leather-covered cushions on rubber straps. Chairs can be combined to sofas

327 **Antonello Mosca** 1970 Italy

Easy chair "Attico" with frame of chrome-plated tubular steel and leather seat slings

328 **Jan des Bouvrie** 1973 Netherlands

Easy chair "740" with frame of chrome-plated tubular steel and canvas seat slings with polyfoam upholstery

329 + 330 **Arne Jacobsen** 1971 Denmark

Seating range comprising single easy chairs, sofas composed of several elements, and circular sofas; frames of chrome-plated tubular steel, polyfoam upholstery with fabric covers

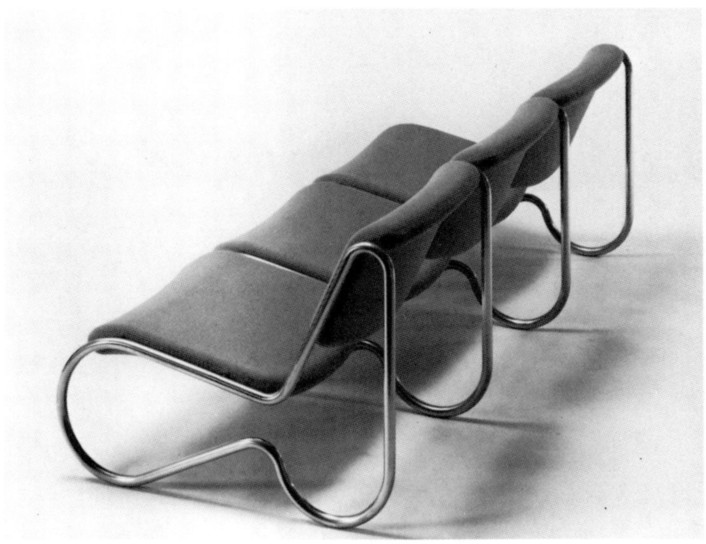

331 **Jonathan De Pas, Donato D'Urbino, Paolo Lomazzi** 1970 Italy

Easy chair "Duecavalli" with frame of chrome-plated tubular steel to which the canvas seat is fixed by rubber rings. Detachable upholstery with fabric covers

332 **Jürgen Lange** 1972 Germany

Easy chair "1011" with frame of chrome-plated tubular steel. Seat sling in black canvas, polyfoam upholstery

334 **Conran Design Group** 1969 Great Britain

Seating range "Terminus Seating" with seat-back unit of molded laminated plywood with polyfoam upholstery, frame of chrome-plated tubular steel. Single chairs, also with armrests and high back, can be linked to units of any length

333 **Gae Aulenti** 1975 Italy

Armchair "54-S1" with frame of aluminum profiles, loose seat and back cushions with fabric or leather cover

335 **Sergio Asti** 1968/70 Italy

Chair "Charlotte" of chrome-plated or lacquered steel tube with seat covered in velvet or oilcloth

336+337 **Gae Aulenti** 1963 Italy

Furniture series "Locus Solus" including lounge chair "P.G. 02", stool/table "P.G. 01", bench "D.G. 05", and table. Frames of steel tubing in lacquer finish, loose cushions with printed patterns

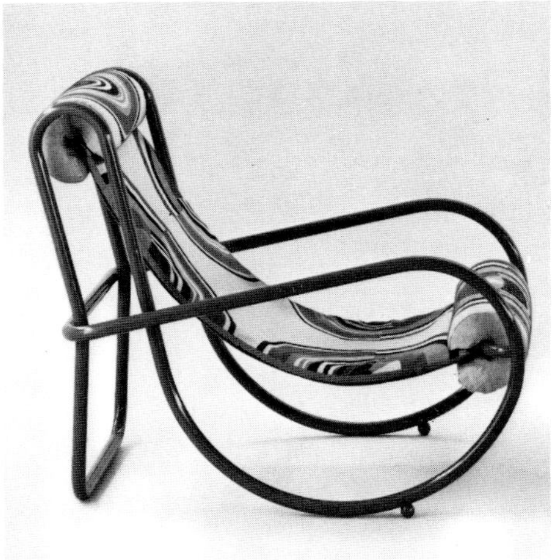

337

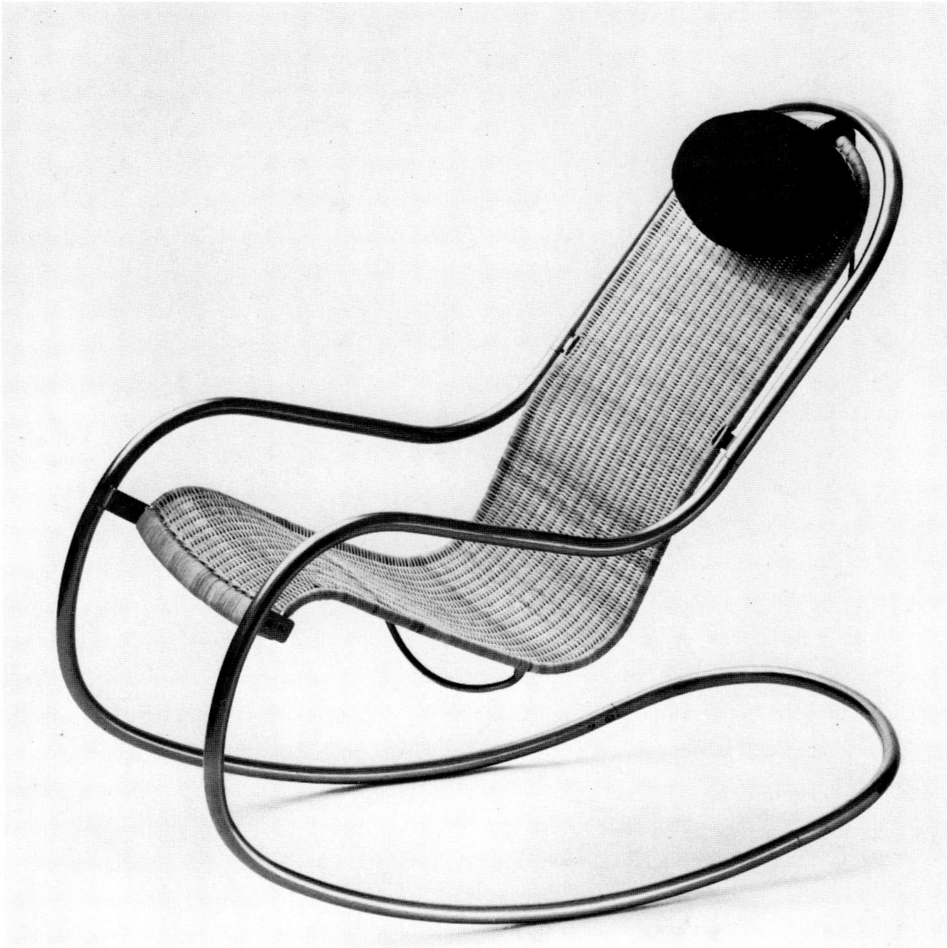

338 **Sigurd Persson** 1967 Sweden
Rocking chair with tubular steel frame and rattan seat

339 **Bartolucci, Waldheim** c. 1950 USA
Lounge chair with aluminum tube frame and canvas slings

340 **Pierre Guariche** 1963 France
Collapsible lounge chair with frame of chrome-plated steel tubing and black imitation leather slings

342 **George Nelson** 1957 USA

Armchair with chrome-plated tubular steel frame, seat and high back of molded plywood with polyfoam cushions

341 **Eero Saarinen** 1945–48 USA

Armchair "Womb 70" and ottoman "74" with chrome-plated tubular steel frame and molded plastic shell, fabric-covered polyfoam upholstery, loose cushions

343 **Charles Eames** 1957 USA

Lounge chair "670" and ottoman "671" on cast aluminum swivel base, rosewood veneer molded plywood frame with leather covered polyfoam and down upholstery

344 **Jørn Utzon** 1969 Denmark

Easy chair "8101" and footstool "8110" of molded laminated wood; chrome-plated tubular steel frame, polyfoam upholstery with fabric cover

345 **Yrjö Kukkapuro** 1965 Finland

Lounge chair "Karuselli" with seat shell and swivel base of fiberglass; seat suspended by means of a steel spring. Polyfoam upholstery with leather cover

346 **Charles Eames** 1960 USA
"Lobby Chair 675" with chrome-plated cast aluminum frame, black leather upholstery

347 **Charles Eames** 1958 USA
Lounge chair "682" with cast aluminum frame and plastic-covered upholstery

348 **Richard Sapper** 1978/79 Germany ▷
"Sapper Collection" multiple seating system. Seat frames of molded steel profile, polyfoam upholstery covered with fabric or leather; steel bases, height adjustable, revolving and tipping devices, casters; with or without armrests

349 **Charles Pollock** 1965 USA

Armchair "1255" on aluminum pedestal with or without swivel. Black plastic seat shell, polyfoam upholstery

350 **Mauser – Hircheteam** 1976 Germany

Office chair "Serie 180", multiple seating system, with our without swivel, height adjustable; spring frames to be combined with different types of bases; polyfoam upholstery covered with leather or fabric

351 **Hircheteam – W. Müller-Limmroth** 1978 Germany

"Ergomat 190", office chair developed according to medical and ergonomical researches. Inside mechanism of hinges, each position can be fixed

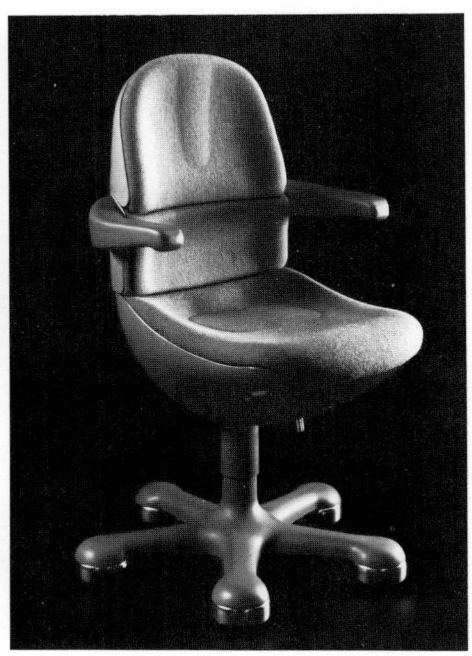

352+353 **Charles Eames** 1962 USA

"Eames Tandem Seating 2600", multiple seating system with two to ten seats for single and double rows. Legs and seat frames of polished cast aluminum; T-shaped support beam and back spreader of black painted steel. Suspended upholstery of black plastic

354 **Richard Sapper** 1978/79 Germany

"Sapper Collection" multiple seating system. Seat frames of molded steel profile, polyfoam upholstery covered with fabric or leather; legs of polished cast aluminum, support rails of black painted steel. Also with armrests and matching table tops (see also ill. 348)

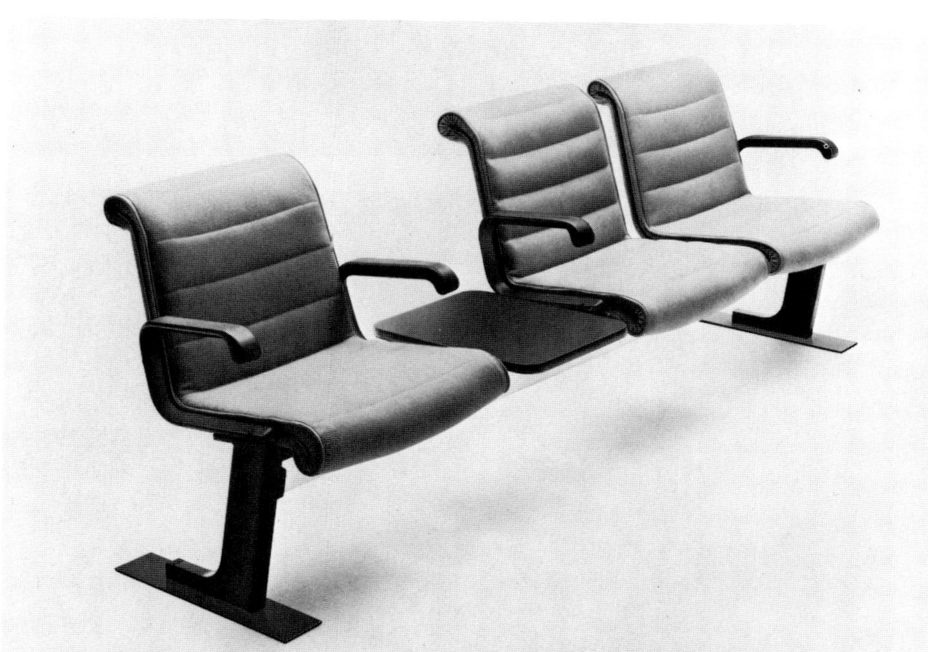

356 **Friso Kramer** 1968 Netherlands ▷

Seating system "1200" combined of two-seated shells of glass-reinforced polyester which can be linked to any length by means of tubes incorporated in the cast aluminum frames

△ 355 **Geoffrey D. Harcourt** 1969 Great Britain
"Multiple Seating" range with seat shells of molded plywood and polyfoam upholstery, covers in leather or fabric. Anodized aluminum fixtures, support rails of black painted steel. Also with armrests and matching table tops

▽ 357+358 **Giancarlo Piretti** 1969 Italy
Seating system "Axis 3000" with frames of cast aluminum; seat and back veneered in oak, walnut, beech, rosewood, or with upholstery. Matching table tops. Elements are fixed to a supporting steel rail by means of clips and special screws

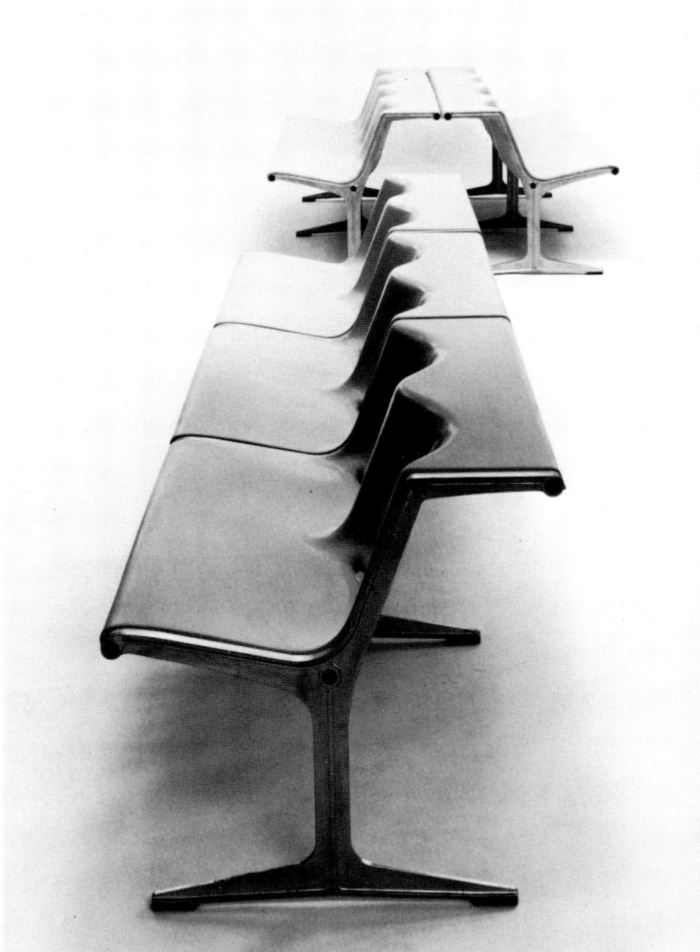

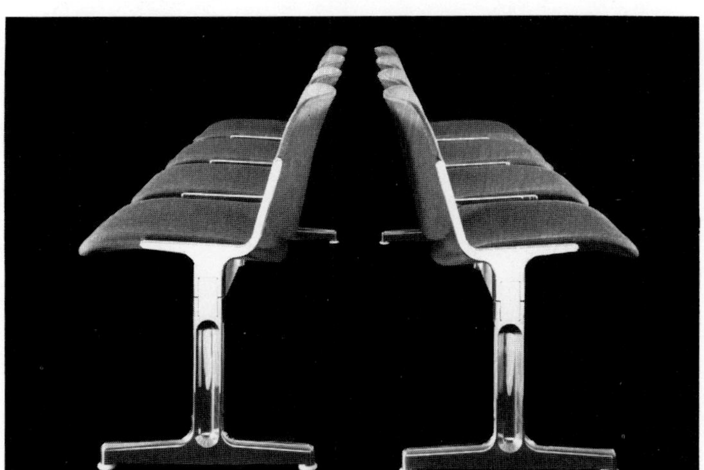

359 **George Kasparian** 1960 USA

Modular seating arrangement "Multalum" with frames of anodized aluminum, polyfoam upholstery. Seats with or without backs

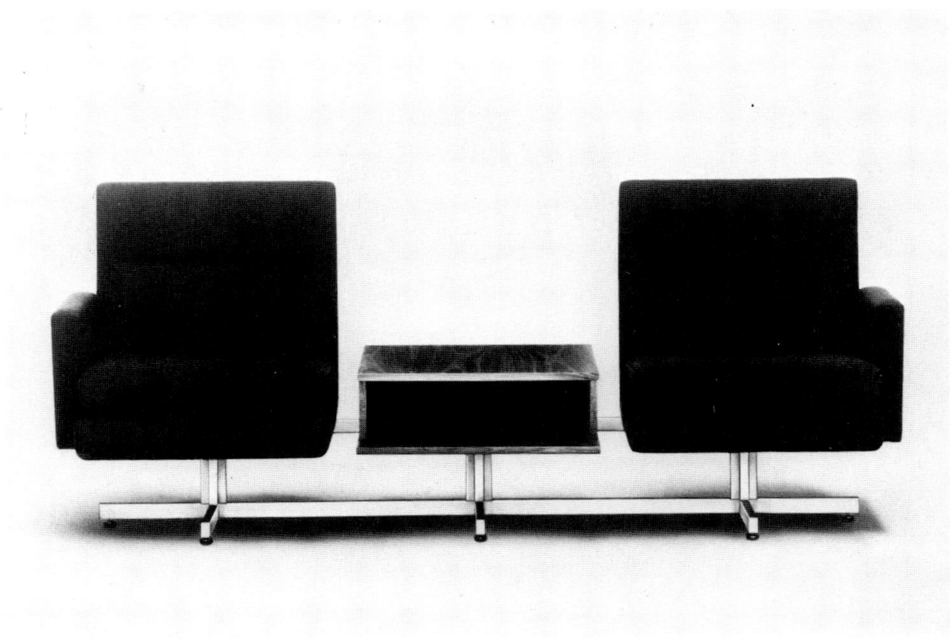

360 **George Kasparian** 1962 USA

Modular seating arrangement "X-ALUM" with cross-shaped frames of anodized aluminum, polyfoam upholstery over rubber webbing, loose cushions. Various components: seats with or without backs and armrests, table tops, and drop-in units

361 **Werner Heumann, George Kasparian** 1964 USA

"Kolum Series" multiple seating allowing a great variety of combinations. Bases of anodized aluminum, seat shells of fiberglass with polyfoam upholstery, loose cushions

362 **Verner Panton** 1959 Sweden

Seating range "853/854" with frames of chrome-plated flat steel and upholstery

363 **Ernst Moeckl** 1962 Germany

Range of combination furniture with bases of anodized flat oval aluminum tubing and linking devices. Wooden parts of walnut or rosewood, polyfoam upholstery over springs

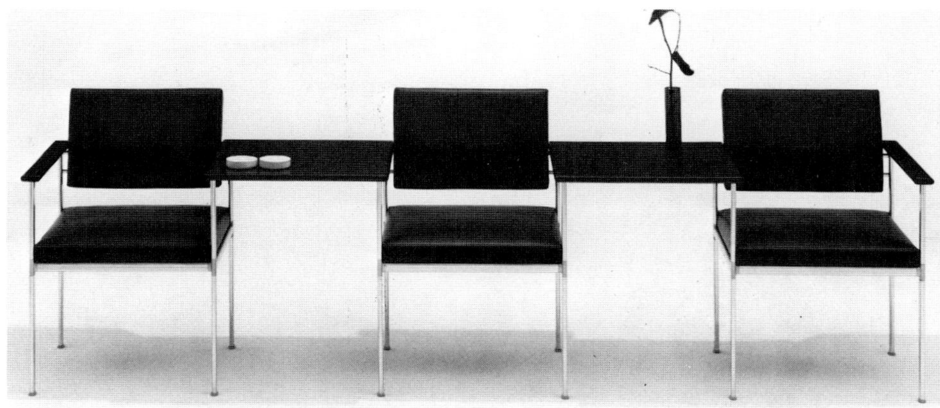

364+365 **Andrew Ivar Morrison, Bruce R. Hannah** 1971 USA

Seating range with four basic types: easy chairs with and without headrest, easy chair with a more upright position for offices, and stools. All models can be assembled to two-, three-, and four-seaters. Suspension seating held together by extruded aluminum edges with plastic-covered cast aluminum frame. Polyfoam upholstery with fabric or leather covers

366 **Pierre Paulin** 1959 France

Easy chair "437" with chrome-plated steel tube frame and double shell of molded laminated wood upholstered in polyfoam

367 **Poul Kjaerholm** 1953 Denmark

Chair with steel tube legs and aluminum seat, also with polyfoam upholstery

368 **Herbert Hirche** 1957 Germany

Chair with tubular steel frame and plastic seat with polyfoam upholstery

369–371 **Arne Jacobsen** 1958 Denmark
"Egg" and "Swan" easy chairs with swivel frames of aluminum or with teak veneered wooden legs, shells of plastic upholstered in polyfoam, covered with fabric, leather, or plastic

372 **Arne Jacobsen** 1958 Denmark
"Bow" easy chair with tubular steel frame, shell of plastic upholstered in polyfoam and covered with leather

369
370 | 371 | 372

373+374 **Günter Ferdinand Ris, Herbert Selldorf** 1969/71 Germany

Easy chair "Sunball" for open-air use. The sphere which can be completely closed consists of two segments, easily movable by balance springs, and a basic shell of fiberglass-reinforced polyester. Seat for one or two persons of polyfoam with fabric cover, can be changed into a daybed. Clamp-on trays, built-in lamp and loudspeakers

375 **Pierre Paulin** 1967 France

Easy chair "300" with glass-fibre shell and removable polyfoam upholstery covered with stretch fabric

376 **Angelo Mangiarotti** 1961 Italy

Easy chair "1110" with cast metal base and shell of foamed polystyrole with fabric cover

377 **Joe Colombo** 1964 Italy

Swivel easy chair "Elda 1005" with plastic shell molded in one piece, detachable upholstery of black leather

378+379 **Dieter Rams** 1962 Germany

Seating range "RZ 62" with shells of fiberglass-reinforced polyester in plastic laminate finish on casters. Loose down cushions with removable leather or fabric covers

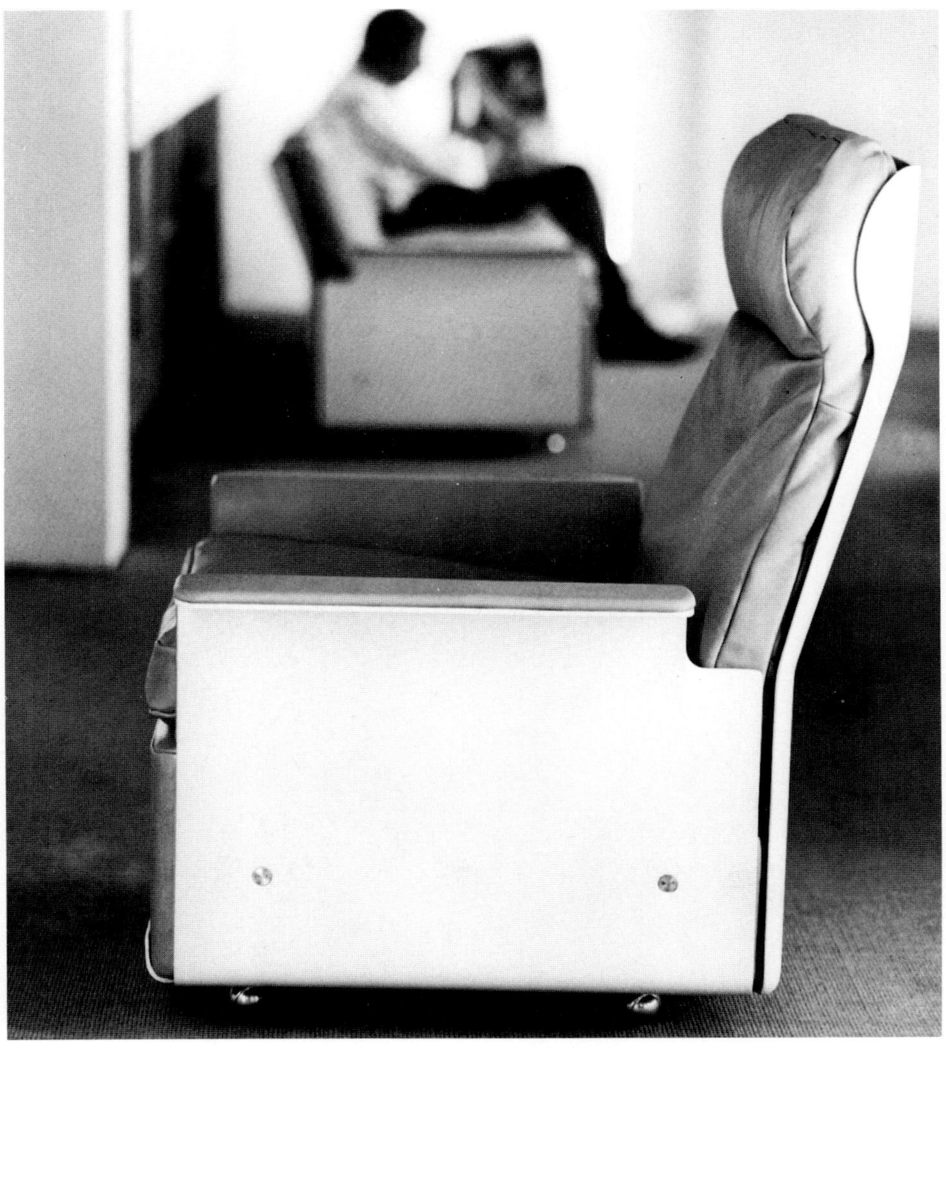

380 **Estelle and Erwine Laverne** 1962
USA

"Champagne" chair and coffee table with cast aluminum pedestals; swivel chair with seat shell of clear transparent plastic and loose cushion, table top of marble

381+382 **Estelle and Erwine Laverne** 1960
USA

Chairs "Daffodil", "Jonquil", "Buttercup", and "Lily" of clear transparent plastic, loose cushions

383–385 **Eero Saarinen** 1956/57 USA
Single pedestal armchair "150", chair "151", and stool "152" with cast aluminum bases, seat shells of fiberglass-reinforced polyester with polyfoam upholstery, loose cushions

386 + 387 **Helmut Bätzner** 1964 Germany

Stacking and linking chair "BA 1171" of fiberglass-reinforced polyester

388 + 389 **André Vandenbeuck** 1967 France

Chair and easy chair "Unica I and II" of fiberglass

391 + 392 **Joe Colombo** 1965 Italy ▷

Stacking and linking chair "4868" of plastic with added feet of several heights to meet varying needs

393 **Vico Magistretti** 1971 Italy ▷▷▷

Chair "Gaudi" of reinforced resin

390 **Vico Magistretti** 1968 Italy
Stacking chair "Selene" of fiberglass-reinforced polyester

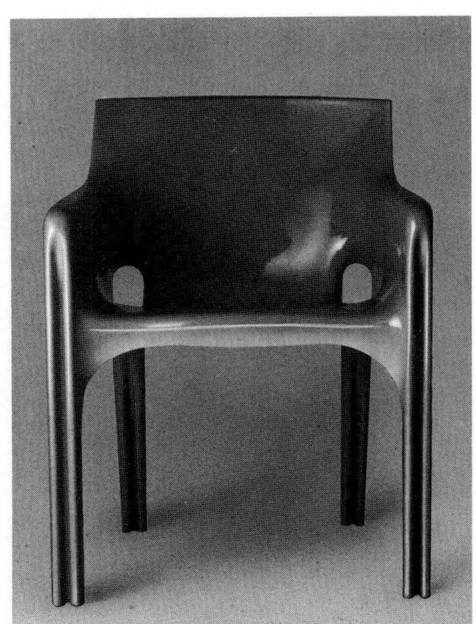

394 **Verner Panton** c. 1954 Denmark
Chairs "275/276" of molded laminated wood, stained or lacquered

395 **Verner Panton** 1960 Denmark
Stacking chair of fiberglass-reinforced polyester

396 **Walter Papst** 1964 Germany
Stackable garden bench "1000" of fiberglass-reinforced polyester

397 **Eero Aarnio** 1967 Finland
"Pastilli" chair of glass-reinforced polyester

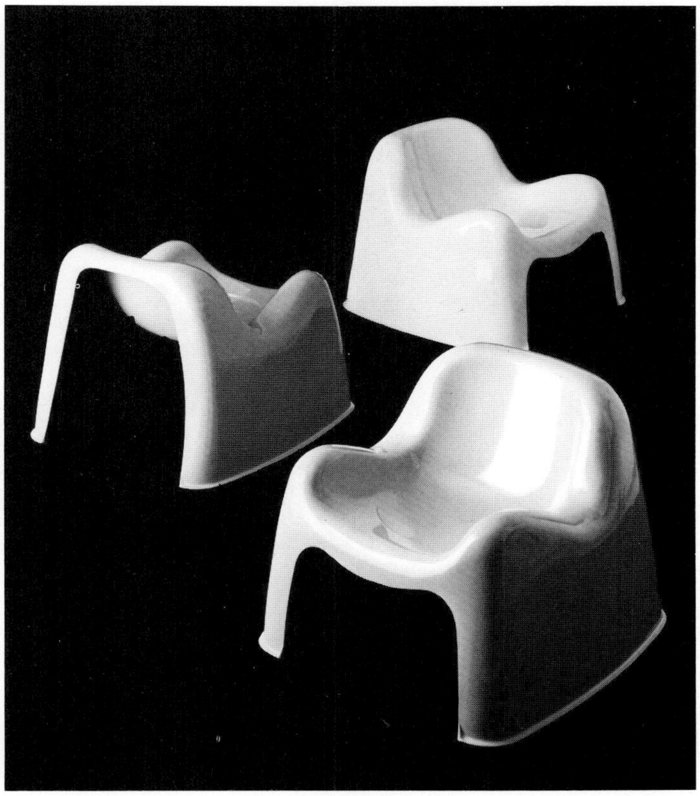

398 **Pierre Paulin** 1969 France
Polyester chair "305"

399 **Sergio Mazza** 1968 Italy
Easy chair "Toga" of fiberglass-reinforced polyester

400 **Sori Yanagi** 1956 Japan
Stacking stool of plastic

401 + 402 **Stacy Dukes** 1970 USA
Stool "Efebo" of plastic

403 **Verner Panton** 1968 Denmark

Seating range "270/271" composed of identical parts of molded laminated plywood with lacquer finish which can be assembled as desired

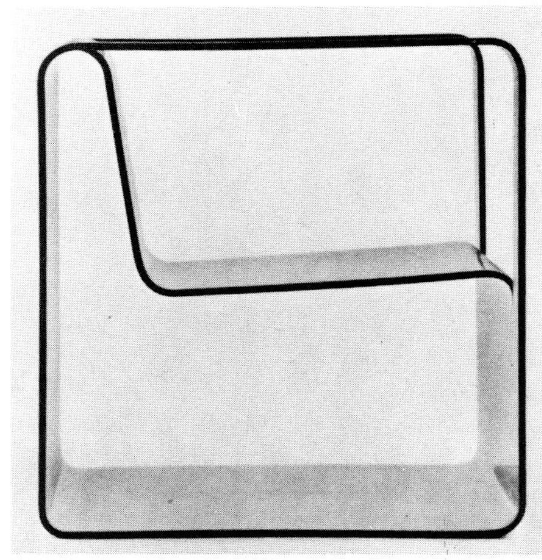

404 + 405 **Heinz Witthoeft** 1967 Germany

"Tail 13", a thermoplastic panel cut molded to form armchair or table

403	404
	405
406	

406 **Grete Jalk** 1963 Denmark

Chair of molded laminated oak, also upholstered

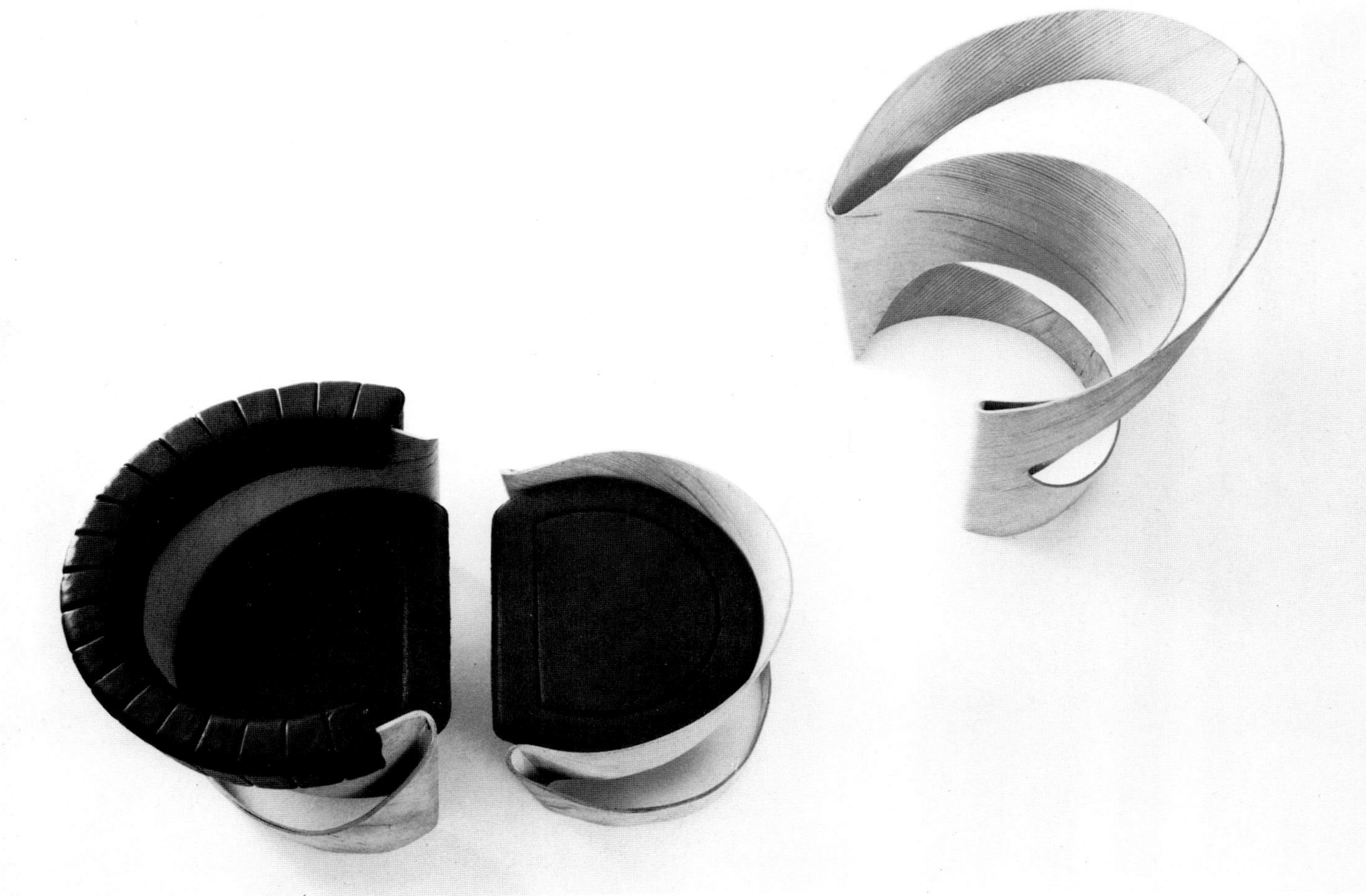

407 **Grete Jalk** 1963 Denmark

Armchairs and ottoman of molded laminated Oregon pine, upholstered

408 **Joe Colombo** 1963 Italy

Easy chair "4801" assembled of three interlocking parts of molded plywood

409 **Motomi Kawakami** 1968 Japan

Lounge chair "Florenza" of molded plastic

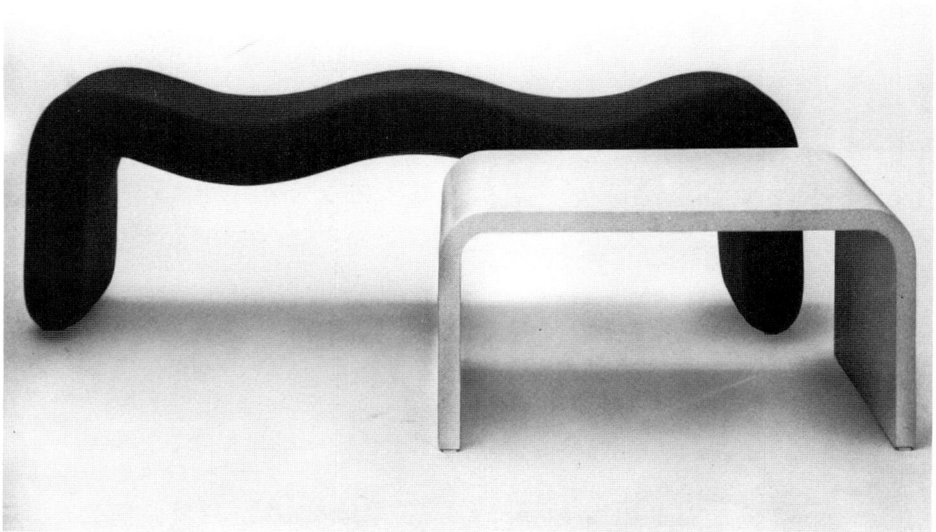

410–412 **Olivier Mourgue** 1965 France

Daybeds and easy chair "Collection Domino" with metal frames, polyfoam upholstery and detachable fabric covers

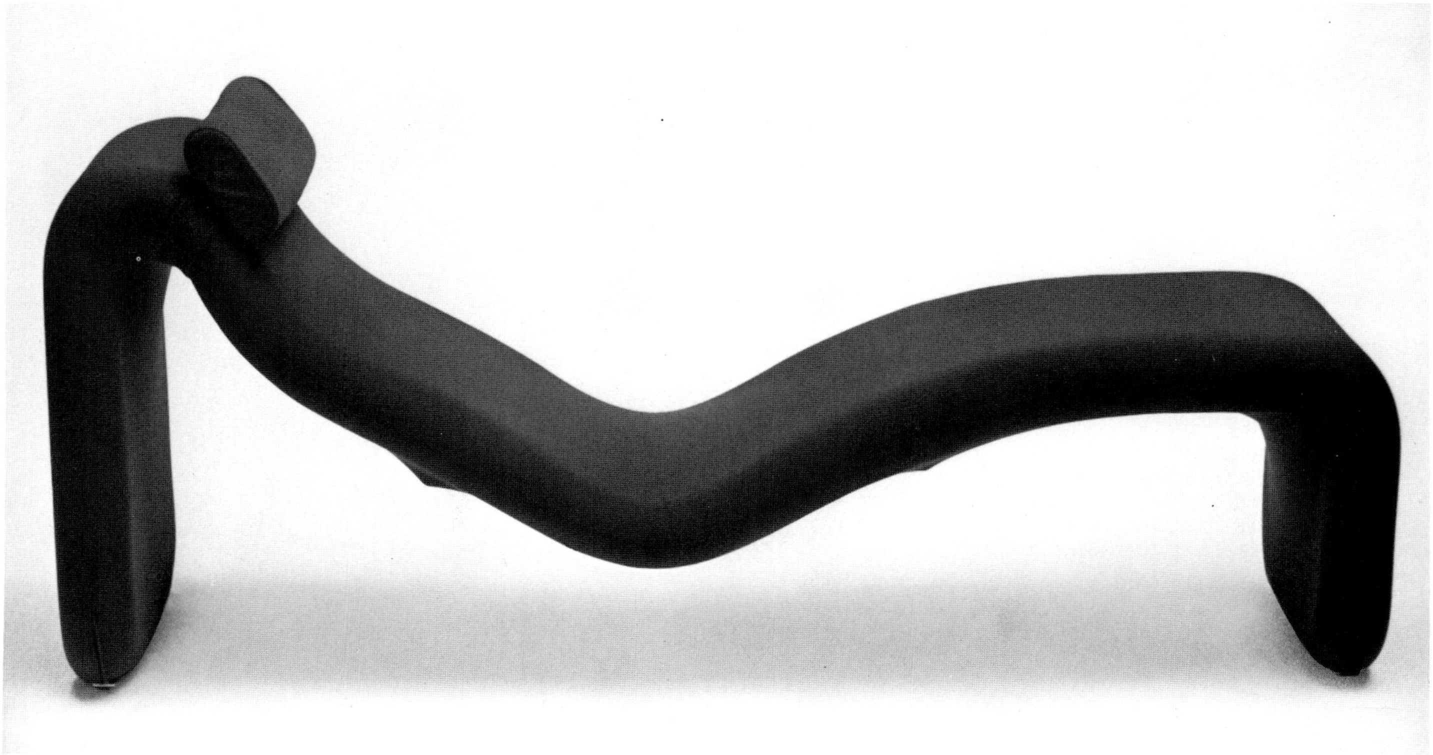

413+414 **Pierre Paulin** 1967 France

Easy chair "577" with frame of metal tubing and rubber straps, polyfoam upholstery

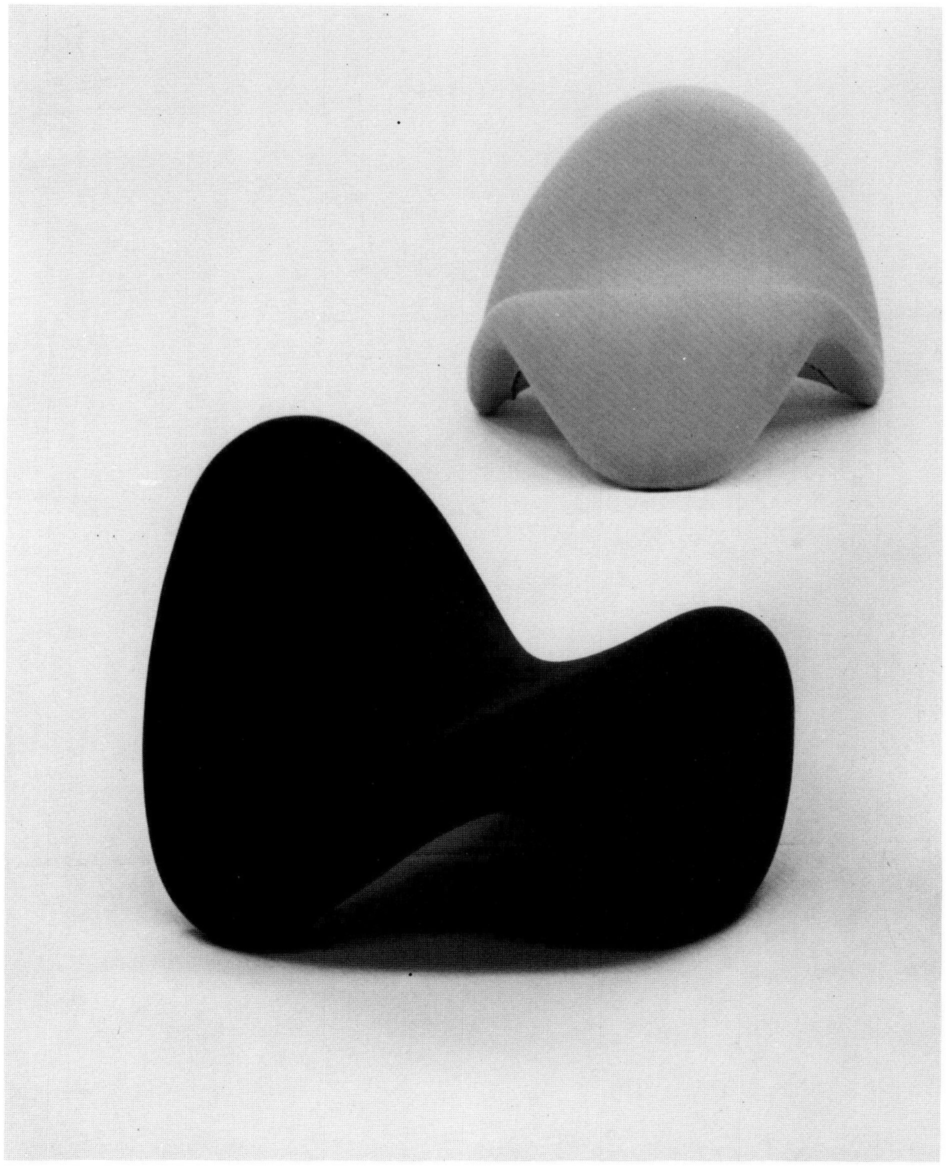

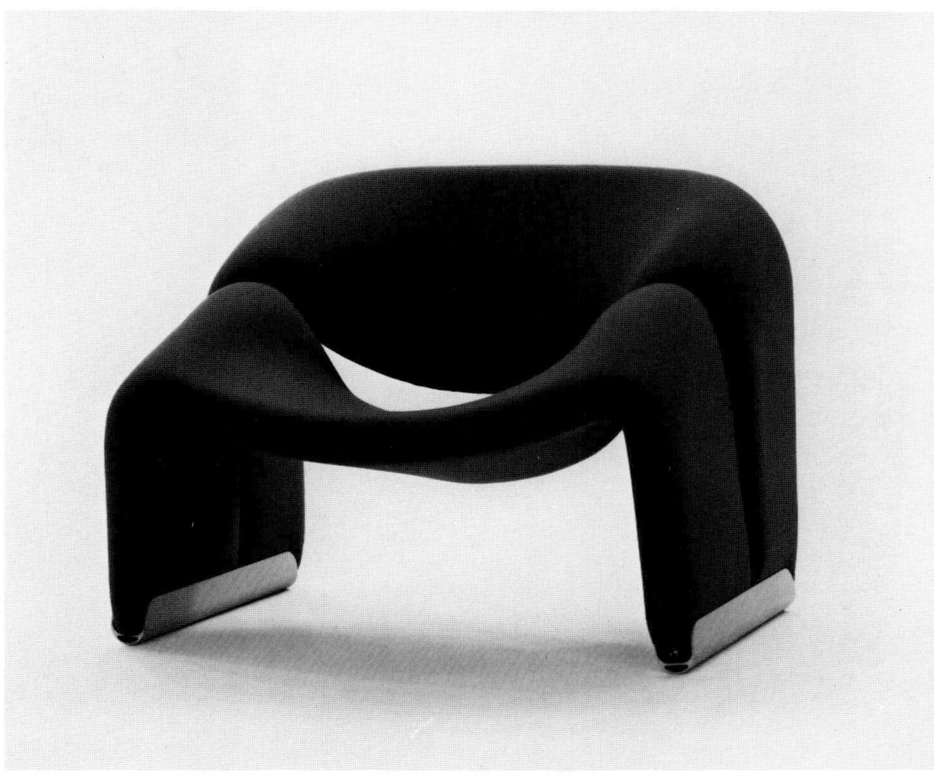

415 **Pierre Paulin** 1972 France

Easy chair "598" with metal chassis and polyfoam upholstery, zip-fastened covers of stretch material. Foot glides in extruded aluminum couple the two elements of the chair. Linking device for connection of several chairs

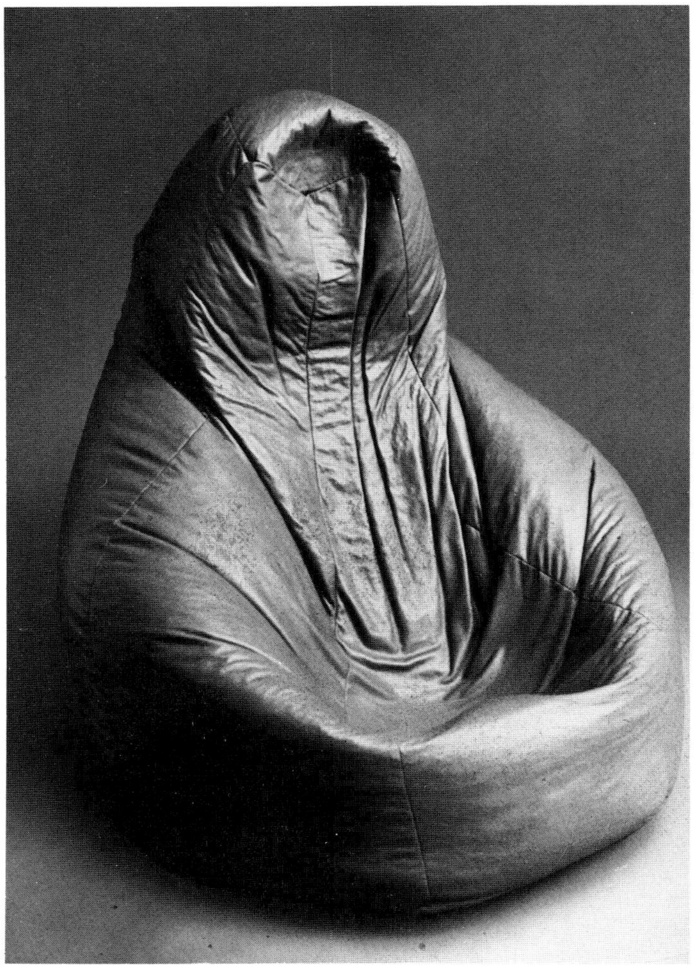

416 **Piero Gatti, Cesare Paolini, Franco Teodoro** 1969 Italy
Bag chair "Sacco" of leather, filled with plastic beads conforming to the body in any position

417 **Carla Solari, Paolo Lomazzi, Jonathan De Pas, Donato D'Urbino** 1967 Italy
Inflatable armchair "Blow" of plastic with electronic welding, suspended seat and headrest

▽ 418+419 **Günter Sulz** 1973 Germany
Seating combination "Canvas" of inflatable plastic cushions with canvas covers. All parts are connected with cords and eye-lets

420 **Gaetano Pesce** 1969 Italy

"Serie UP" seating range consisting of six designs of polyurethene foam covered in stretch fabric. Seats come in a compressed air-tight container and instantly expand into their proper shape when case is opened

421 + 422 **Roger Dean** 1968 Great Britain

"Sea Urchin", a truncated seating sphere of fabric-covered polyfoam

423 **Gruppo A.R.D.I.T.I.** 1972 Italy

Easy chair "Memoria" with basic structure of polyurethene foam and air-tight layer; inside air cavity can be regulated by adjusting valve for optimal sitting position. Various fabric covers

420
421
422
423

424 **George Nelson** 1963 USA
Sofa "Sling" with frame and base of chrome-plated steel. Sections of underframe are joined by epoxy resin. Loose down and polyfoam cushions with leather cover

Seating Arrangements, Sofas, and Beds

In the past three decades the sofa has changed from the familiar classic model into a seating landscape. This means that it has developed from the exactly contoured piece of furniture on four legs into an amorphous and variable collection of elements that can be grouped according to one's needs and mood. No other type of furniture has experienced a comparable metamorphosis. More important than the changes in construction and materials that can be noticed here is the completely different use that one of the oldest items of furniture we know has been put to. The change in lifestyle during recent years can be seen very clearly in the sofa. Like the table but unlike the chair, the sofa is an object meant for use by several people; it is therefore a "communal piece of furniture". A sofa only fulfills its purpose properly when at least two people are using it at the same time. New customs are reflected in such a piece of furniture faster than elsewhere. The preference for a more relaxed attitude and for less constrained behavior, but also the sacrificing of "conversation" in favor of free attitudes-all this can been seen in the example of the sofa. Because the seating height has been reduced, we have placed ourselves lower, and the item of furniture naturally as well. It is no longer the symbol of an important ritual activity that it once was. On the contrary, its new form represents a very direct expression of modern customs. The interchangeable order of movable seating elements can be interpreted as being a result of the increasing dismantling of hierarchies and as a simile of continuous change in our society. Even if one does not want to go that far, it must be admitted that the way we deal with each other in private is different from what it used to be and this aspect of our lives is characterized in the furniture we use.

The sofa designed by George Nelson in 1963 (ill. 424) was still very much indebted to the classic form. For a long time it was exhibited in the Museum of Modern Art in New York as one of the very few modern articles of furniture. The object is without doubt beautiful and, as regards its structure, logical as well. It expresses convincingly that it is a technically conceived object.

Its aesthetics are those of an object coupling two sorts of sensuality: the cold, dominating sensuality of steel tubes with the warm sensuality of dark leather. However, the large, encompassing bow form, which subordinates everything, not without strictness, to a structural idea, remains dominant. It is a matter for consideration whether this is really a good idea and if it does not give the impression of being superimposed. This design is, however, a clear attempt at connecting the traditional idea of a sofa with modern preferences and ways of thinking. At the same time it was not possible for it to avoid giving the impression that the basic idea behind this piece of furniture came from elsewhere, from architecture and car design for instance.

The example of the adjustable car seat has had a stimulating effect; several items indicate this clearly (ills. 485, 486, 499, 501, 502).

The seating snake by JOrn Utzon (ills. 466,467) was a new departure for the sofa. The principle of serial arrangement surprises at first but it also makes sense. The idea that a piece of furniture can grow and decrease in size and that it can behave like an organic being was unusual and led to a revision of old attitudes. Organic associations had already been included covertly, but never as directly as here.

425 **Peter Hvidt, Orla Mølgaard Nielsen** c. 1952 Denmark

Sofa with wooden frame and polyfoam upholstery

426 **Alf Svensson** c. 1953 Sweden

Ottomans "Corner", also to be used as tables, with wooden frame and polyfoam upholstery

427 **Peter Hvidt, Orla Mølgaard Nielsen** 1955 Denmark

Sofa with frame of wood and seat support of rubber straps, metal fittings, seat and back upholstered, removable arm-rests

428 **Karl Erik Ekselius** c. 1957 Sweden

Sofa with wooden frame, can be converted to a bed

429 **George Kasparian** c. 1951 USA
Sofa/bed "700" with wooden legs, upholstered seat and back of wood

430+431 **Hans Olsen** 1955 Denmark
Bench system with removable polyfoam upholstered seats and table tops

432 **Edward J. Wormley** c. 1951 USA
Sofa with detachable legs of brass or aluminum, polyfoam upholstery

433 **Florence Knoll** c. 1950 USA

Settee and sofa with black lacquered metal tube frame and polyfoam upholstery

436 **George Nelson** c. 1957 USA ▷

"Modular Combination" with chrome-plated metal bases and interchangeable inserts: upholstered chairs, table tops of white plastic, chests of drawers in walnut or rosewood

434 **Norman Cherner** c. 1951 USA

Sofa/bed "300" with metal frame and polyfoam upholstery

435 **Florence Knoll** c. 1955 USA

Sofa "67" and lounge chair "65A" with chrome-plated square steel frame, polyfoam cushions over springs

▷ 437 **George Nelson** 1952 USA

Seating range with metal bench frame and interchangeable elements: seats with rubber webbing and loose cushions, table tops with plastic laminate

▽ 438 **Nanna and Jørgen Ditzel** 1961 Denmark

Modular seating range with benchlike frames of wengé and black square tubular steel legs. Polyfoam upholstery, L-shaped seating elements on fiberglass frames, detachable trays of wengé

439 **Edward J. Wormley** 1949 USA
Sofa "4907 A" with frame of maple, metal legs, loose cushions with silk covers

440 **William Katavolos, Ross Littell, Douglas Kelley** c. 1952 USA
Sofa with frame of chrome-plated steel, black-enamelled steel rail and polyfoam upholstery

441 **Hans J. Wegner** 1957 Denmark
Sofa "A.P.35/3S" with steel legs, polyfoam upholstery and woolen fabric cover

442 **George Kasparian** 1960 USA
Sofa "KM/108", three- or four-seater, metal or wood frame, loose cushions

443 **Theo Tempelman** 1959 Netherlands
Sofa "18" with frame of square steel or in teak, loose polyfoam cushions with cover in leather or fabric

444 **Pierre Paulin** 1962 France
Sofa "442" with wooden frame on chrome-plated metal base. Loose polyfoam cushions covered in leather or fabric over springs

445 **Charles Eames** 1954 USA

Sofa with folding back and chrome-plated steel base

446 **Charles Eames** 1962 USA

Sofa "RE-204" with base of polished cast aluminum, polyfoam upholstery with black plastic cover

447 **Poul Kjaerholm** 1958 Denmark

Sofa "31" with frames of chrome-plated steel, leather-covered seat, back, and armrests, loose down cushions

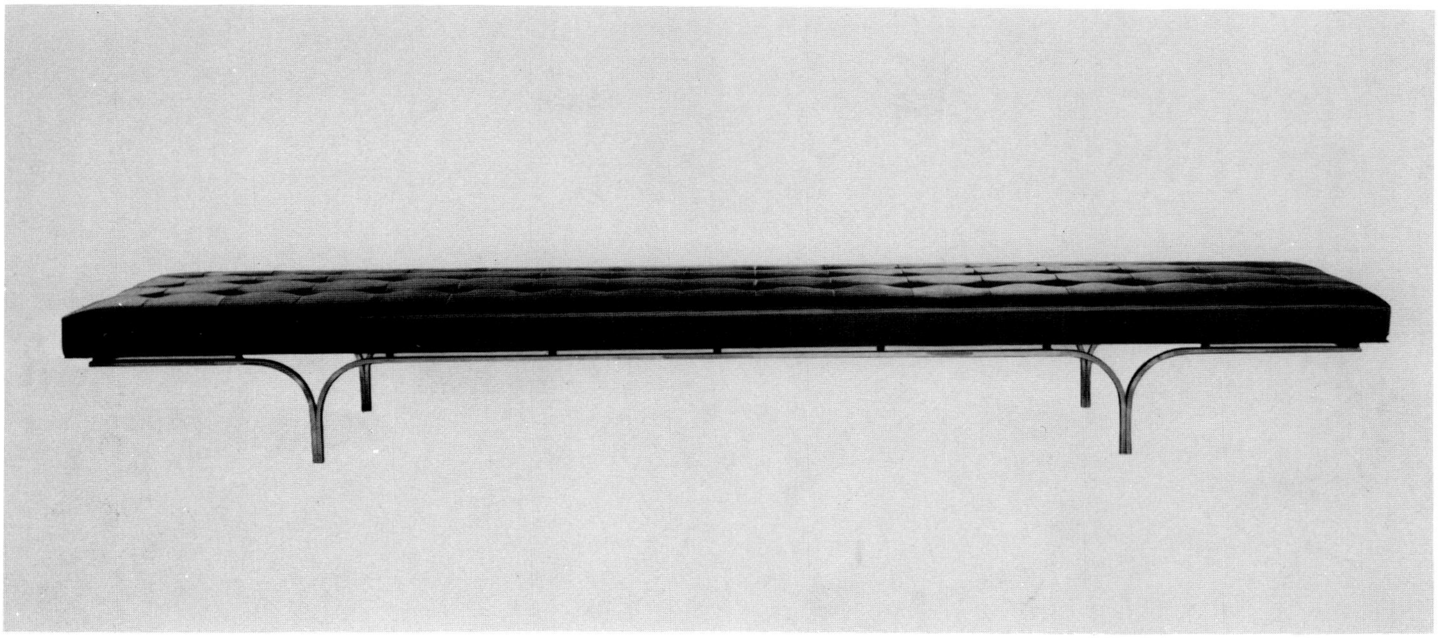

448 **Estelle and Erwine Laverne** 1962
USA
"Philharmonic Suspension Bench" with polished steel frame, polyfoam upholstery with leather or plastic cover

449+450 **Horst Brüning** 1969 Germany
Sofa ".6915" and bench "Systembank" with frames of chrome-plated flat steel hoops, upholstery covered in leather or fabric, table tops in marble, glass, wood, or white plastic laminate. Seats and table tops can be combined to units of various lengths

451 **Horst Brüning** 1968 Germany

Range of furniture, including easy chair "6910", two- and three-seater sofas "6912/6913" and tables, with frames of chrome-plated flat steel hoops in mat finish, upholstery covered in leather or fabric

452 **Frank Gullie** 1963 Great Britain

"Duo Seating, 300 Group" with seating unit which can be converted to form single or double bed; white plastic-laminated coffee table tops. Seat frames of afrormosia on black metal underframes, upholstered cushions over rubber webbing

455 **Arne Jacobsen** 1957 Denmark

Armchair "3000" and sofa "3003" with chrome-plated tubular steel frames and upholstery

456 **Jørn Utzon** 1968 Denmark

Modular furniture system in knockdown construction. Basic structure of nine sizes of U-shaped hoops of triangular-shaped aluminum tubing. Cushions of polyfoam with covers in oxhide or fabric, table tops of plastic laminate. Pieces can be used separately or linked

◁◁ 453 **Roland Rainer** c. 1956 Austria

Armchair "460S" and sofa "462S" with chrome-plated steel frames, loose seat and back cushions

◁ 454 **Alain Richard** 1960 France

Sofa with chrome-plated square steel frame and upholstery

457 + 458 **Adriano Piazzesi** 1970 Italy

Seating group "Okay" with frame structure of chrome-plated tubular steel into which cushions of soft foam are inserted; covers of fabric, leather or plastic. Ottoman converts into a table when glass top is clipped on

459 **Gianfranco Frattini** 1970 Italy

Sofa and easy chair "Sesann" with upholstery of polyfoam on wooden base, covers of leather or fabric, and chrome-plated steel tube base

460 **Gianni Songia** 1963 Italy

Convertible sofa "GS 195" with frame of rosewood and fittings of brass. Polyfoam upholstery covered in leather or fabric

461 **Tobia Scarpa** 1971 Italy

Easy chair and Sofa "Bonanza" with dacron fibres upholstery on plastic seating shell, covers in leather or fabric

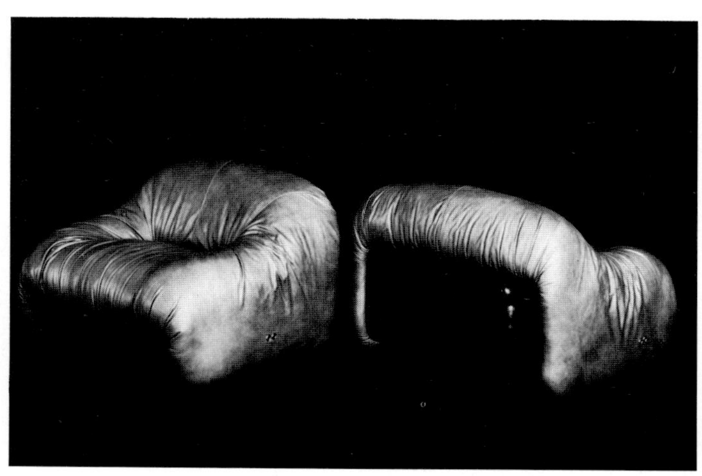

462 **Afra and Tobia Scarpa** 1970 Italy
Seating group "Soriana" with polyfoam upholstery and leather or fabric covers, frame of chrome-plated steel

463–465 **Works Design** 1971 Italy
Sofa "Anfibio" with substructure of steel and polyfoam upholstery, covers in fabric or leather. Frame and mattress are kept in folded position by nylon zippers and leather straps, by opening it changes to a bed

466 | 467
468
469

468 **Dieter Schempp** 1968 Germany

Polyfoam elements that may be combined to form all kinds of seating units and furniture landscapes, removable covers with zippers

469 **Burkhard Vogdherr** 1970/71 Germany

Seating system "VarioPillo" for straight or curved arrangements. Five different elements of polyfoam with varying density on plastic shells with handles. Elements are linked by plastic coupling devices, clamp-on trays

472+473 **Pierre Paulin** 1969 France ▷

Easy chair and ondulating sofa of three fiberglass units which are separately upholstered in polyfoam and are then joined and mounted on a base with casters

474+475 **Joe Colombo** 1969 Italy ▷▷

"Additional System", a seating program consisting of upholstered polyfoam segments in six different sizes, each covered in stretch fabric and mounted on a steel rail to form chairs and sofas of any desired length and shape

◁ 466+467 **Jørn Utzon** 1968 Denmark

Seating system consisting of three basic elements of polyfoam with fabric covers for arrangements in straight or curved lines

470+471 **Marco Zanuso** 1967 Italy ▷

Seating element "Lombrico" with units of fiberglass-reinforced polyester upholstered in polyfoam and covered in fabric may be combined to any length

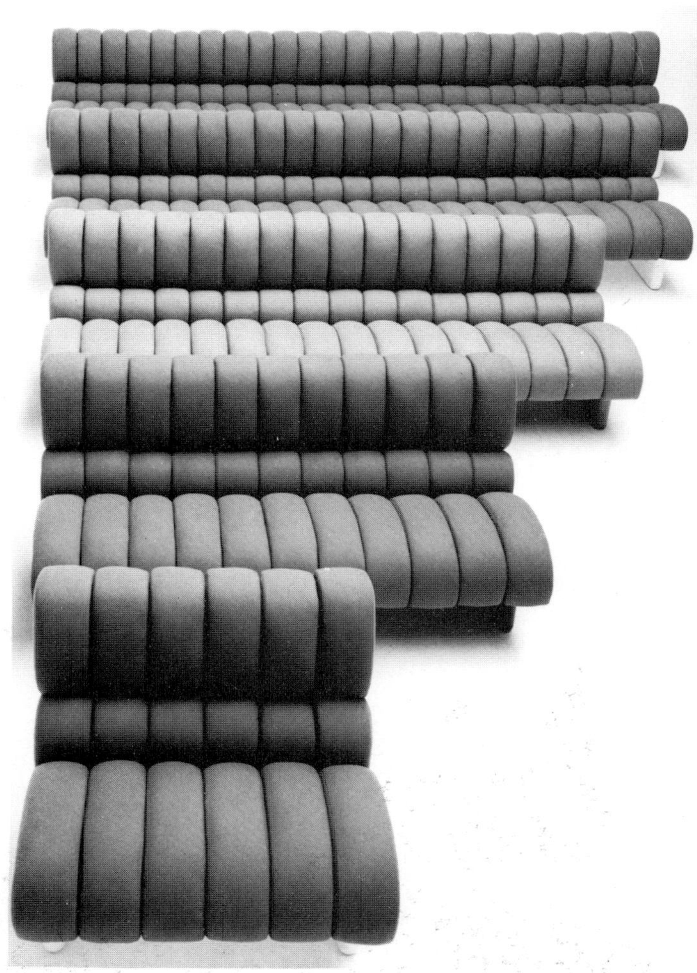

470	471
472	473
474	475

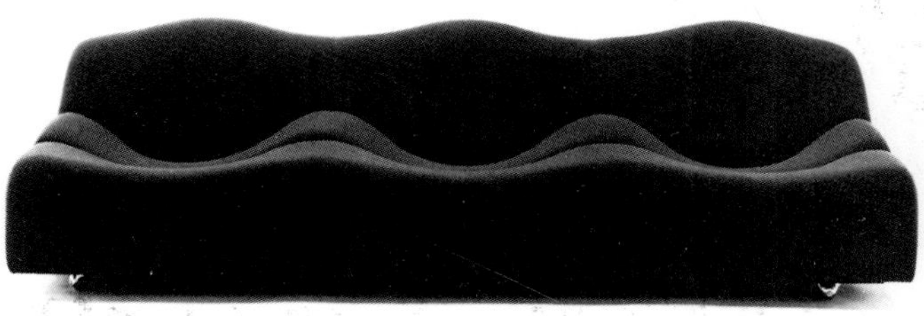

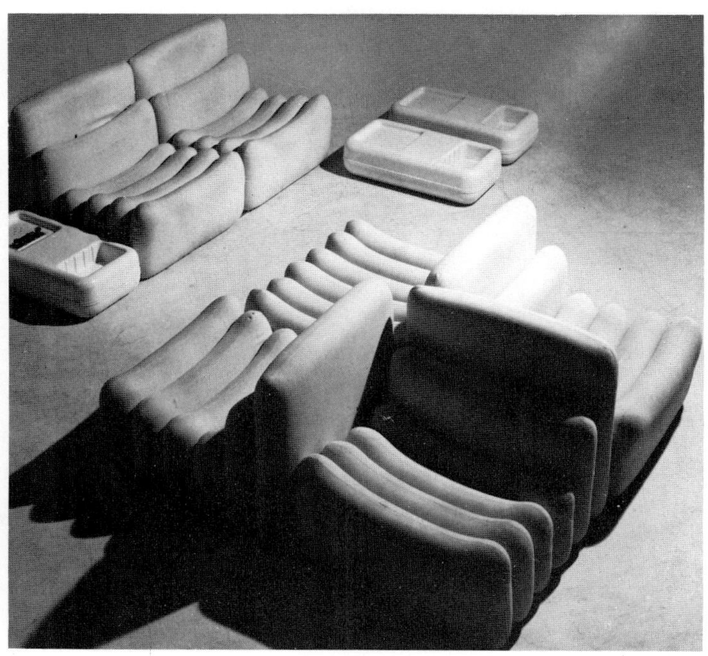

476 **Kazuhide Takahama** 1965 Italy
Easy chair and sofa "Marcel" with polyfoam cushions on aluminum frame

477 **Kazuhide Takahama** 1965 Italy
Easy chair "Suzanne" of polyfoam cushions with base of chrome-plated steel; matching sofa and single chair

478 **Works Design** 1970 Great Britain
"F" range of chairs and ottomans of polyfoam with removable plastic covers. Chairs can be linked by special zipping device

480+481 **Rodolfo Bonetto** 1971 Italy ▷
Linking easy chair "Boomerang" with chrome-plated steel frame, polyfoam upholstery and covers in fabric

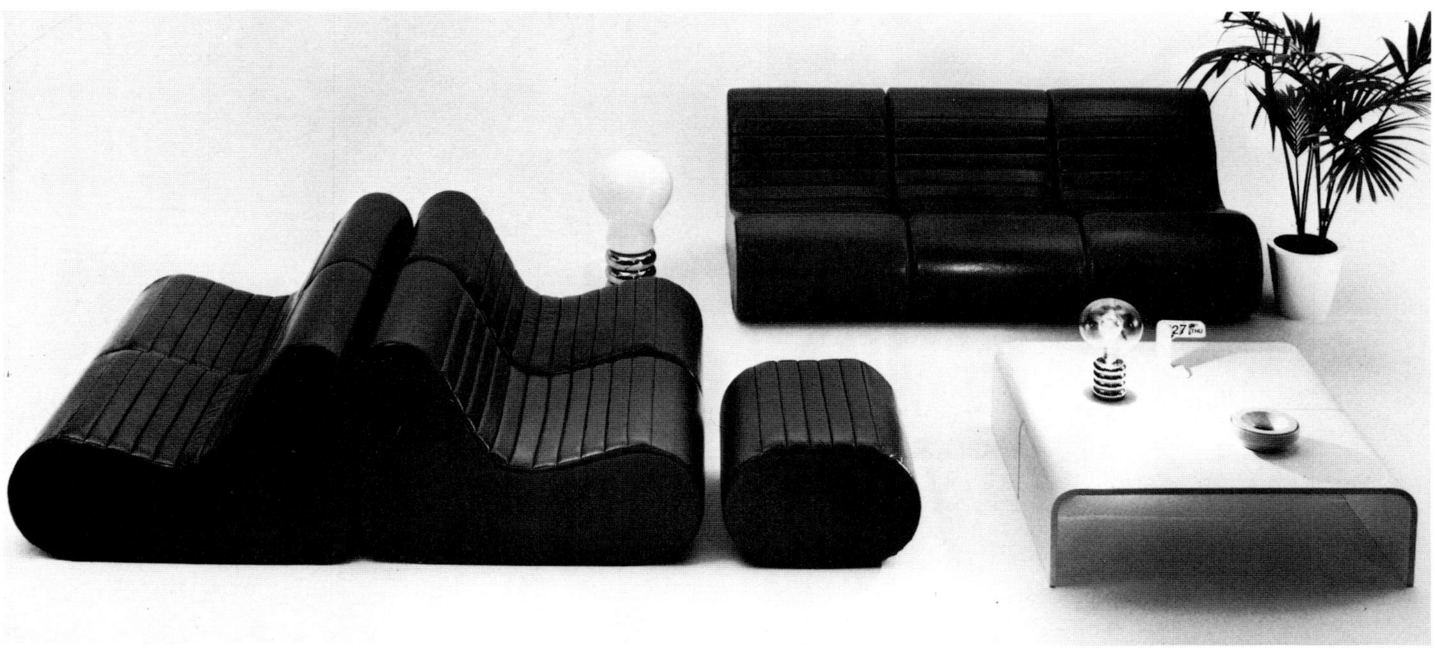

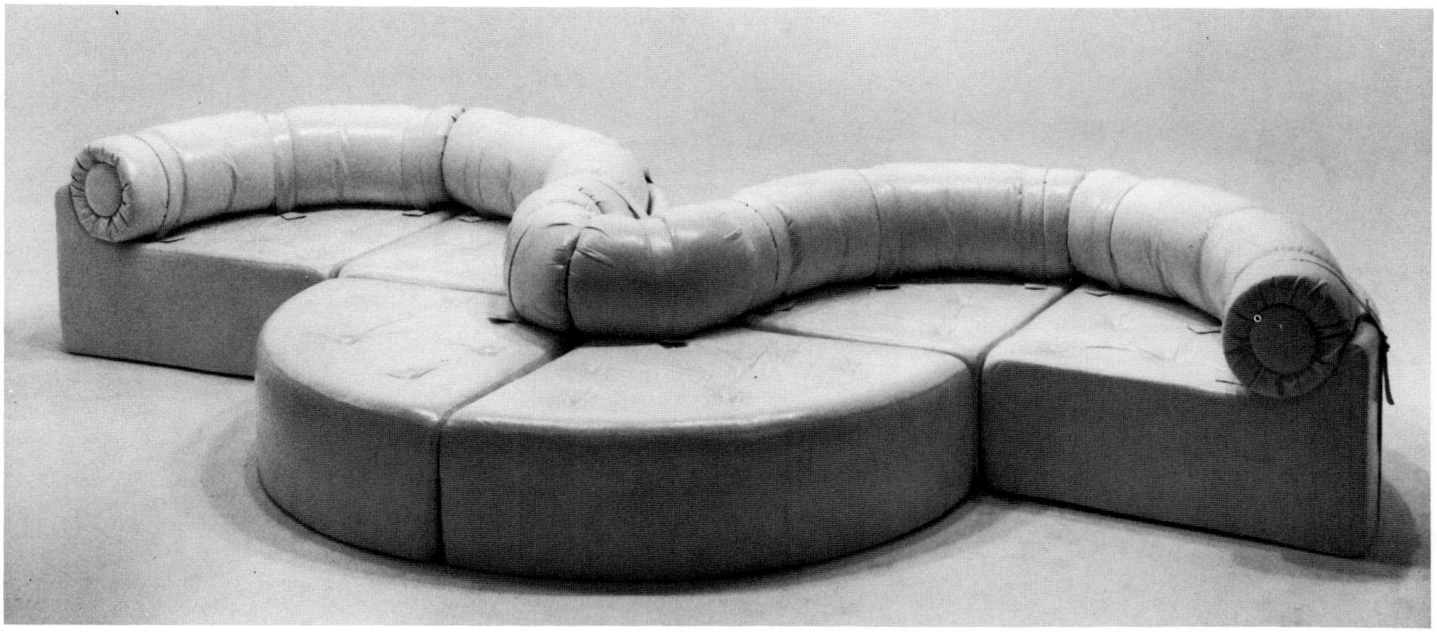

479 **Hughes Steiner** 1969 France
Sofa complex "Swany" of three units of polyfoam allowing a wide variety of arrangements, covered in plastic or fabric

482 **Ueli Berger** 1968 Switzerland
"Multi-Soft" seating unit of polyfoam with fabric cover; can be used as chair, sofa, bed, or daybed

483 **Luigi Colani** 1970/71 Germany

Living pad "Pool" consisting of square ground, border, and corner elements of polyfoam with detachable covers in various fabrics. Supplementary cushions and black or white slide-tables

484 **Bernard Govin** 1967 France

Furniture elements "Asmara"; four basic elements of polyfoam with removable fabric covers can be combined to form seating units or landscapes

485+486 **Joe Colombo** 1971 Italy

Furniture range "Livingcenter" consisting of daybeds with angular cushions, a "dinner element" and a "service element" Daybed with frame of chrome-plated tubular steel with gliders and casters, plastic-laminated extensible shelves. The angular cushions can be used as foot- or headrest or be put on the daybed as raised seat during the meals. Polyfoam upholstery with fabric covers.
Cabinet elements plastic-laminated in various colors, on casters. Dinner element with electric plate-warmer and refrigerator, extensible lids and pull-out sides to enlarge table top. Service element with shelves behind grey plastic tambour doors and built-in loudspeakers

487 **Jonathan De Pas, Donato D'Urbino, Paolo Lomazzi** 1972 Italy

Cushion system "Ali Baba" consisting of square seat and back cushions with removable canvas covers, additional table top

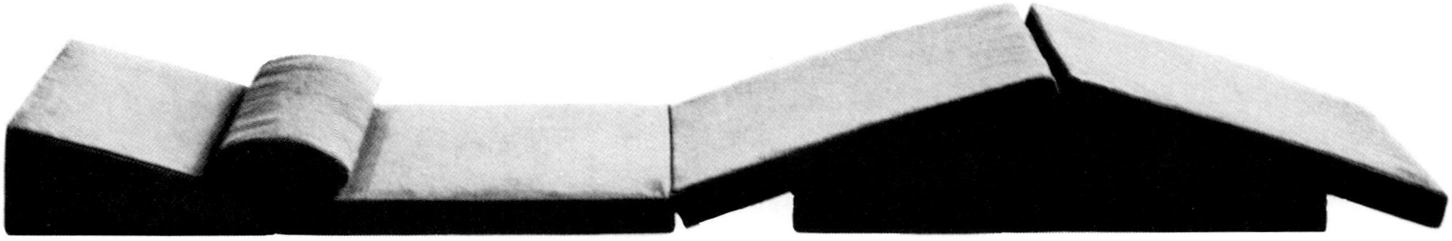

488+489 **Torsten Johansson** 1953 Denmark

Seating furniture with wooden frame and various polyfoam elements, can be combined as desired

▽ 490+491 **Verner Panton** 1962 Denmark

Modular seating range with chests of wengé or teak with hinged lids and casters, fabric-covered polyfoam cushions

▽ 492+493 **Roland Gibbard** 1963 Great Britain

Knockdown "Plus Unit Seating" of plywood panels veneered in larch, joined by anodized aluminum angles and fixed by bolts to any desired combination. Loose polyfoam cushions with detachable fabric covers

488	
489	
490	492
491	493

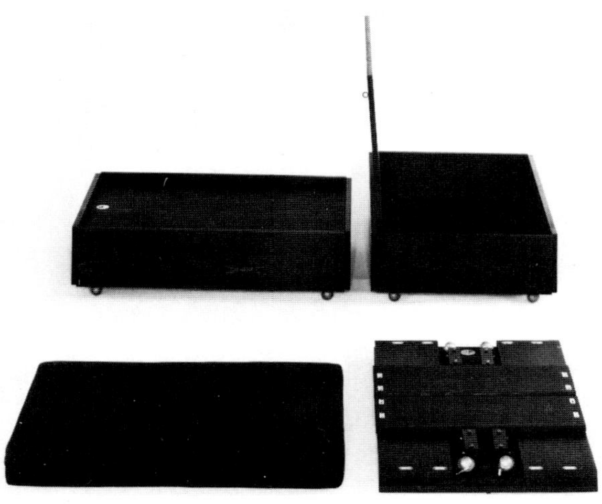

494 **Heinz Witthoeft** 1959–70 Germany
Modular furniture system "Tail 4" with frames of pinewood and inserted panels; seat slings of canvas or leather. An earlier designed group has been considerably expanded and now comprises chairs, tables, beds, and shelving, all easily assembled and suited for living rooms, studios, children's rooms, students' hostels, among others

495 **Rolf Heide** 1975 Germany
Terrace furniture. An easily assembled construction of wood with canvas covers, which can be used either indoors or out

496–498 **Studio B.B.P.R.** 1950 Italy

Daybed with movable frame of metal tubes and wood, polyfoam mattress

499 **Hans Gugelot** c. 1951 Switzerland

Easy chair with wooden frame and movable seat

500 **Friso Kramer, Jaap Penraat** c. 1952 Netherlands

Adjustable lounge chair with steel tube frame and polyfoam upholstery

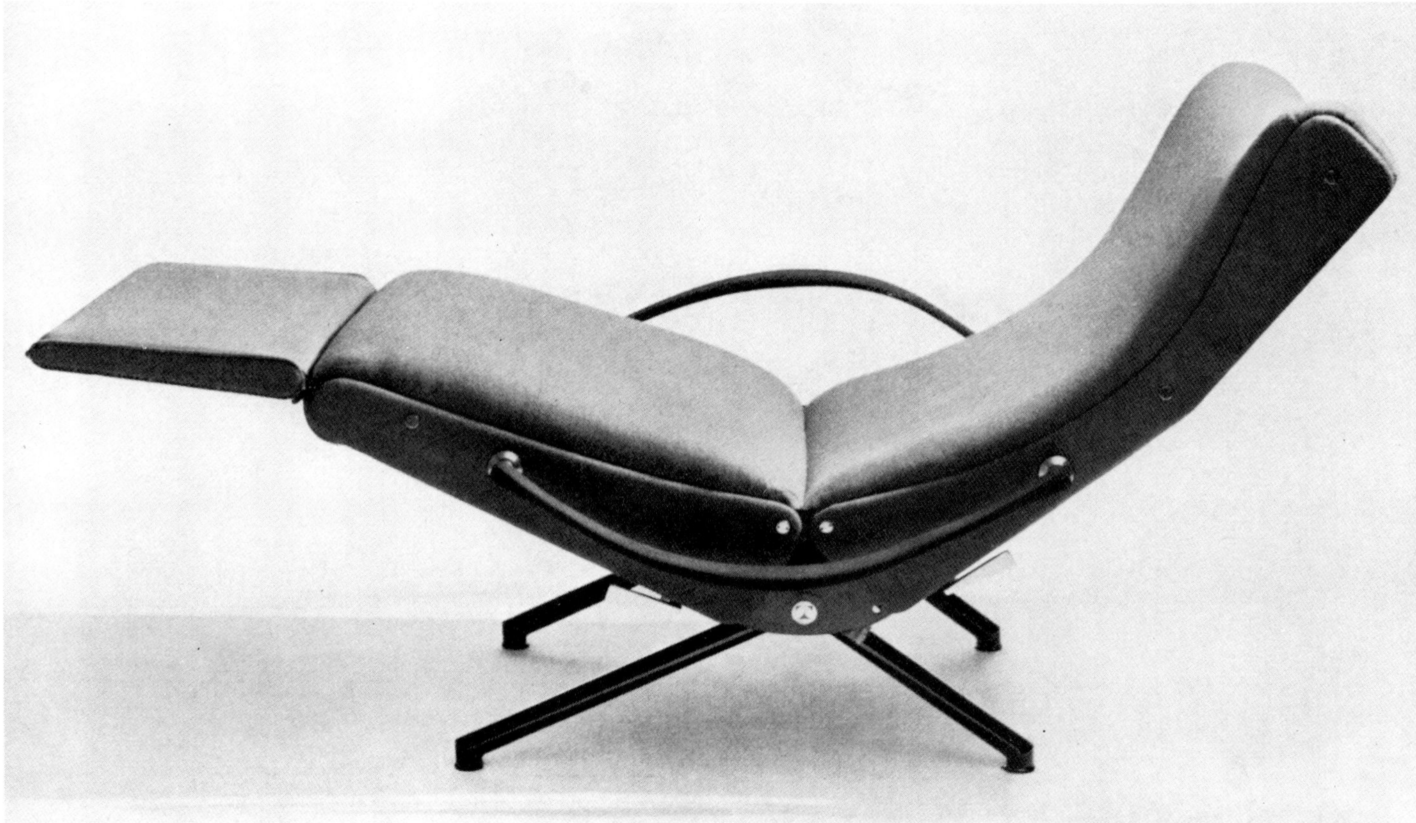

501 + 502 **Osvaldo Borsani** 1956 Italy
Adjustable lounge chair "P 40" with metal frame, elastic armrests and polyfoam upholstery, hinged footrest

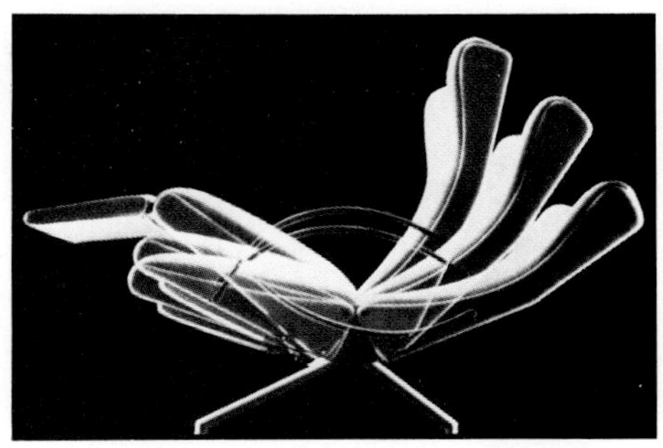

503–505 **Osvaldo Borsani** 1957 Italy
Adjustable daybed "L 77" with metal frame and polyfoam mattress on straps

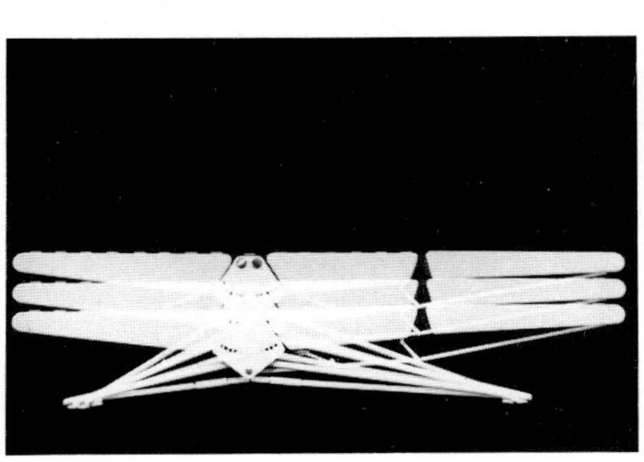

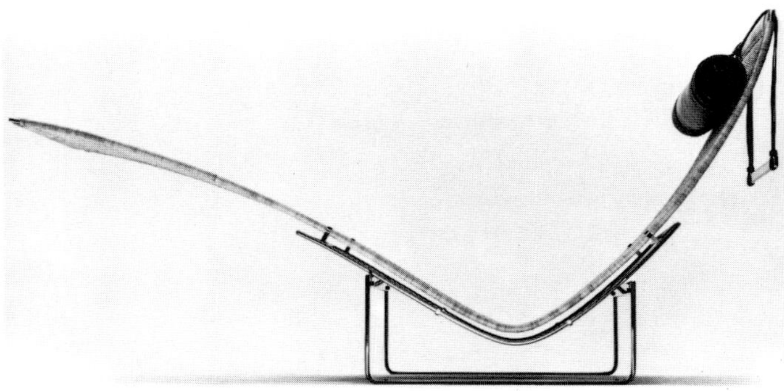

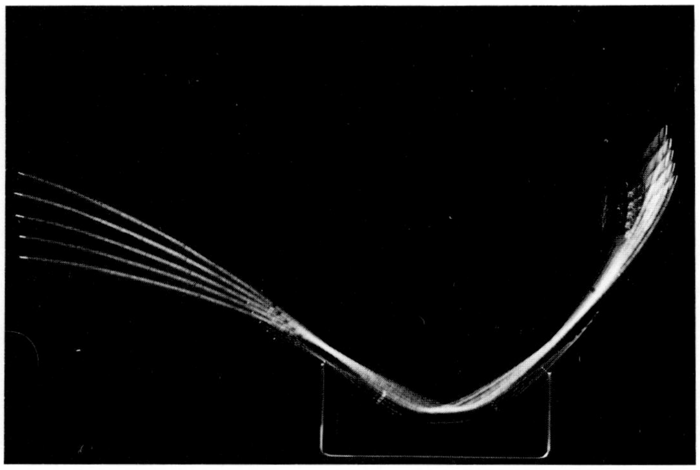

506+507 **Hendrik van Keppel, Taylor Green** c.1952 USA
Daybed with adjustable frame of wood and polyfoam mattress

508+509 **Poul Kjaerholm** 1966 Denmark
Adjustable lounge chair "24" of rattan with base of stainless steel, neck-cushion covered in leather

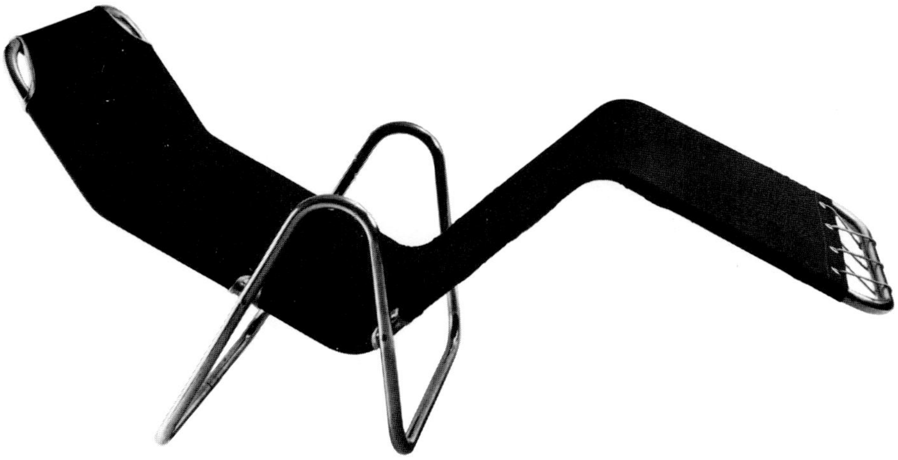

510 **Julien Hébert** 1951 Canada
Lounge chair "Sun-Lite" with aluminum tube frame and nylon slings

511 **George Nelson** c. 1953 USA
Chaise "5490" with base of chrome-plated steel and polyfoam upholstery

512 **Charles Eames** 1969 USA
Chaise "ES 106" from "Soft Pad" group. Black base of epoxy-coated aluminum; six soft, foam-padded, leather-covered cushions joined by zippers

513 **Richard Schultz** 1966 USA
"Outdoor Program", for indoor use as well, including chair and easy chair with or without arms, lounge chair, tea and dining tables. Frames of cast and profile aluminum in mat white lacquer finish with white plastic gliders. Seats of a special white synthetic fabric with side strips of brown plastic

514 **George Nelson** c. 1950 USA
Upholstered easy chair and stool with metal legs, small removable table

515 **Edward J. Wormley** c. 1950 USA
Daybed with wooden frame, detachable brass legs and polyfoam mattress

516 **Works Design** c. 1951 USA
Hotel bed "Tourinns" on metal legs with casters, innerspring mattress, upholstered headboard

517 **Harvey Probber** c. 1951 USA
Beds with frame and matching corner cabinet of wood

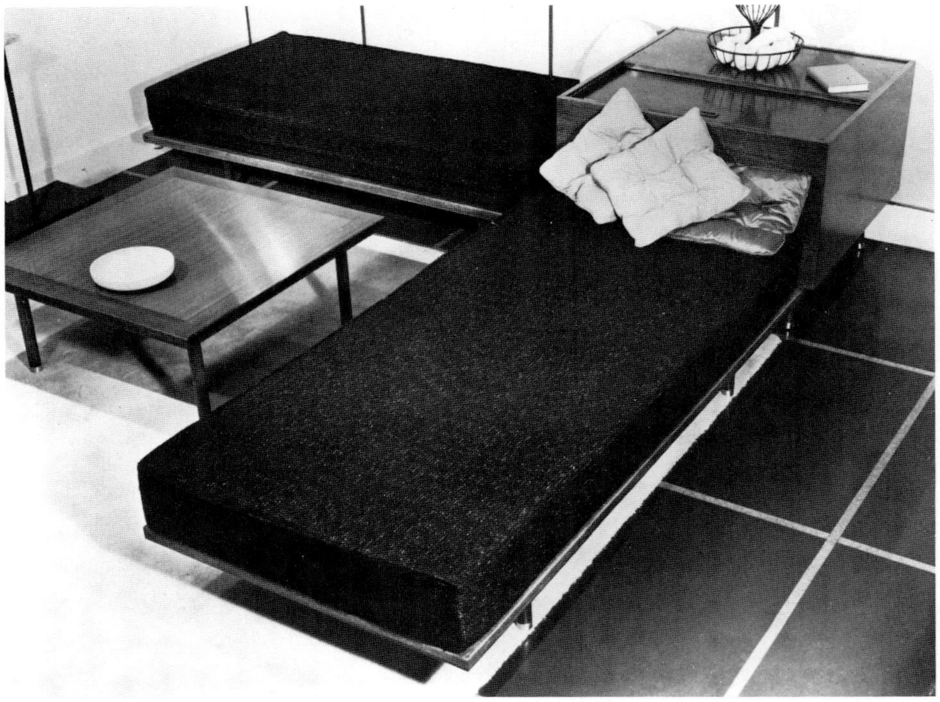

518 **Carlo Pagani** c. 1952 Italy
Bed with frame of wood and cabinet section

519 + 520 **Hans Olsen** 1955 Denmark
Daybed with one or two frame parts of wood and adjustable polyfoam cushions

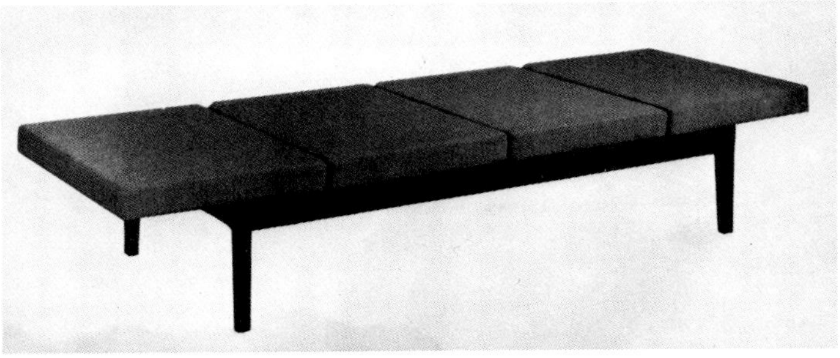

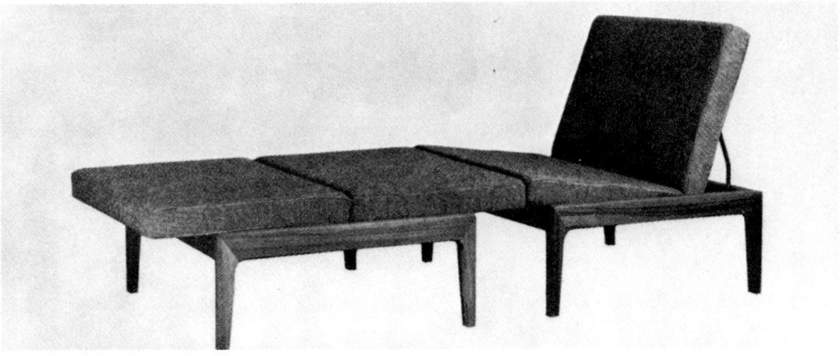

521 + 522 **Eduard Ludwig** c. 1953 Germany
Demountable daybed with innerspring mattress

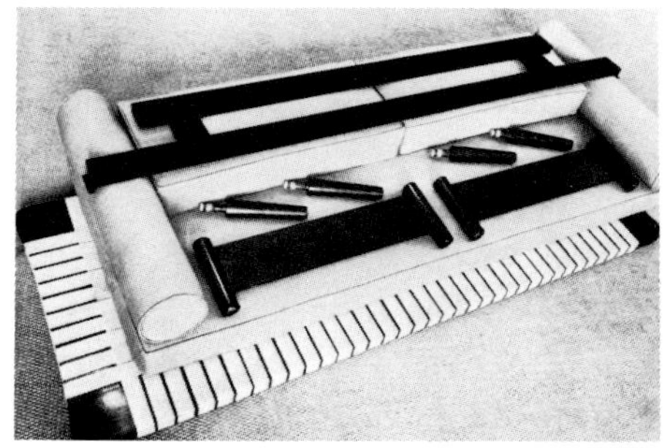

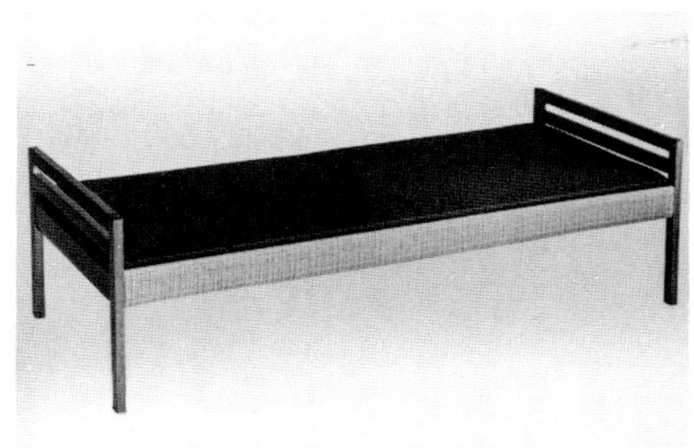

523–525 **Erik Berglund, Uno Swalen** 1956/57 Sweden
Daybed with convertible back upholstered in polyfoam, beech frame

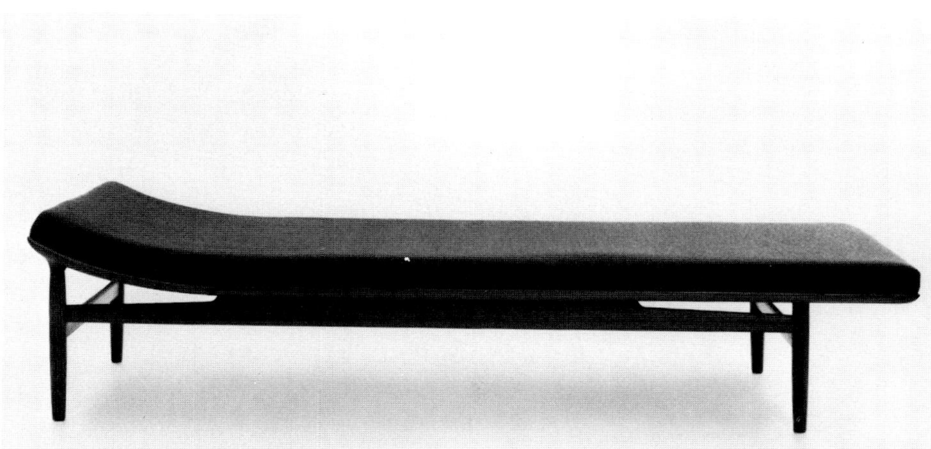

528 **Herta-Maria Witzemann, Wolfgang Stadelmaier** 1960 Germany
Bed "Dagmar" with frame of teak

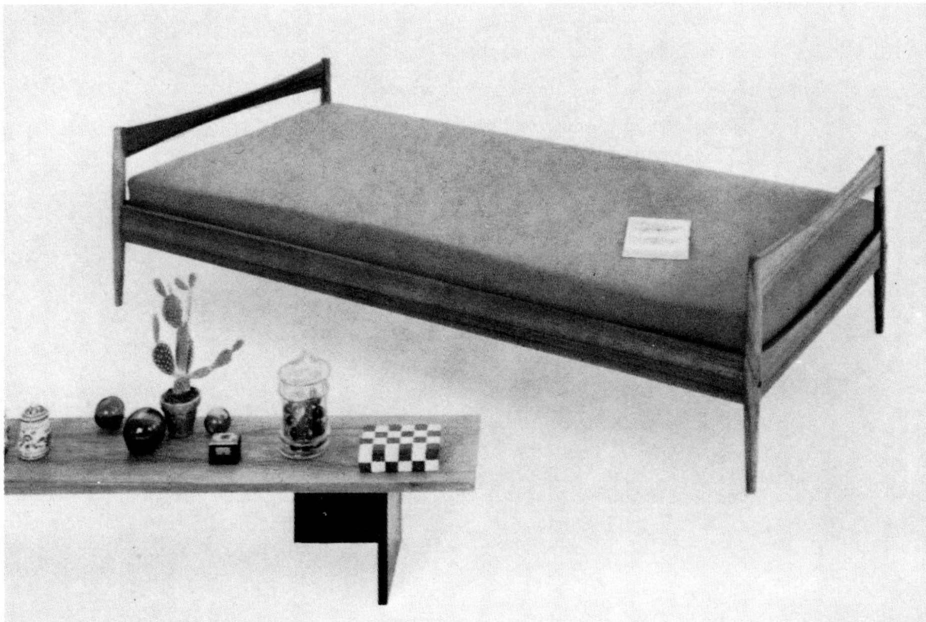

529 **Carl Bjørn** 1960 Sweden
Bed "Triva-Snark" with oak frame, foam rubber upholstery over No-sag springs

530 **Pertti Aalto** 1963 Finland
Bed "Silja" with frame of white lacquered wood, head- and footboards covered in black imitation leather

◁◁ 526 **Kurt Østervig** 1958 Denmark
Bed "311" with teak frame, rubber webbing, and polyfoam mattress

◁ 527 **Robin Day** 1962 Great Britain
"MK II" bed settee with steel frame, legs and armrests of afrormosia, polyfoam upholstery over rubber webbing

531–533 **Peter Hjorth, Arne Karlsen** 1958 Denmark

Collapsible bed consisting of two parts and a case for bedclothes, with oak frames, panels of the case black lacquered

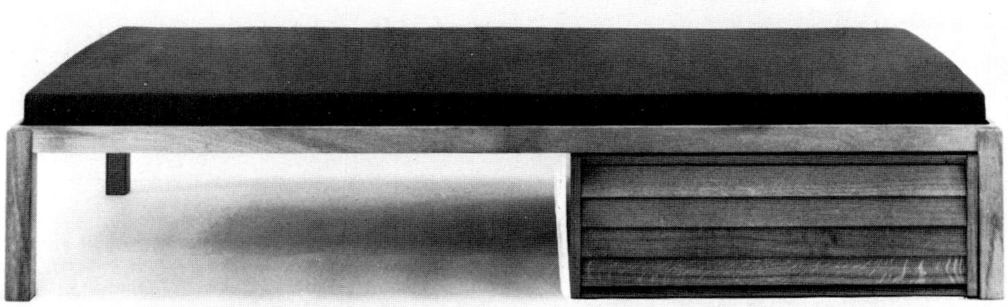

534 **Reino Ruokolainen** 1958 Finland

Bed "H" and attached wood case for bedclothes, polyfoam mattress on perforated plywood plank

535 + 536 **Bard Henriksen** 1970 Denmark

Reversible sofa/bed with attached chest for bedclothes serving as bedside table; frames of chipboard stained in various colors

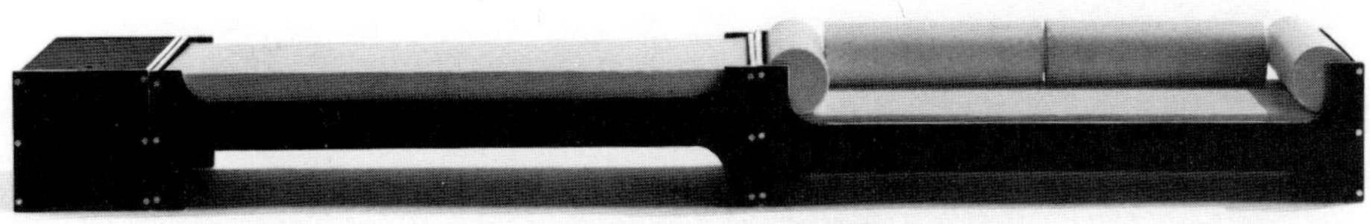

537 **Rolf Heide** 1969 Germany

Stacking beds "3001–3006" (in different sizes) and matching chest "3007" for bedclothes, made of laminated wood stained in various colors or of chipboard laminated in white plastic

538 **Fred Ruf** c. 1951 Switzerland
Bed of wood with metal legs

539–541 **Hans Gugelot** 1955/56 Switzerland

Bed with wooden frames and polyfoam mattress on metal base; convertible into twin-beds by pulling out the single beds

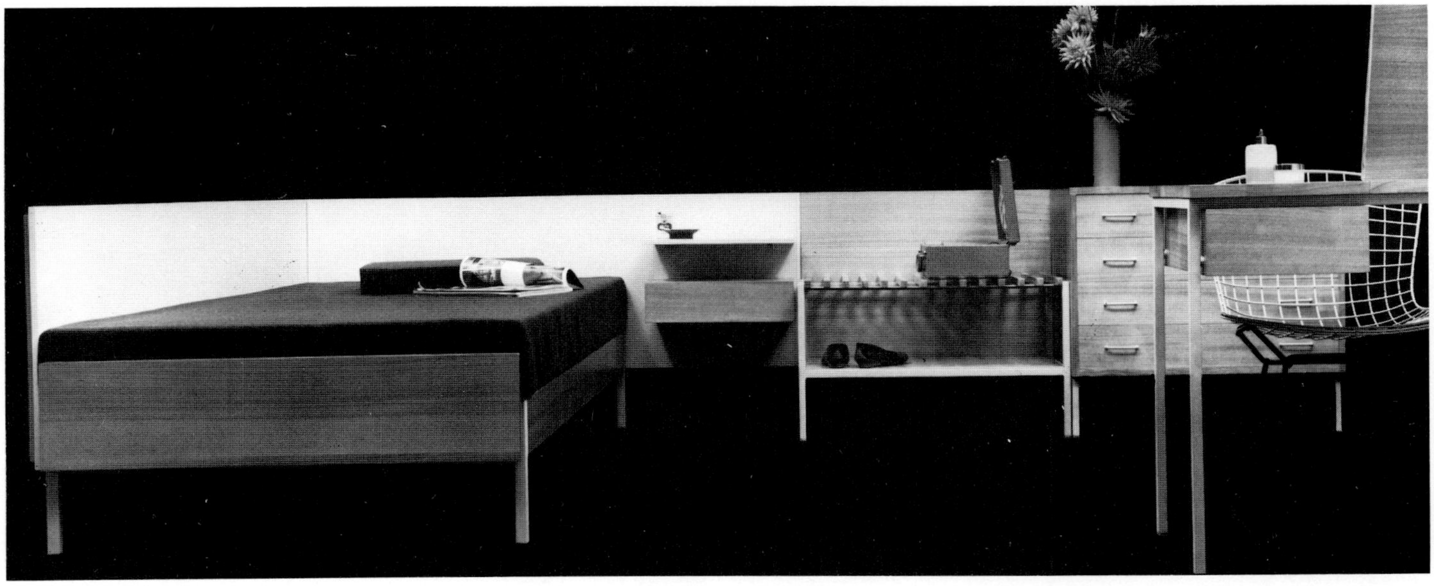

542+543 **Herbert Hirche** 1961 Germany
"MOL" bedroom furniture series of cherrywood, interiors white maple, white lacquered steel frames, headboard of white plastic

544 **Rudolf Lübben** 1963 Germany
Bed with matching case for bedclothes and chest, made of oak and white plastic with aluminum edgings and cubical linking devices

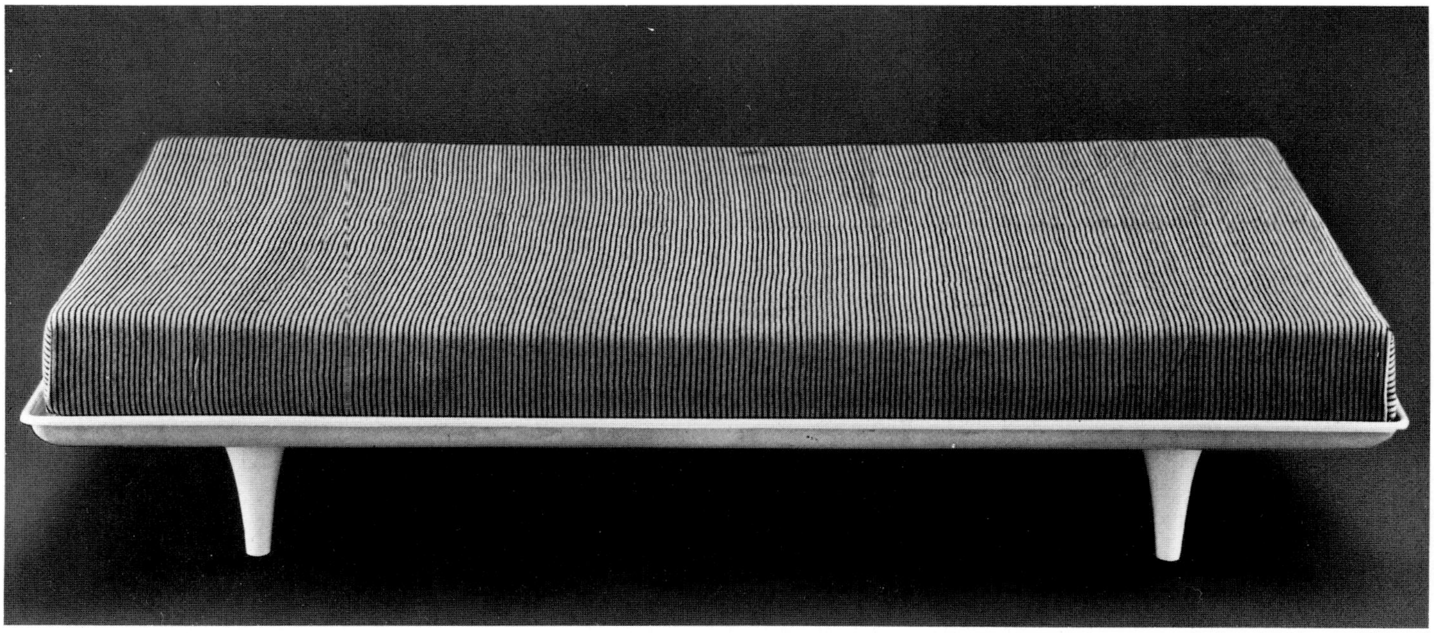

545+546 **Andreas Christen** 1960 Switzerland
Stacking bed of polyester

547 **Wolfgang Feierbach, Manfred Vitt** 1967 Germany
Daybed "fg 2003" with frame of fiberglass and polyfoam mattress

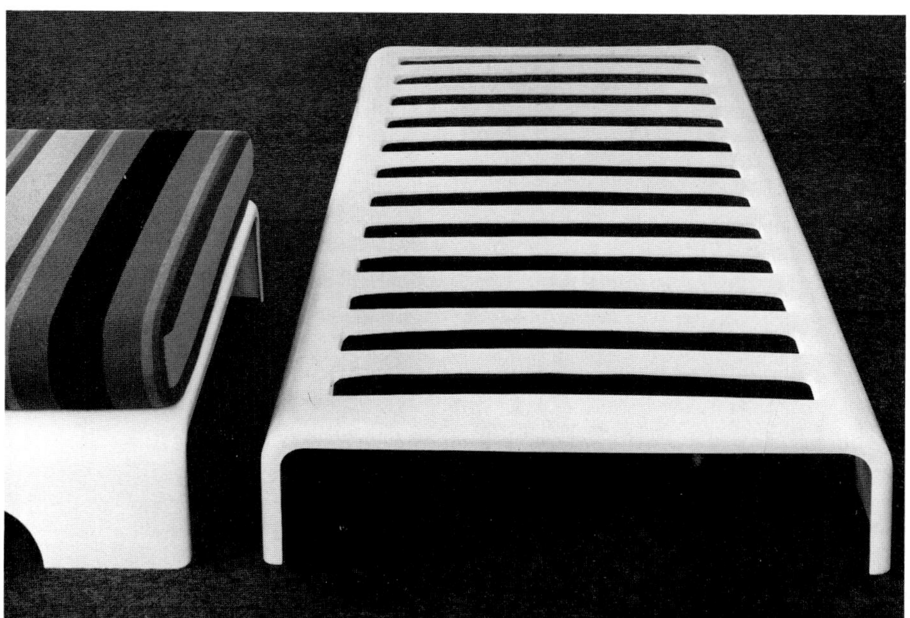

548 **Anna Castelli Ferrieri, Ignazio Gardella** 1969 Italy ▷
Bed "4550" with two identical parts of fiberglas-reinforced polyester in red or white, mounted on casters

549+550 **Vittorio Parigi, Nani Prina** 1972 Italy ▷
Bed of vacuum-formed ABS in various colors, metal grill resting on two chests for bedclothes. The chests can be pulled out

551 **Ennio Chiggio** 1971 Italy ▷
Bed "Luka" with frame of chrome-plated steel tube

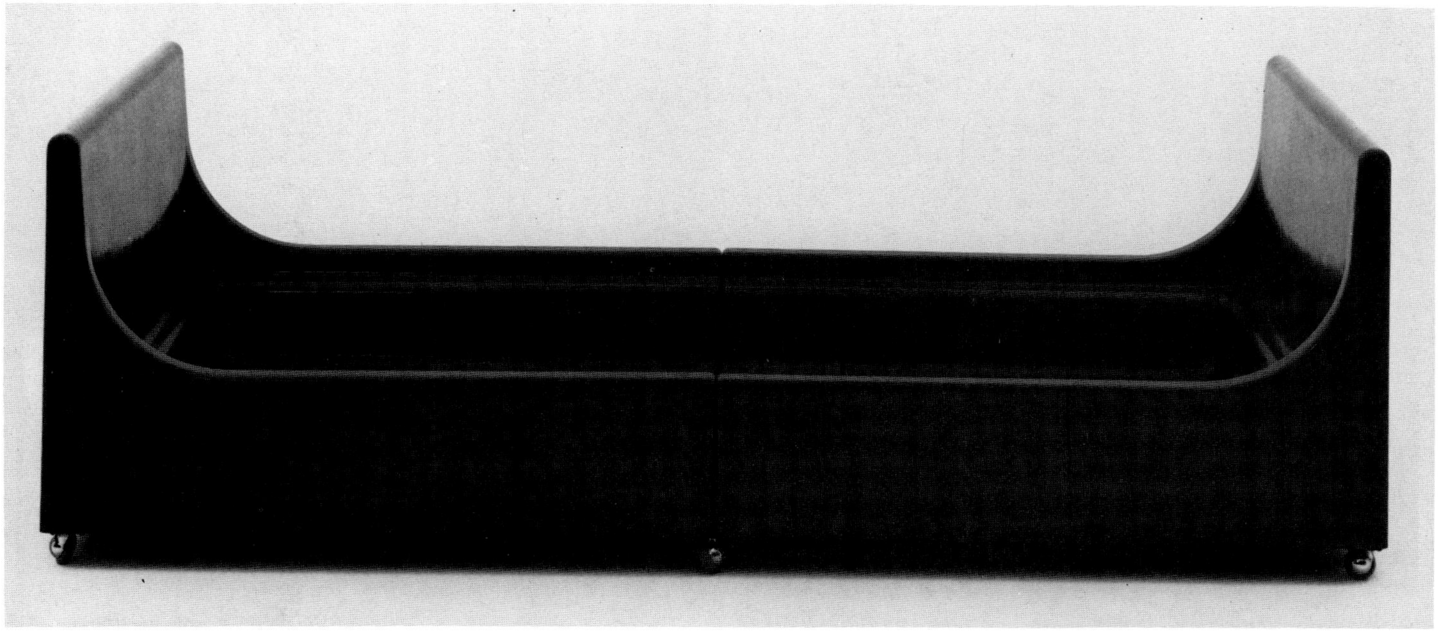

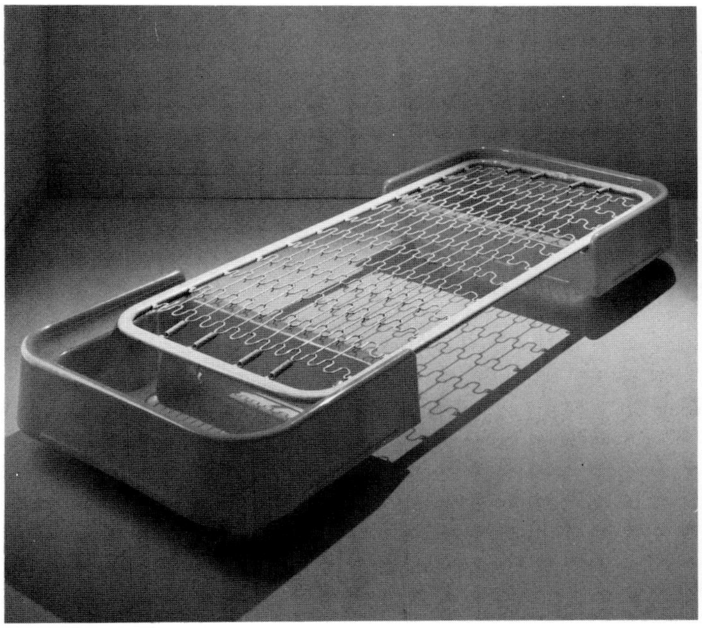

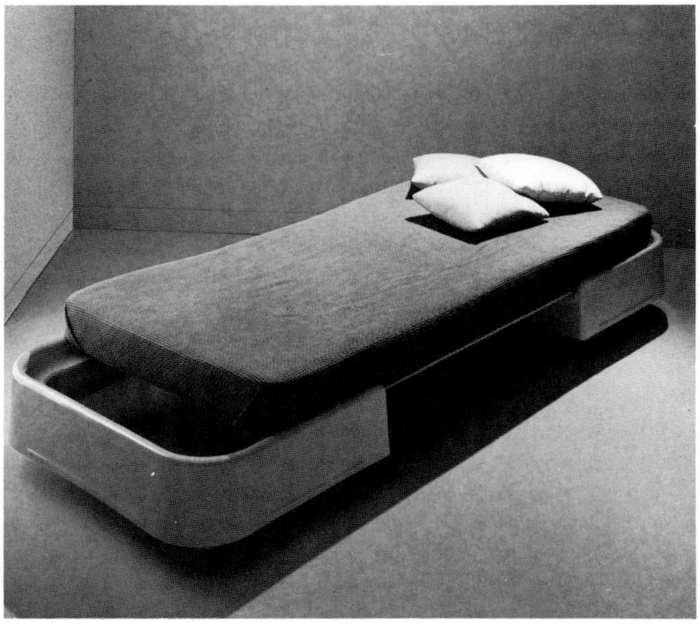

552 **Mogens Koch** 1960 Denmark
Folding table "ambassade" with beech frame, top in teak, legs held by leather straps

Tables

One should really start the chapter on tables by stating that there are no longer any normal, sensible tables. By this is meant a robust wooden top with a veneered edge on four sturdy legs, connected by a frame. Basically the construction of this piece of furniture is one of the simplest in the world, but this seems to be exactly the reason why it can no longer be applied.

Instead, what one comes across are examples that have dimensions that are much too weak, giving the impression of being delicate mixtures made out of squared iron and wood set on extremely thin legs. The only tables that have looked in any way convincing recently have come from the Ikea range. A reason for this shabby treatment may be the fact that there are hardly any separate dining-rooms these days and the "classic" dining tables have been condemned to extinction. Their modest successors seem to suffice for the eating areas in today's living space. If one happens to come across a decent table, one can be sure that it is an old one. It may be that a solid design does not correspond with the requirements and expectations of the furniture trade, which would like to sell furniture that is light and can be taken apart.

But a basic model could be developed which, despite its robust dimensions, could be delivered in pieces. The suspicion remains that tables of a normal height have become cinderellas among furniture.

The folding table developed by the Danish designer Mogens Koch (ill. 552) to go with his previous folding chair (ill. 13) is excellent proof that it is worth rethinking a traditional form. This is a resurrection of the classic garden table, although the iron frame has been replaced by a wooden one. The process has not produced a hybrid-that is, a piece of furniture that is neither really simple nor sufficiently convincing as regards its worth-but just the best appearance this kind of table can attain. What is also very sensible about it is the shape of the top, which does without curved edges where this would have been only possible with the help of an extra structure. One feels that one is looking at a traditional model, or at least at a table that can stand as a light-legged, movable substitute for its missing brothers.

The situation as regards coffee tables is better than for dining tables. By far the most intelligent model was designed by Harald Roth in 1958 (ills. 584, 585). It is inspired by the idea that by changing the position of the legs the height can be altered from low to middle height. To do this, all one has to do is raise the top gently and the frames forming the lower structure automatically do the rest. The pieces slide quietly and effortlessly from one position to the other. This ingenious mechanism, which is somewhat mysterious, has such a sensible form that it is always a pleasure to operate it.

The table looks "Japanese", although it is not directly based on a specific model; the effect is produced above all by its inner philosophy. It is, if one can express it like this, the result of meditation on the job of designing a table. Most of the other designers are merely satisfied with creating a table.

553 **Børge Mogensen** 1952 Denmark
Dining table "121" with oak frame, top in teak

554 **Ejner Larsen** c. 1953 Denmark
Coffee table of wood

555 **Lewis Butler** 1954 USA
Wooden table

556 **Works Design** 1953 Sweden
Table of wood

557 **Bruno Mathsson** c. 1952 Sweden
Table with teak top

558 **Grete Jalk** 1957 Denmark
Teak table "03" with loose anodized aluminum plate

559 **Ib Kofod-Larsen** 1958 Denmark
Teak table

560 **Hans J. Wegner** 1951 Denmark
Drop-leaf table of wood

561 **Basil Spence** c. 1951 Great Britain
Drop-leaf table

562 **Folke Sundberg** 1952 Sweden
Drop-leaf table with red beech frame and teak top

564+565 **Michel Mortier** c. 1950 France ▷
Extension top table of wood

566+567 **Fred Ruf** c. 1951 Switzerland ▷
Extension table

568+569 **Roberto Mango** 1954 Italy ▷
Extension double top dining table "T 48" of plywood with hinge-joints, fittings of black lacquered metal

570+571 **Franco Albini** 1954/55 Italy ▷
Folding table with wooden frame, top of polished wood with removable woolen cloth cover

563 **Arne Jacobsen** 1957 Denmark
Drop-leaf dining table "4606" with beech base and teak top

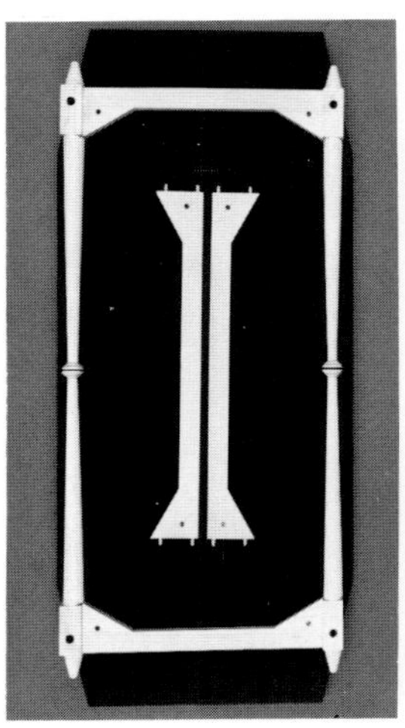

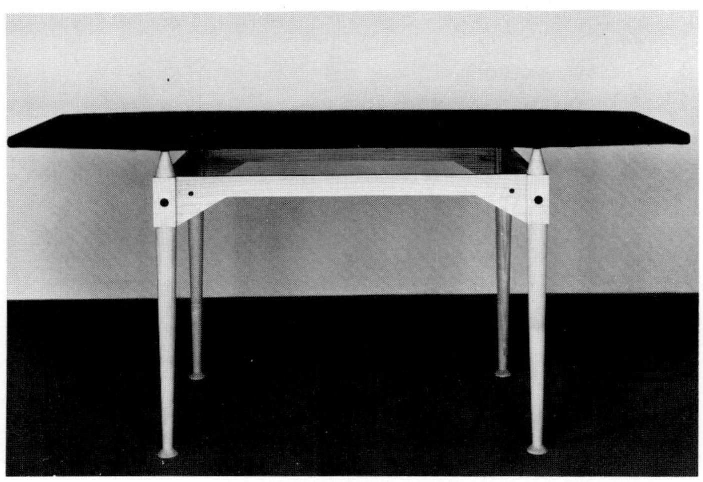

564	565
566	567
568	569
570	571

575 + 576 **Carl Auböck** 1960 Austria
Stacking table in beech, grey plastic-laminated top

577 **Finn Juhl** 1958 Denmark
Tables "533/531/536" of various sizes with one or two tops in teak
Tables can be combined

578 **Marco Zanuso** 1974 Italy
Table "Forrestal" with top of solid ash or bay oak bands, glued together at high frequency; removable legs

◁ 572 **Ejner Larsen, A. Bender Madsen** 1957/58 Denmark
Extension table "1631" with teak top

◁ 573 **Ejner Larsen, A. Bender Madsen** 1959 Denmark
Dining table "1636" in teak with one extension leaf

◁ 574 **Ejner Larsen, A. Bender Madsen** 1962 Denmark
Dining table "1736" in oak or teak with extension leaf

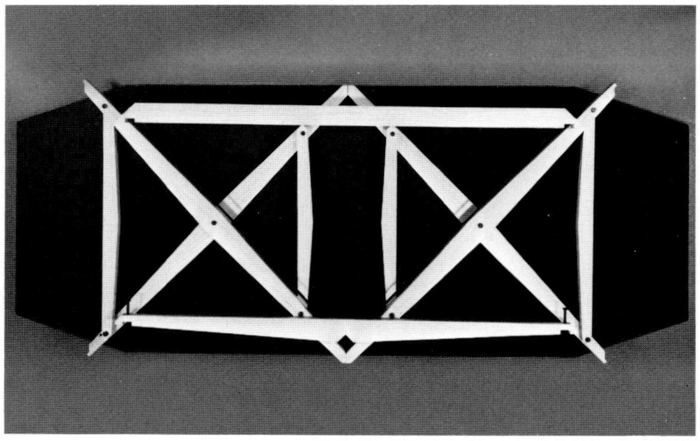

579+580 **Mirko Romih** 1958 Yugoslavia
Folding table in beech

581+582 **Franco Albini** 1954/55 Italy
Folding table with wooden frame, top of polished wood with removable woolen cloth cover

583 **Jonathan De Pas, Donato D'Urbino, Paolo Lomazzi** 1976 Italy
Folding outdoor table "Merenda" of solid bay oak

584 + 585 **Harald Roth** 1958 Germany
"Mandarin" table in teak, height adjustable

586 **Franco Albini** c. 1951 Italy
Folding dining table of wood

587 **Achille and Pier Giacomo Castiglioni** 1968 Italy
Working desk "Leonardo" with top of white plastic laminate or glass

588 **Eduard Ludwig** c. 1951 Germany
Demountable shelves and coffee table of wood

589 **Vico Magistretti** c. 1952 Italy
Coffee table with top in birch plywood and mahogany legs

590 **Angelo Mangiarotti, Bruno Morassutti** 1955 Italy
Small tables and stools of molded plywood elements in birch with glass tops or cushions

591 **Hans Bellmann** c. 1950 Switzerland
Demountable table of wood

592 **Jürg Bally** 1952/57 Switzerland
Table with black lacquered metal base, adjustable height, black plastic top with maple edges

593 **Bruno Mathsson** c. 1951 Sweden
Coffee table with base of bentwood and teak veneer top

594 **Max Bill** 1949/50 Switzerland
Table with three legs

595 **Ico Parisi** c. 1953 Italy
Table with steel tube frame and wooden top

596 **Florence Knoll** 1956 USA
Table with chrome-plated metal base and crystal glass top

597 **Alberto Rosselli** c. 1951 Italy
Table with steel tube frame and crystal glass top

598 **Robin Day** c. 1952 Great Britain
Table with steel frame and plywood top

599 **Florence Knoll** 1961 USA
Conference and dining table "2480/81" with oval top of teak or rosewood and base of chrome-plated steel

600 **Giancarlo Piretti** 1974 Italy
"SBC" component system for tables. The interchangeable components fit together to provide unlimited possibilities for a vast range of tables. Bases: columns of chrome-plated steel tube, spider attachements of die-cast metal enamelled white, assembly rods of steel, blades available in three lengths; tops in plastic laminate, walnut or rosewood veneer, treated with self-hardening polyester resins (see also ill. 618)

601 **Poul Kjaerholm** 1957 Denmark

Dining table "51" with frame of chrome-plated steel and wooden top

602+603 **Poul Kjaerholm** 1967 Denmark

Table with chrome-plated steel base and ash top

604 **Alfred Altherr** c. 1958 Switzerland

"Team" dining table with base of square tubular steel and plastic top

605 **Hans Eichenberger** 1956 Switzerland

Table with chrome-plated tubular steel base and plastic-laminated top

606 **William Katavolos, Ross Littell, Douglas Kelley** c. 1952 USA

Table with legs of chrome-plated steel tubes and marble top

607 **J.M. Thomas** 1959 Germany

Table "WR 194" with collapsible metal pedestal, adjustable height; top in various woods

608 + 609 **J.M. Thomas** 1962 Germany

Double pedestal, height-adjustable table "WR 247" with charcoal lacquered steel tube columns and chrome-plated legs. Folding/sliding top of natural walnut, teak or rosewood

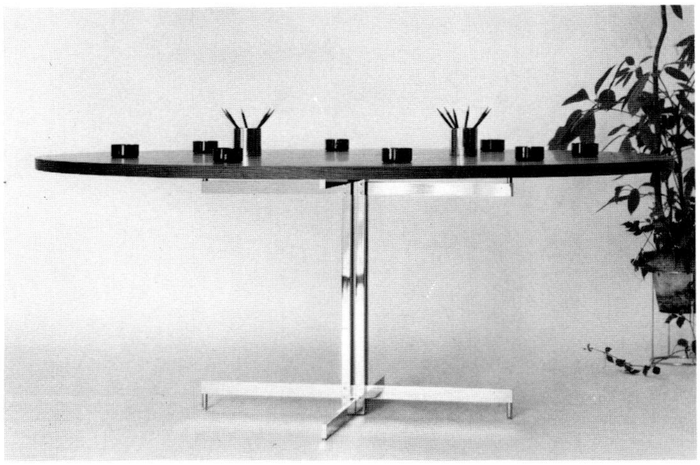

610 **Hugh Acton** 1962 USA

Round or oval table with chrome-plated steel base and walnut top

611 **Knud Joos** 1958 Denmark

Table "601" with collapsible chrome-plated steel frame, teak or rosewood top

612 **Jørgen Høj** 1960 Denmark

Circular dining table "53" with three legs of mat finished anodized aluminum, top of laminated wood veneered in oak or rosewood

613 **Arne Jacobsen** 1962 Denmark

Table "3609" with aluminum base and top of teak

614 **Osvaldo Borsani** 1964 Italy

Circular dining table "T69" with top of teak, rosewood, or other woods. Base of nickel-plated steel

◁ 610

611	612
613	614

615	616 ▷
	617
618	619

615+616 **Eugenio Gerli, Mario Cristiani** 1961 Italy

Dining table "T92" with black lacquered or nickel-plated metal base. For extension the square wooden top is turned and the triangular drop-leaves are unfolded

617 **Osvaldo Borsani** 1958 Italy

Table "T41" with lacquered metal base, height adjustable, wooden top

618 **Giancarlo Piretti** 1974 Italy

"SBC" component system for tables (see ill. 600), round table

619 **Works Design** 1978 Italy

Folding table "Plano" with round or square top of rigid polyurethane in various colors, base of polished die-cast aluminum alloy with adjustable nylon glides. A patented locking mechanism ensures stability when table is erected, special hinges allow the table sections to be folded together

620+621 **Robert Haussmann** 1956 Switzerland

Drop-leaf dining table with base of black lacquered steel, top with linoleum cover

625 **Uli Wieser** 1959 Switzerland ▷

Dining table "WI 1035" with extensible metal base and three-part walnut top. The central leaf can be stored in the frame

622+623 **Fred Ruf** c. 1952 Switzerland

Extension table with iron frame, top in maple with linoleum cover

624 **Ernst Kirchhoff** 1959 Germany

Extension table "T-60" with square tubular steel frame, top in wood or plastic

626 + 627 **Jørgen Høj** 1960/63 Denmark ▷

Circular table "54" with four legs and cross-bar of mat finished anodized aluminum, top veneered in oak or rosewood on both sides. The table can be extended by four ring sections with light frame constructions, grey plastic laminate and edging of oak or rosewood

628 + 629 **Poul Kjaerholm** 1963 Denmark ▷

Table "54" with base of satin finished chrome-plated steel and top of marble. Can be extended by attaching six ring sections of solid maple

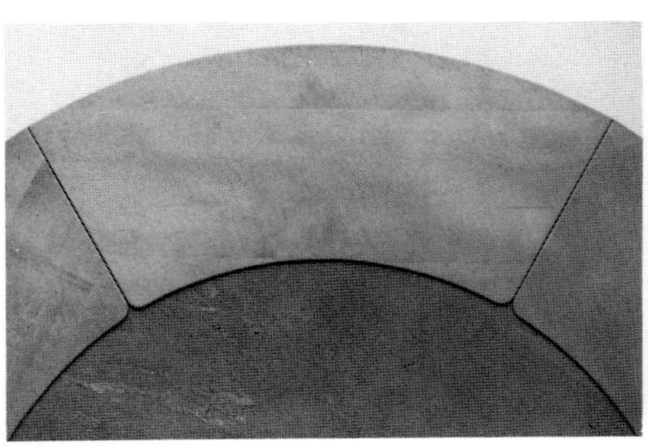

630+631 **Wolfram Elwert** 1976 Germany

Table with base of chrome-plated tubular steel, twin top of black or white oak veneer finish or white formica, height adjustable

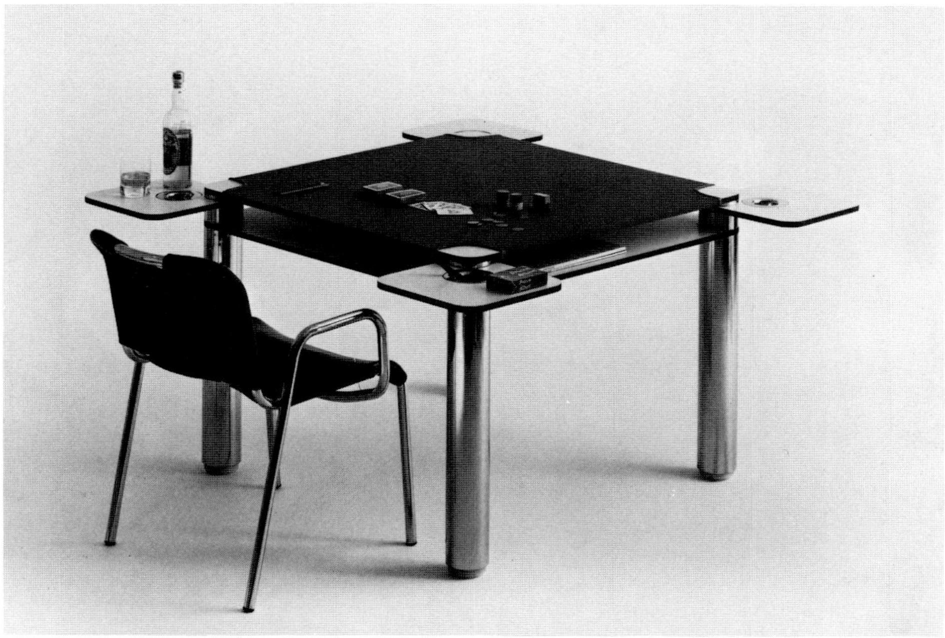

632 **Joe Colombo** 1967 Italy

Game and dining table "Poker" with twin top laminated in plastic, height-adjustable legs of chrome-plated steel. A green cloth can be snapped to underside of upper top when needed. At corners, four small shelves with stainless steel ashtrays can be pulled out

633 **Carlo Viganò** 1968 Italy

Low table of lacquered wood with sliding tops, flap doors, drawers, and recesses that can be used for various purposes

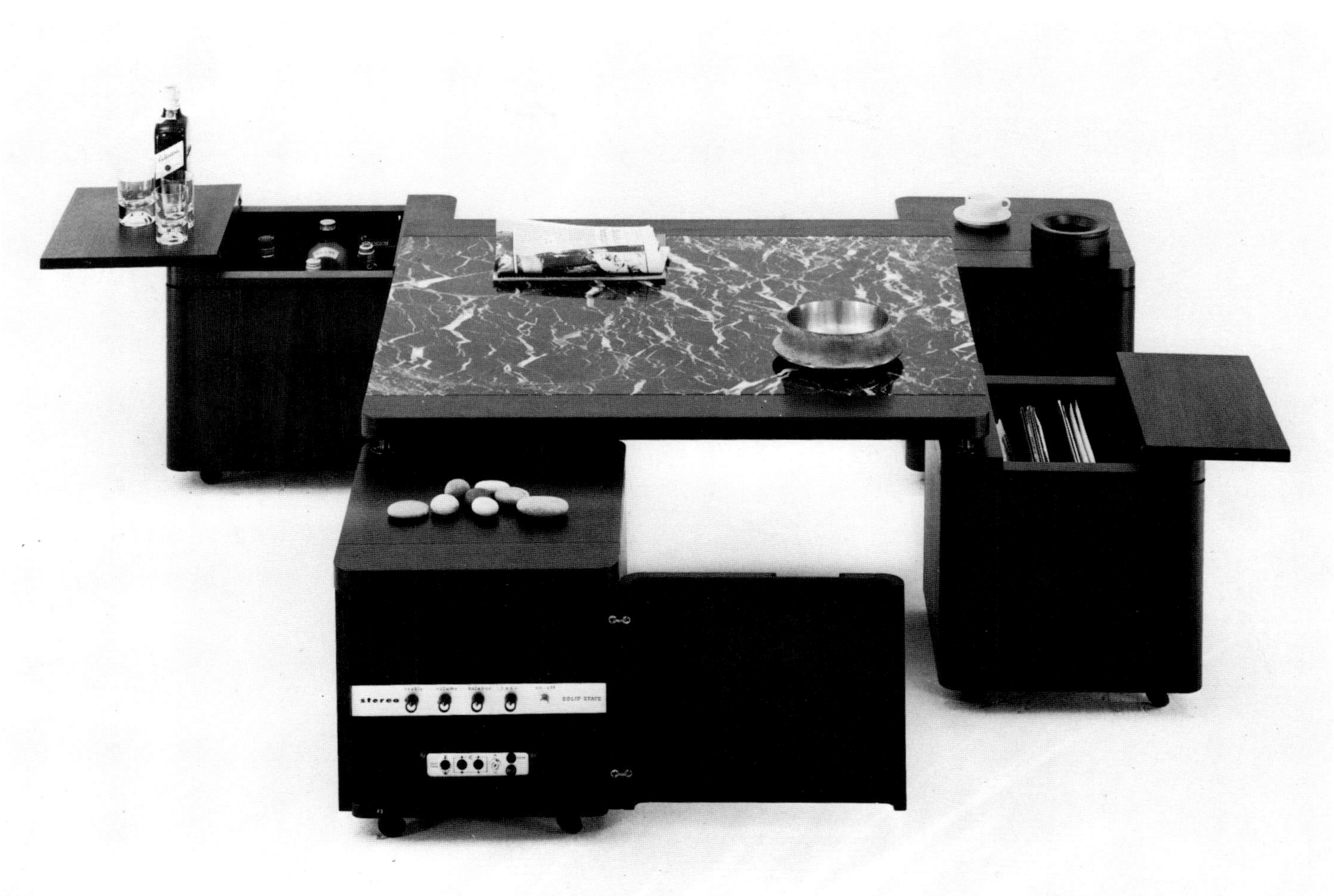

634 **Angelo Mangiarotti** 1967/68 Italy

Dining table "Idilor" with four attached containers on casters fitting under the central top when not in use. Made of rosewood with table top of green marble or white granite

635 **Roberto Pamio, Renato Toso, Noti Massari** 1967 Italy

Storage furniture "Lara B/G/LS" of wood, partly laminated in white plastic, with revolving compartments. "Lara" consists of two parts of which one is fixed and the other is mounted on casters, with a built-in extensible table top. Various variations for living and dining area

636 **Isamu Noguchi** 1946 USA
Coffee table with demountable wood base in walnut and glass top

637 **Herbert Hirche** 1953 Germany
Coffee table with chrome-plated steel tube base and glass top

638 **Jørgen Høj** 1954 Denmark
Table with steel base and glass top

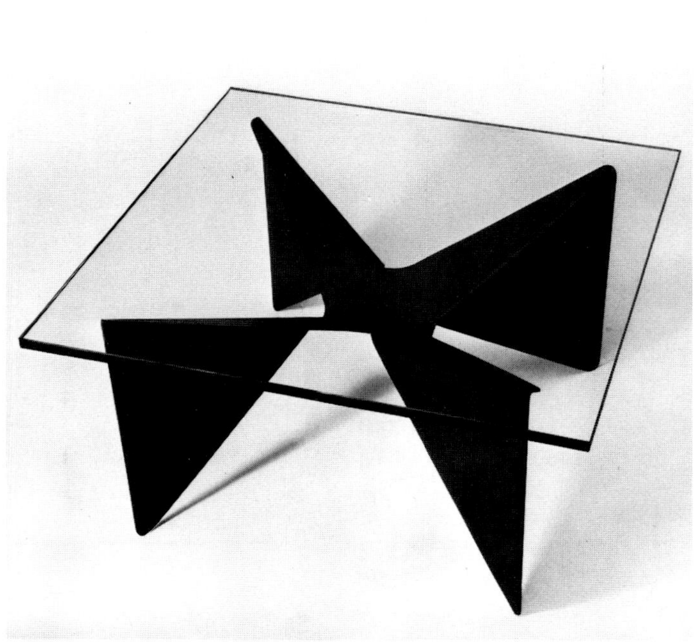

639 **Nicos Zographos** 1960 USA
Table "406" with frame of polished stainless steel and glass top

640 **Nicos Zographos** 1960 USA
Low table "TA 35 G" with frame of polished stainless steel and glass top

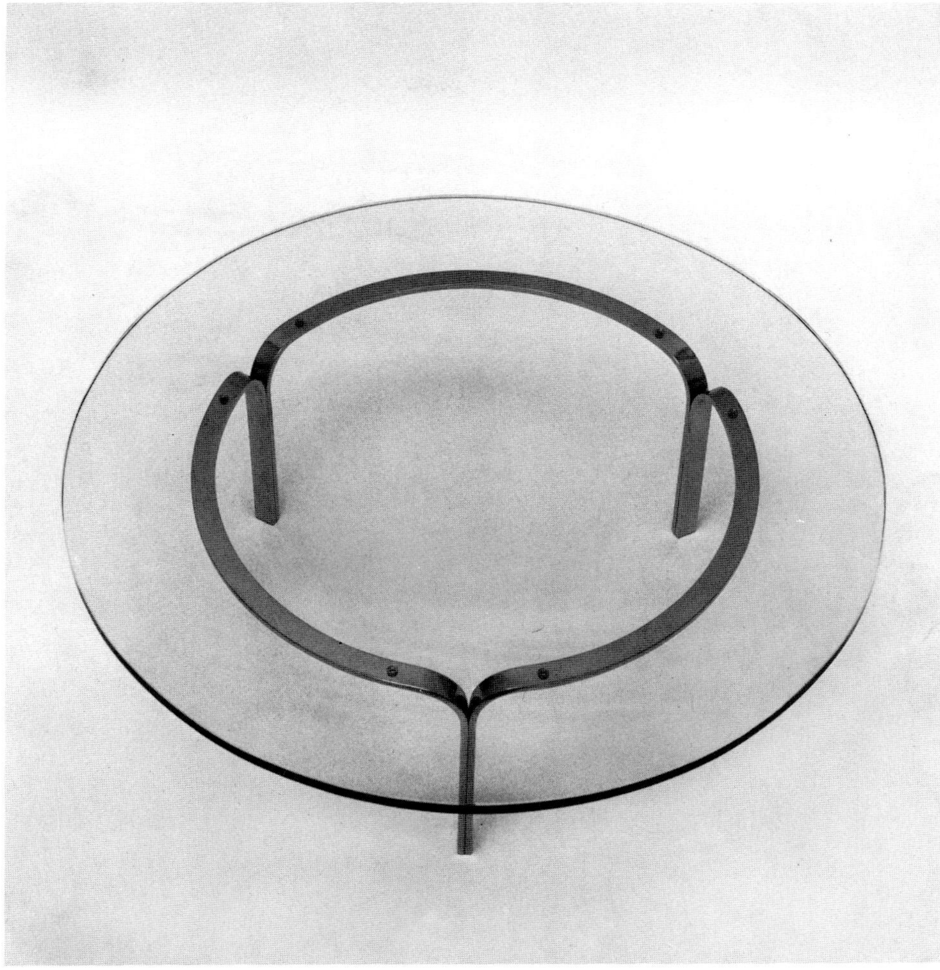

641 **William Armbruster** 1937 USA
Coffee table with steel frame and glass top

642 **William Armbruster** 1937 USA
Small table with steel base and glass top

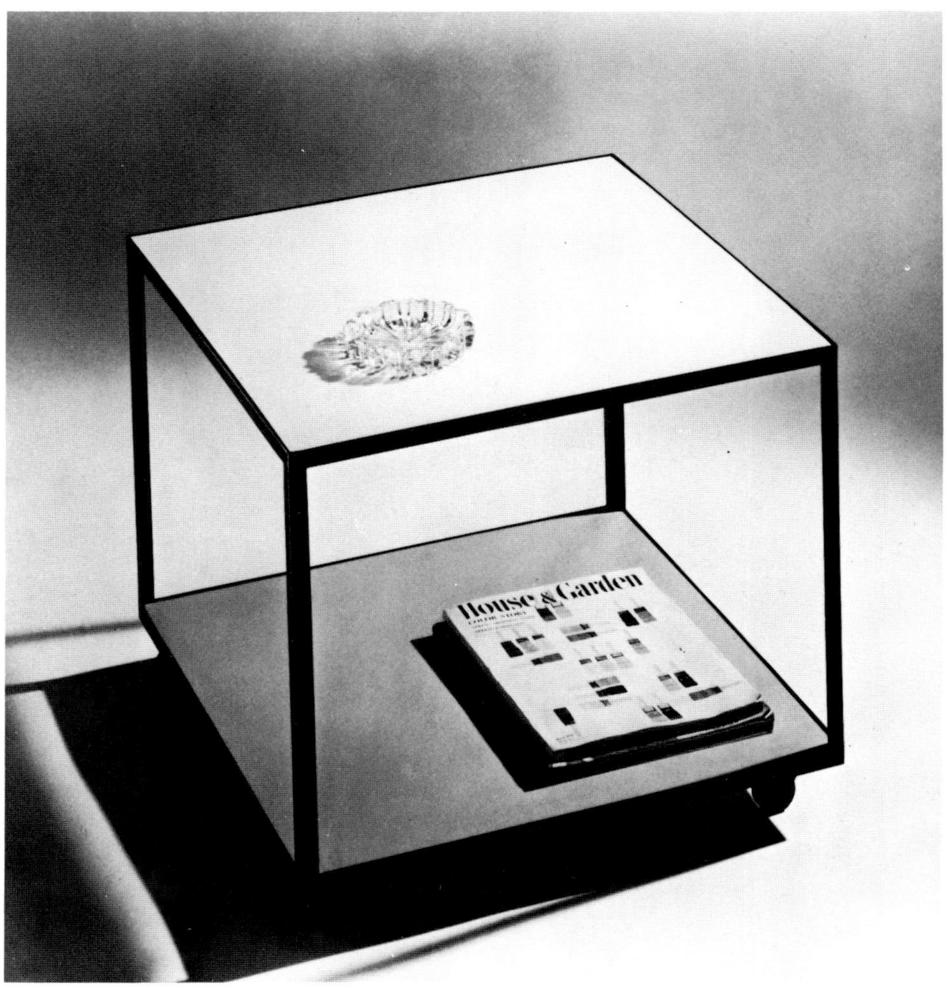

643 **George Nelson** c. 1951 USA
Tea trolley with angle-iron frame and plastic tops

644 **Herbert Hirche** 1959 Germany
Tea trolley with square tubular steel frame and tops in wood or plastic

645 **Florence Knoll** 1953 USA
Tables with iron bases and tops of wood

646 **George Nelson** c. 1951 USA
Small table with angle-iron frame and plastic top

647 **George Nelson** c. 1951 USA
Coffee table with angle-iron frame and plastic top

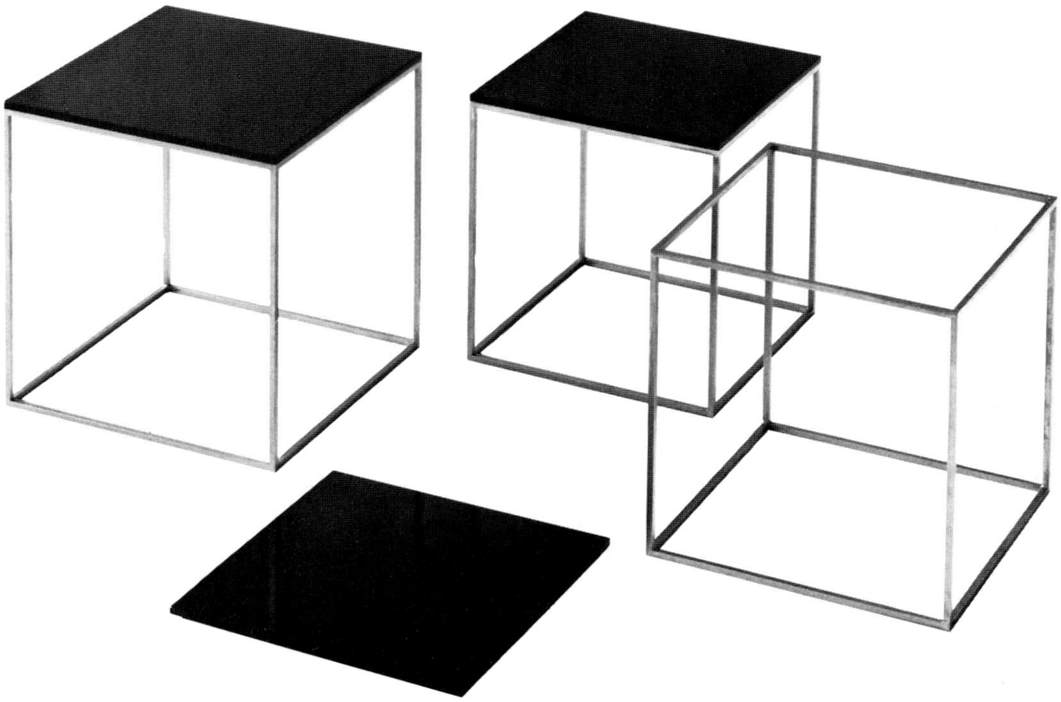

648 **Poul Kjaerholm** 1957 Denmark

Small stacking tables "71" with metal bases and plastic tops

649 **Team Form AG** 1963 Switzerland

Nesting tables "K 1" with frames of square tubular steel and inserted tops of crystal glass or marble

650 **Works Design** 1972 Germany

Nesting tables "121" with frames of chrome-plated steel tubes and tops of plastic

653 **Gae Aulenti** 1971 Italy ▷

Series of dinner and coffee tables "Festo" with frames of anodized aluminum and joints of injection-molded aluminum, tops of crystal glass or plastic laminate

651 **Poul Kjaerholm** 1956 Denmark
Table "61" with steel base and glass top

652 **Jørgen Høj** 1959 Denmark
Coffee table "157" with legs of mat finished anodized aluminum; top of laminated wood veneered in oak or rosewood on both sides

654 **Nardin & Radoczy** c. 1951 USA

Coffee table "TL-1" of solid ash or mahogany with legs of chrome-plated steel tubes

655 **Florence Knoll** 1955 USA

Table with chrome-plated steel base, birch or walnut top

656 **Jørgen Høj** 1962 Denmark

Circular coffee table "154" with legs of mat finished anodized aluminum; top of laminated wood veneered in oak or rosewood on both sides

658 **George Nelson** c. 1953 USA ▷

Coffee table "5452" with base of cast aluminum enamelled in black or white with plastic top and natural birch edgings

△ 657 **Eero Saarinen** 1957 USA
Table series with single pedestals of aluminum and marble or plastic tops

▽ 659 **Robert Haussmann, Fred Hochstrasser** 1960 Switzerland
Tables "T 304" with pedestals of anodized aluminum and wooden or marble tops

660 **Vico Magistretti** 1969 Italy
Demountable table "Stadio" of reinforced resin in various colors and sizes

661 **Helmut Bätzner** 1969 Germany
Stacking table of fiberglass-reinforced polyester, designed to match "Bofinger" chair (see ill. 386+387)

662 **Giovanni Offredi** 1968 Italy
"Gruppo Carola" including cupboard of molded plywood in lacquer finish, and matching demountable table composed of three identical parts

663 **Vico Magistretti** 1967 Italy

Square occasional table "Demetrio 70" of fiberglass-reinforced polyester

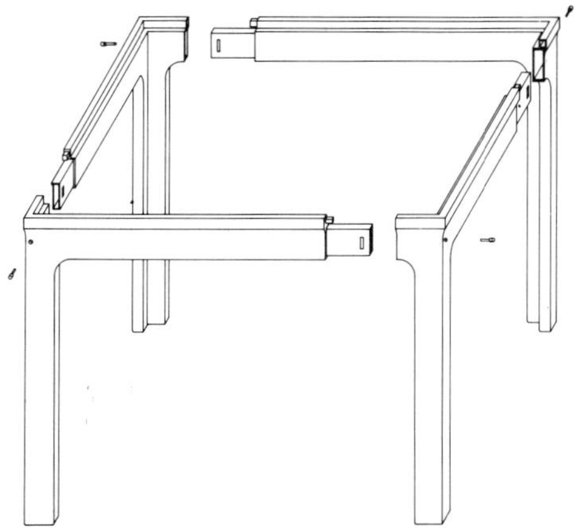

664+665 **Olaf von Bohr** 1971 Italy

Collpasible tables in various sizes and heights. Frame of four identical parts in ABS resin, simply put together and screwed. Top of plastic laminate in various colors

666 **John Mascheroni** 1968 USA

Stacking tables "422/18" of acrylic plastic

667 **Wolfgang Feierbach** 1965 Germany

Side tables "fg 2001" of fiberglass in various sizes, shapes, and colors; some with casters

668 + 669 **Rodolfo Bonetto** 1969 Italy

Plastic table "700 Quattroquarti" in four units which can be stacked and grouped as desired

670 **Giotto Stoppino** 1969 Italy

Stacking table "Scagno" of injection-molded plastic. Tables may also be arranged horizontally

672 **Mario Bellini** 1966 Italy
Stacking tables "I quattro gatti" of plastic

671 **Kenneth Brozen** 1968 USA
"Highlight" magazine table of plexiglass with joints of chrome-plates steel

673 **Alberto Rosselli** 1972 Italy
Open container elements in plastic on casters. Can be put together to various heights with corner elements of different lengths and built-in slots

674 **Verner Panton** 1965 Denmark

"Barboy" of molded wood on casters in lacquer finish

674	
675	676
677	678

675 **Emma Schweinberger-Gismondi** 1967 Italy

Small cylindrical table "Giano" and "Giano Vano" (with or without recess) of fiberglass-reinforced polyester

676 **Chiara Briganti** 1968 Italy

Small cylindrical table on casters with storing space and two drawers; molded plywood lacquered white

679+680 **Verner Panton** 1965 Denmark
"Party Set" of molded wood, to be used as stools (with loose cushions), occasional tables, and bar. Being of varying diameter, tables stack inside each other

681 **Anna Castelli Ferrieri** 1970 Italy
Range of cylindrical plastic containers "4953–4956" in two sizes, with or without sliding doors and casters; can be combined as desired

682 **Eugenio Gerli** 1967 Italy
Bar "Jamaica B.106" on casters in veneered wood or lacquer finish

◁ 677+678 **Sergio Mazza** 1968 Italy
Bar "Bacco" of fiberglass-reinforced polyester

683 **Works Design** c. 1952 Switzerland
Desk with steel tube legs and separate cabinet units on casters

Office Furniture

Most office furniture today is made of metal. This form has a long tradition, as can be seen from the fact that filing cabinets at the turn of the century were usually made of this material.

If one views the development in the past thirty years, the most convincing examples are those that operate most clearly within this tradition and whose merit is contained in their robust inconspicuousness. This is especially true of the office furniture of Pohlschroder (ills. 727-731).

When one comes across these articles of furniture in places where they are still being used, in the offices of the publisher Hatje, for instance, one feels that the correct form for office furniture has been found. These objects were, of course, never beautiful in the proper meaning of the word, just always sensible and therefore a pleasure to look at. One had the impression that they had been developed by a well trained expert but not especially by a designer. At the time they were planned they could manage without any "styling", which is often somewhat superfluous in objects that have to serve a quite ordinary purpose. Subsequent developments always seemed rather ambitious. They had overtones of elegance that were unsuitable for the way they were to be used.

The system designed by the group of architects B.B.P.R. and produced by Olivetti is an exception (ills. 734-738). The details were styled so precisely that an impression of great functionality was produced. A good deal of thought went into the distinct structure of the furniture. It was easy to see how the individual elements could be put together in different ways. At first sight they appeared old-fashioned but the special intelligence of this Italian system could be seen in the conscious recourse to traditional details (in the formation of the legs, for example). Just as convincing was George Nelson's idea in 1964 of resurrecting the old standing-desk (ills. 743-745). This object, together with the characteristic detail of the roll-top, served to evoke the atmosphere of a "classic" office. However, it could not quite resolve the problem that the object's styling, although excellent, seemed overdone in relation to the simple purpose it was supposed to serve.

In the category of more straightforward office furniture, the table with its movable box elements that Wohnbedarf in Zurich produced (ill. 683) is still very convincing today. The principle behind it was often used afterwards with variations. One cannot help wondering why it was necessary to modify this uniquely successful design. In comparison with its maturity, all the others appear conspicuously affected. In this design the elements are coordinated excellently without any inset or projecting parts; the composition of the materials is extremely sensitive: chrome-plated steel tubes, light wood and black linoleum. A perfect piece of furniture of great precision; an ingenious piece of furniture.

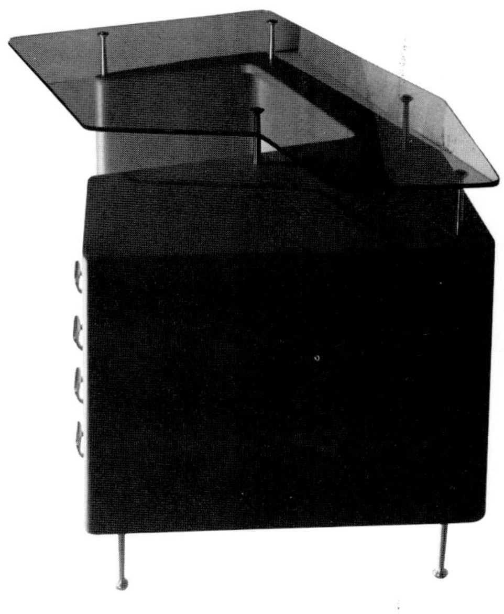

684	685
686	687
688	689

690 **Alfred Altherr** c. 1954 Switzerland
Desk in white maple, sliding doors and pulls with dark veneer

691 + 692 **Alberto Rosselli** c. 1953 Italy
Desk of molded wood with plastic laminate, glass top

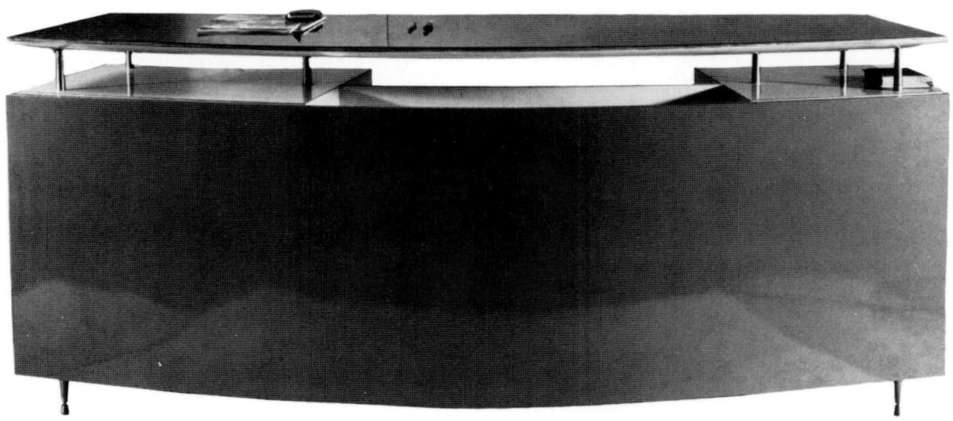

◁ 684 **Franco Albini** c. 1950 Italy
Desk with metal frame and glass top

◁ 685 **Gianemilio, Piero and Anna Monti** 1954 Italy
Desk with metal frame, opaque glass top, plastic-laminated drawer units

◁ 686 + 687 **Alberto Rosselli** c. 1950 Italy
Desk with steel tube frame, top and drawer fronts of glass

◁ 688 + 689 **Jens Risom** c. 1953 USA
Office furniture series "Group Eight" in birch or walnut with brass handles

693 + 694 **Florence Knoll** c. 1950 USA
Desks of wood with square steel tube frames and attached drawers

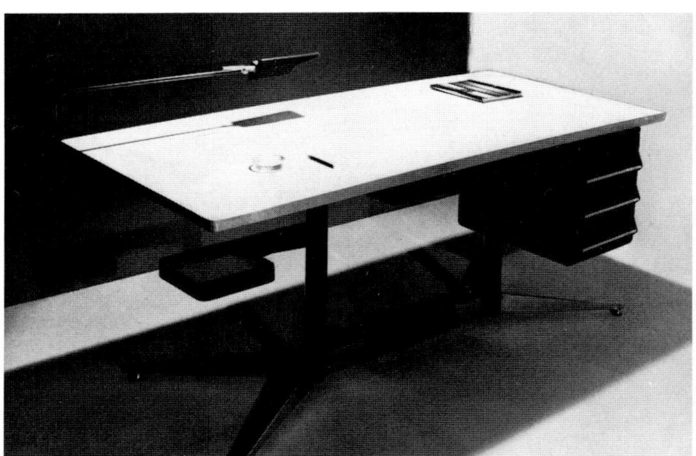

699+700 **George Nelson** 1947/1955 USA
"Executive Office Group" of walnut with wooden or plastic tops, chrome-plated legs

◁◁ 695 **Luisa Castiglioni** c. 1952 Italy
Desk with steel frame, wooden drawer unit and plastic-laminated top

◁ 696 **Oliver Lundquist, Julian von der Lancken** 1958 USA
"Architective Furniture" desk with walnut top and drawer fronts, two pedestals of ebonized walnut

◁◁ 697 **Gio Ponti** c. 1952 Italy
Desk with steel frame and plastic-laminated top

◁ 698 **Robin Day** c. 1954 Great Britain
Desk with metal legs, wooden pedestals and linoleum covered top

701 **Charles Eames** c. 1952 USA

Desk, part of "Eames Storage Units", with top of walnut or birch, frame of chrome-plated steel

702 **Fred Ruf** 1953 Switzerland

Desk with metal frame, wooden top and drawers

703 **Kurt Thut** 1955 Switzerland

Executive desk "KT 124-34" with interchangeable pedestals in rosewood or walnut and frame of chrome-plated profile steel

704+705 **Jaap Penraat** 1956 Netherlands

Desk and typewriter desk with beech base, colored drawers and linoleum-covered top

702	704
703	705

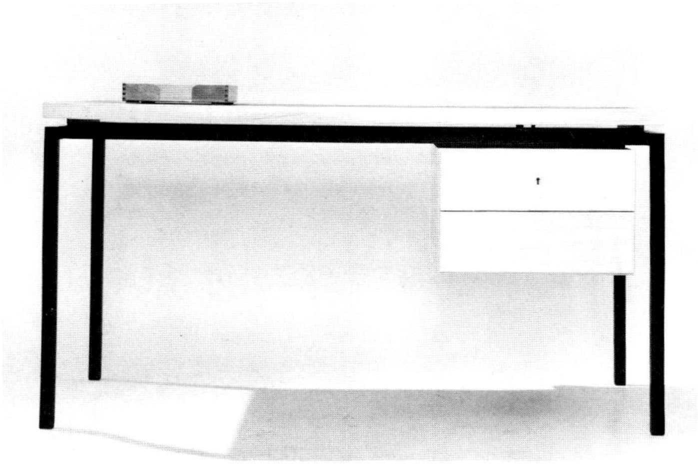

706 **Poul Kjaernoim** 1956 Denmark
Drawing table with flat steel frame, top and drawer of plywood

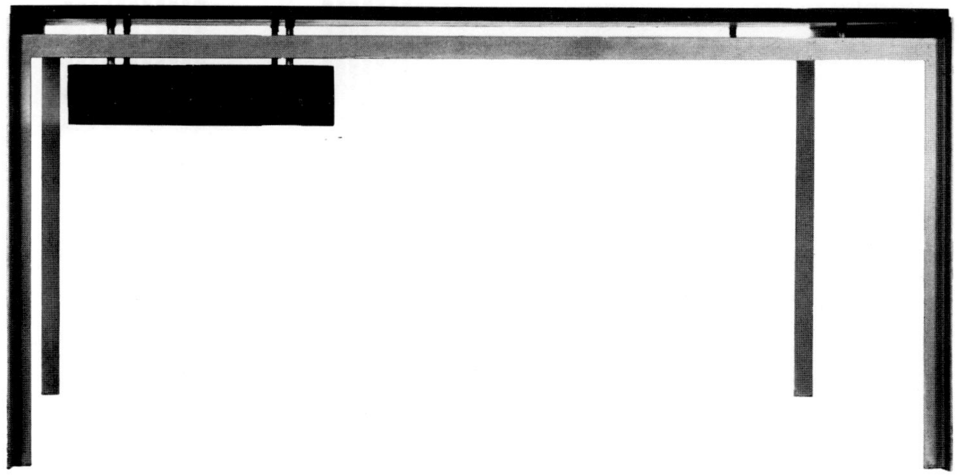

707+708 **Henning Jensen, Torben Valeur** 1961 Denmark
Modular office furniture "M-40"; solid oak, fittings of chrome-plated metal in mat finish

709+710 **Herbert Berry, Christopher Cattle** 1962 Great Britain
Series of office furniture in chipboard slab construction with teak or mahogany veneers, fittings and handles of aluminum. Shown here are double pedestal desk "LD46" and L-shaped work station "LS52/LTY36"

707	709
708	710

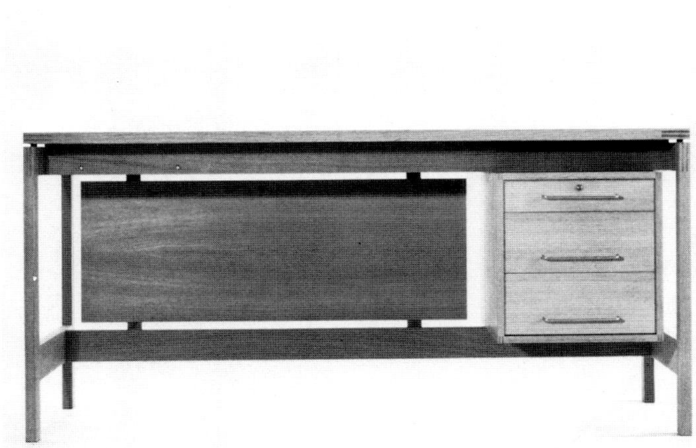

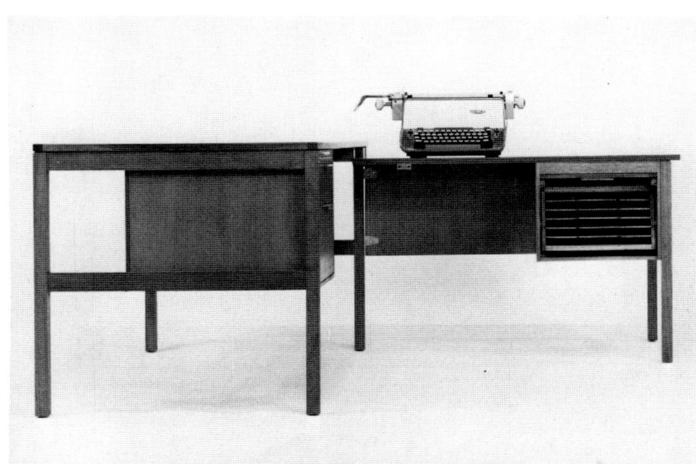

711 **Dieter Rams** 1957 Germany

Double-top desk "RZ57" in beech or walnut veneer; detachable legs of anodized aluminum

712 **Frank Bolliger** 1960 Switzerland

Desk with metal frame in black or grey lacquer finish and rosewood pedestal. Reversible table top of rosewood on one side, plastic on the other

713 **Werner Blaser** 1960 Switzerland

Desk in white plastic with chrome-plated steel frame

716 **Jens Risom** 1959 USA ▷

"Group Nine" office furniture series consisting of desk arrangements and cabinets of walnut with aluminum fittings

717 **Herbert Hirche** 1957 Germany ▷▷

Desk and sideboard in teak, interiors of white maple, bases of square steel tubes

718 **Robin Day** 1958/59 Great Britain ▷

"Status Group" office furniture of walnut, mahogany, or teak, with square steel frames and wooden or plastic tops

719 **Alain Richard** 1960 France ▷▷

"Direction" office furniture series consisting of desk arrangements, filing cabinets, and telephone table in rosewood and plastic, all interiors in oak, frames of black lacquered or chrome-plated steel

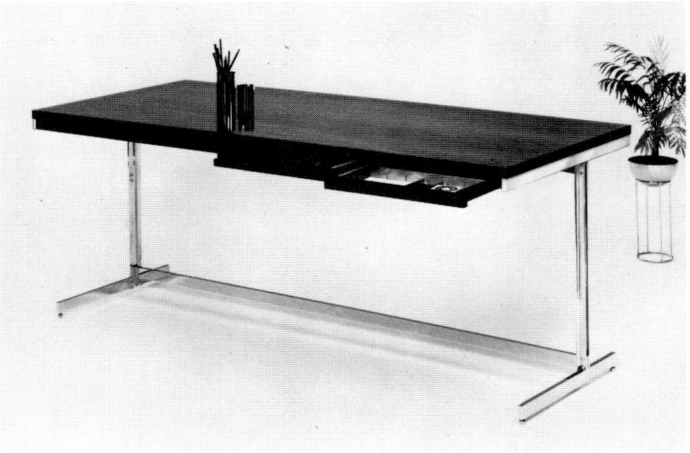

714+715 **Hugh Acton** 1962 USA
Executive desk "ET 3377" with frame of chrome-plated steel and various storage elements

720+721 **Friso Kramer** 1956 Netherlands

"Revolt" desks of pressed sheet steel, frames of square steel tubes, interchangeable drawer units

722 **Works Design** 1958 USA

"Steelcase 1300 Line" desk with lacquered metal frame, colored pedestal and back panel, plastic laminated top

723 **Skidmore, Owings & Merrill** 1957 USA

"Inland Steel Furnishings" desk with black steel frame, baked-enamel steel pedestals, white plastic top

724–726 **Arne Jacobsen, Niels Jørgen Haugesen** 1969/70 Denmark

Office furniture series "Djob". Frames of desks and typing tables of aluminum with rounded foot pieces and angular joints of steel. Typing table changeable into a suspension filing cabinet. Table tops, drawers, and cabinet units in wood with dark blue or ochre plastic laminate

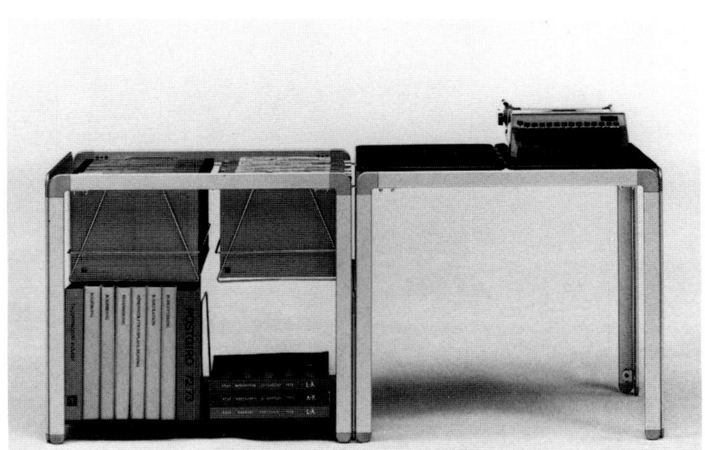

727 + 728 **Georg Leowald** c. 1953 Germany

Desks with frames of chrome-plated steel tubes, interchangeable drawer units of sheet steel, and plastic-laminated tops

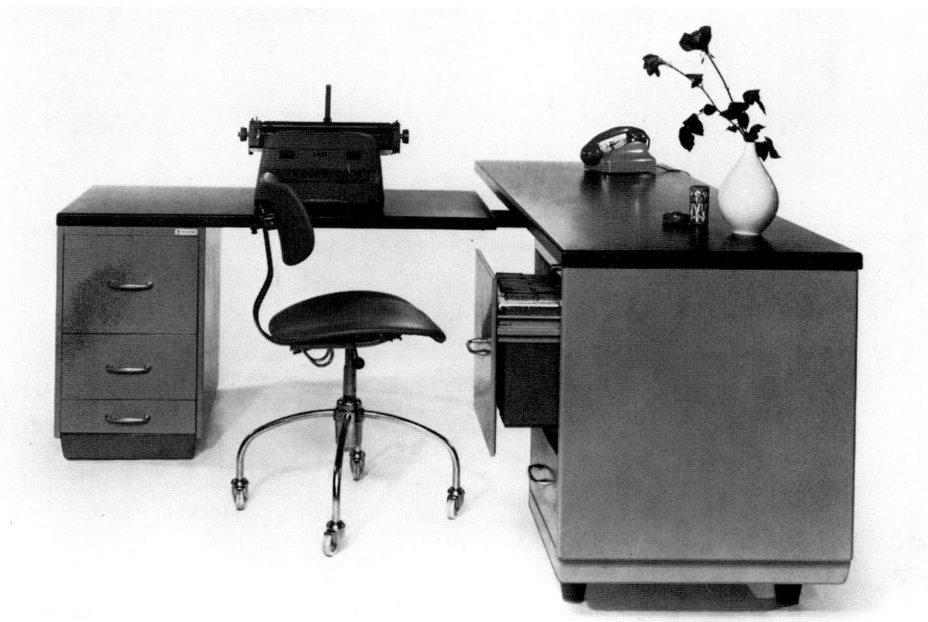

729 + 730 **Georg Leowald** c. 1957 Germany

Desks "3800" with metal legs or bases, lacquered steel pedestals in varying drawer arrangements, plastic tops

731 **Works Design** 1960 Germany
Office furniture "WF-System" with metal bases, lacquered steel pedestals in varying drawer arrangements, plastic tops

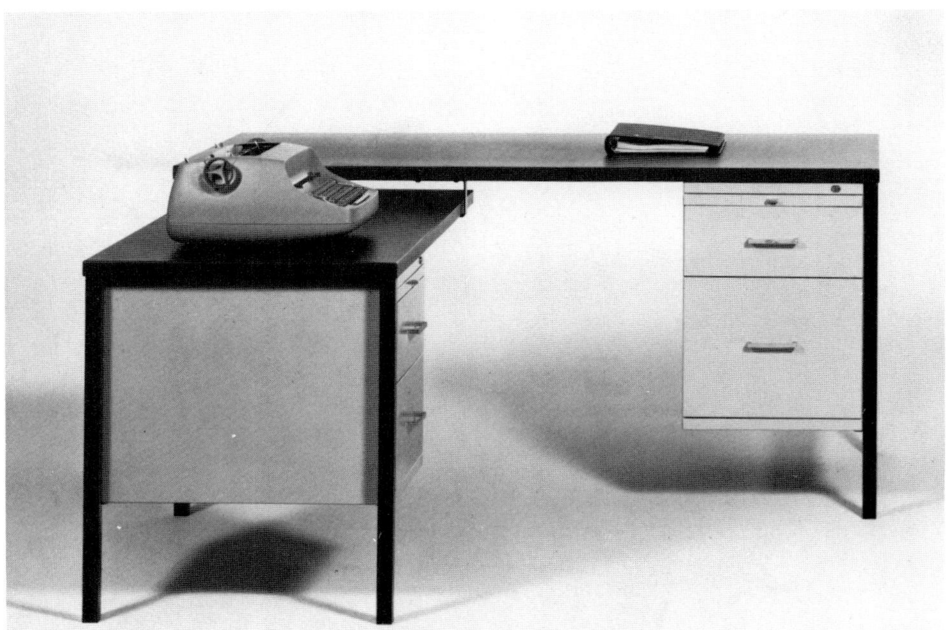

732+733 **Works Design** 1963 Germany
Modular series of office furniture "3900". Table tops in various sizes and pedestals of different depths, with interchangeable drawer units and variable interior equipment, ensure a wide range of combinations. Legs of square profile metal in dark grey lacquer finish; pedestals lacquer-finished in two different states of grey; tops plastic-laminated

734–738 **Studio B.B.P.R.** 1959 Italy

"Spazio" office furniture series composed of interchangeable units. All elements in metal, table tops plastic-laminated

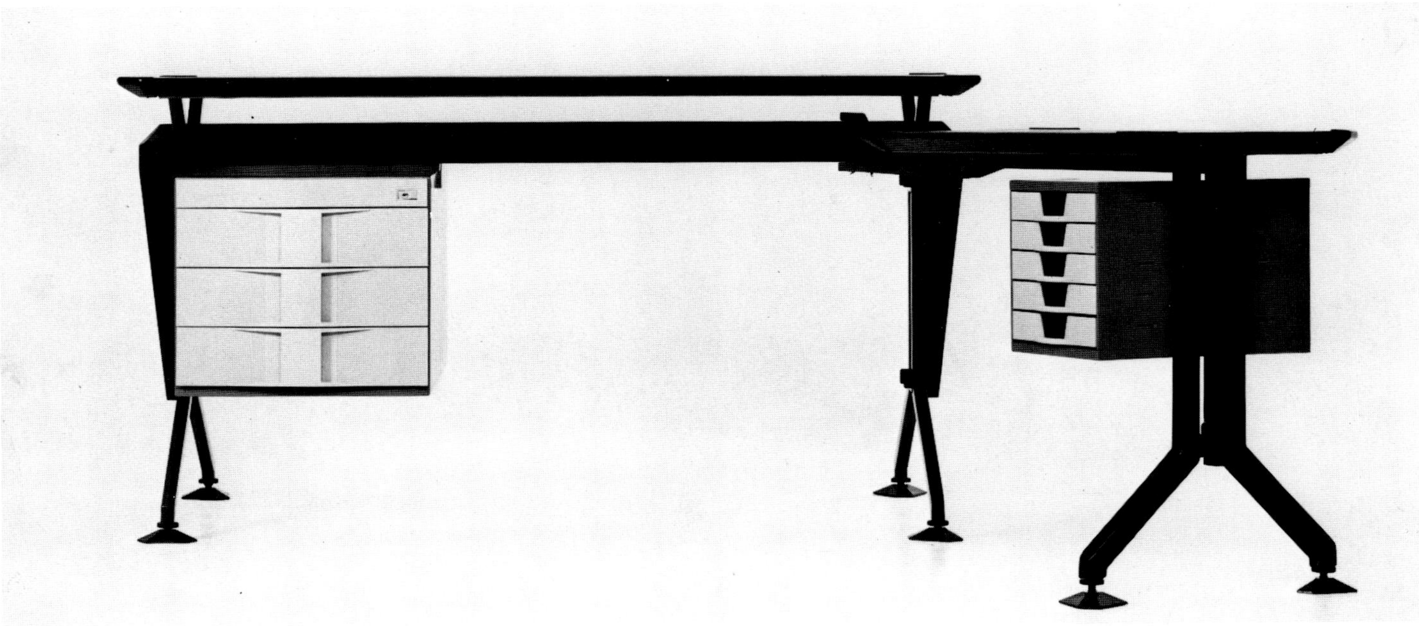

739 **Studio B.B.P.R.** 1963 Italy

Office furniture "Arco" with supporting frames in three sizes and drawers of stove-enamelled steel, tops plastic-laminated or covered with imitation leather or cloth

740–742 **Alberto Rosselli** 1960 Italy

Office furniture series composed of interchangeable units with wooden tops and frames of chrome-plated or black lacquered steel

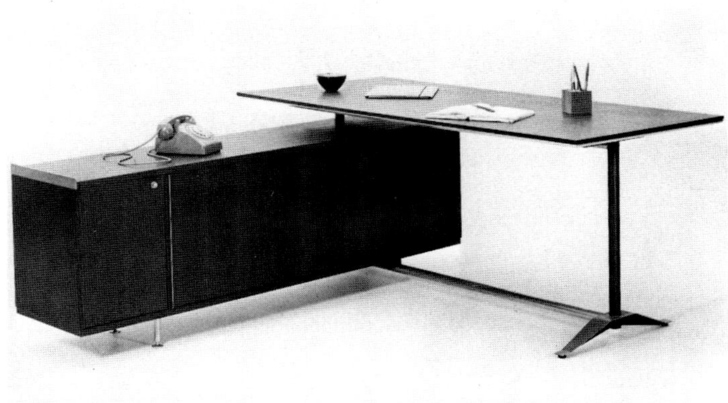

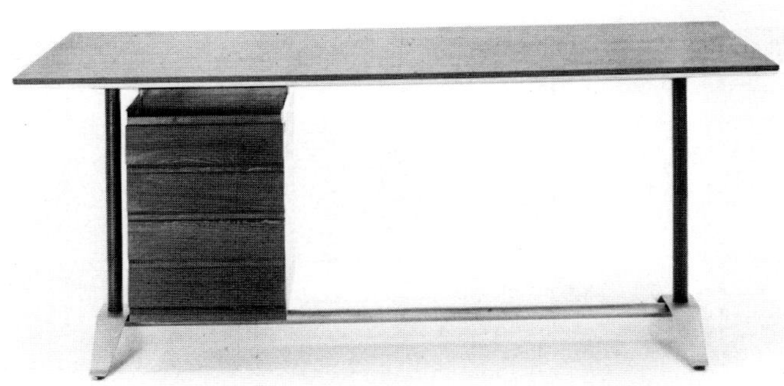

743–745 **George Nelson** 1964 USA

"Action Office" furniture system. Two types of desks with cast aluminum legs and chrome foot rail, molded plastic end panels, filing bins with roll or flipper tops of ash or walnut, writing surfaces of plastic laminate. Matching height-adjustable swivel perch and cabinet unit which can be combined with desks or be hung on a wall

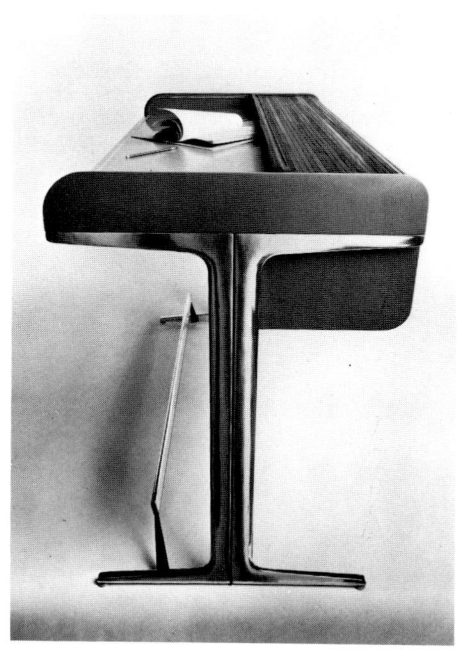

746 **Robert Probst** 1970 USA

"Action Office 2", a wall panel system based on the former "Action Office" with shelves, storage elements and writing tops

747 **Studio Igl** 1970 Germany

All-plastic desk "IGL-Tisch" of cast-molded polyurethane-Duromer foam in various colors, drawer fronts and top in imitation leather or plastic combined with wood. Communication panel can be equipped as desired

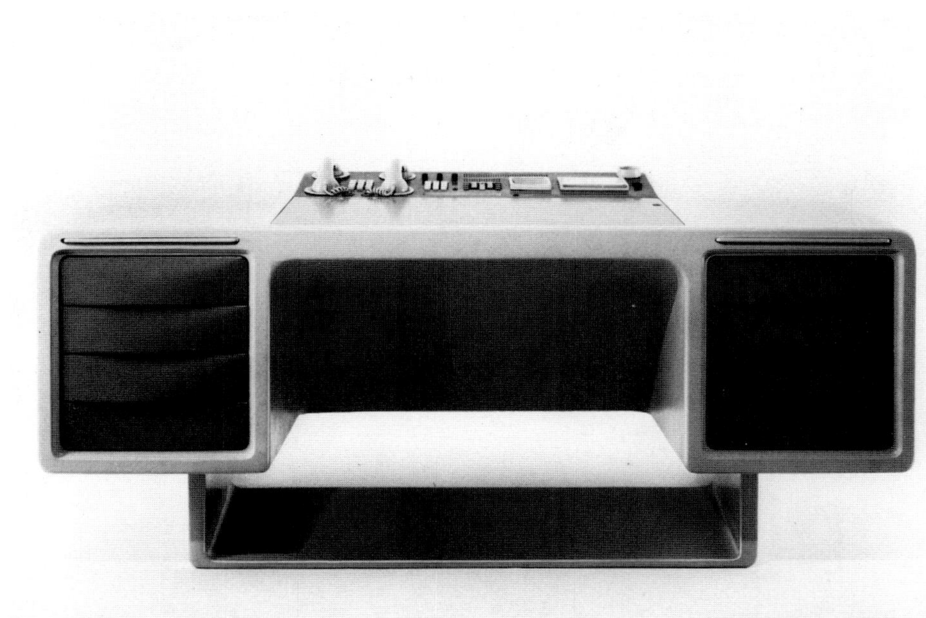

748 + 749 **Works Design** 1971 Germany

Modular office furniture series "exklusiv" with various red colored cabinet elements and grey table tops of polyurethane, supports of grey lacquer-finished cast aluminum. All these components can be assembled in various combinations to form desks, shelves and cabinet units

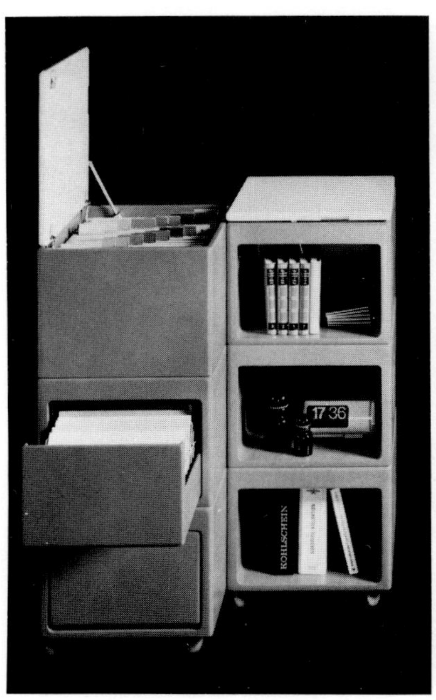

750–754 **Peter Raake** 1958/59 Germany

Office furniture series "ZG-System" composed of interchangeable units; desks, tables, and cabinets of wood, colored steel or plastic, frames of square tubular steel

755 **Fritz Haller** 1964/70 Switzerland

Series of storage furniture for offices with modular frames of chrome-plated steel tubes screwed with spheric joints. Shelves and side panels of lacquer-finished sheet metal or of plastic-laminated wood. Matching table with frame of chrome-plated steel and plastic top

756 **Osvaldo Borsani, Eugenio Gerli** 1968 Italy

Modular office furniture system "Graphis" with three basic elements of sheet steel in white or grey enamel finish: two types of container units, one L-shaped supporting element, and various panels in plastic laminate. The system allows a wide variety of combinations and is particularly suited for open-plan offices

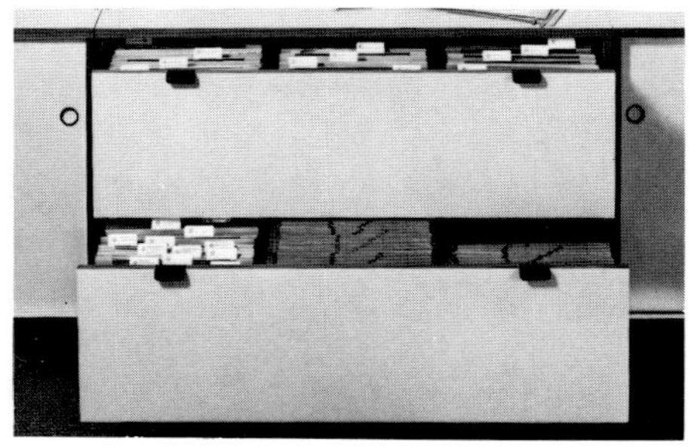

757+758 **Hans Gugelot** 1961 Switzerland

Series of desks "M 125 S" with adjustable interior equipment, designed on the same module as the demountable furniture group "M 125" (see ill. 779). All surfaces covered in dull white plastic, edges in afrormosia. Matching filing cabinets

759 **Walter Wirz** 1960 Switzerland

Desk "WR 403" of walnut with a variety of pedestal elements, metal frame in grey lacquer or chrome finish

760+761 **Works Design** 1962 USA

Office furniture series "Formal Line" with chrome-plated or painted steel frames. Table tops may be selected from a wide range of natural wood finishes or plastic laminates. Cabinets with various drawers and drop-door storage

762 **Marco Zanuso** 1970 Italy

Desk series "Cartesio" of plywood with noise-absorbing white resin laminate; connection of single elements with plastic tenons

763 **Karl-Heinz Teufel** 1974 Germany

Office furniture series "Interfunction", desks in plastic laminate, frames of mat aluminum, tops with resin laminate. Desks and cabinet units are supplied as kits of individual components easily ready for use through a combination of mating joints and threaded fasteners

764 + 765 **Pierre Guariche** 1963 France

Desks and drawing tables of chrome-plated square tubular steel and tops of dull white plastic laminate. Shelves and pedestals of plastic imitation walnut. Cabinet unit in front of window with eight drop-doors

766–768 **Works Design/Karl Dittert** 1972 Germany

Office furniture series "Modulares Element-Programm" with all components for the technologically equipped office. Desk frames of steel in various widths and depths, tops in wood with plastic laminate. Each desk has raceways for electric equipment covered with a metal lid with molded trays of plastic. Larger desks with built-in filing bins. Several desks can be linked by curved elements in different angles or by square elements

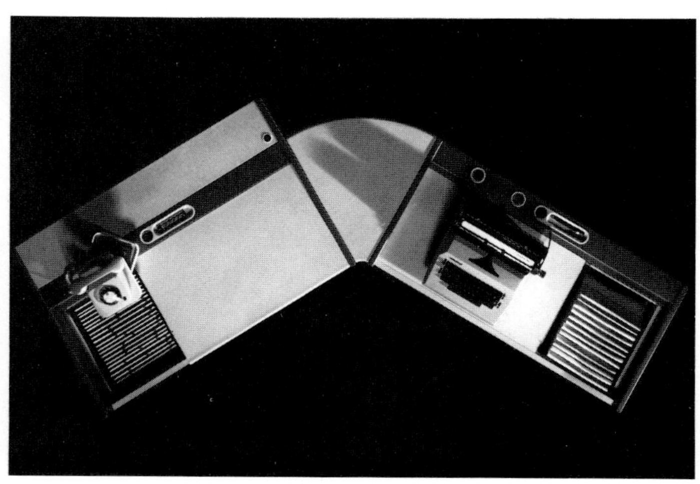

769–772 **Hartmut Esslinger** 1976 Germany

Modular office furniture series "RCO". Frames of tubular steel; tops with rounded corners, cabinet units and shelves of resin laminate in various colors. Tubular supports for telephone or file bins (770), power supply through tubular table legs (771), infinitely variable mechanism for adjusting the height of writing and typing desks (772). The range comprises also such other office furniture items as cabinets, drawers, trolley-type containers on castors, or room dividers

770

771

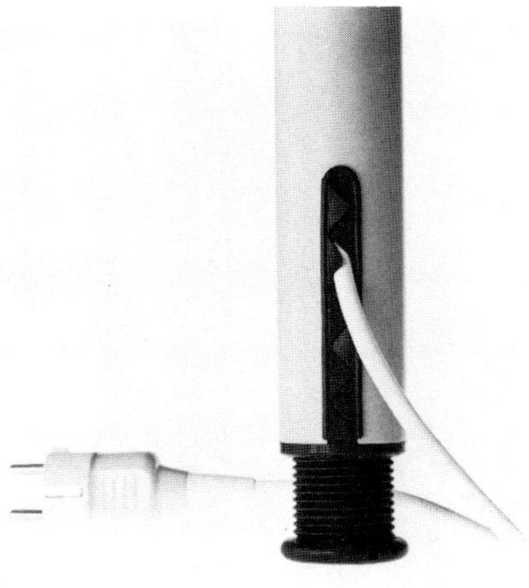

772

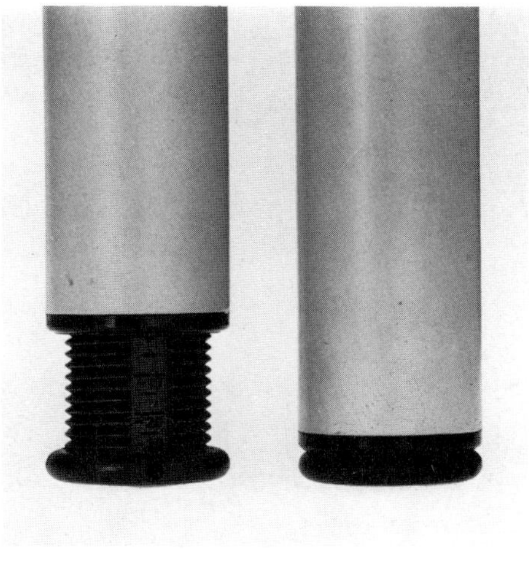

773–775 **Works Design** 1970 Germany

"Raum-in-Raum-System" of office furniture. Wall partitions in two heights of sound-absorbing panels covered with fabric. Connection of panels by posts of anodized aluminum with height-adjustable foot plates. The posts also serve to hang various pieces of office furniture as desk tops, shelves and storage elements

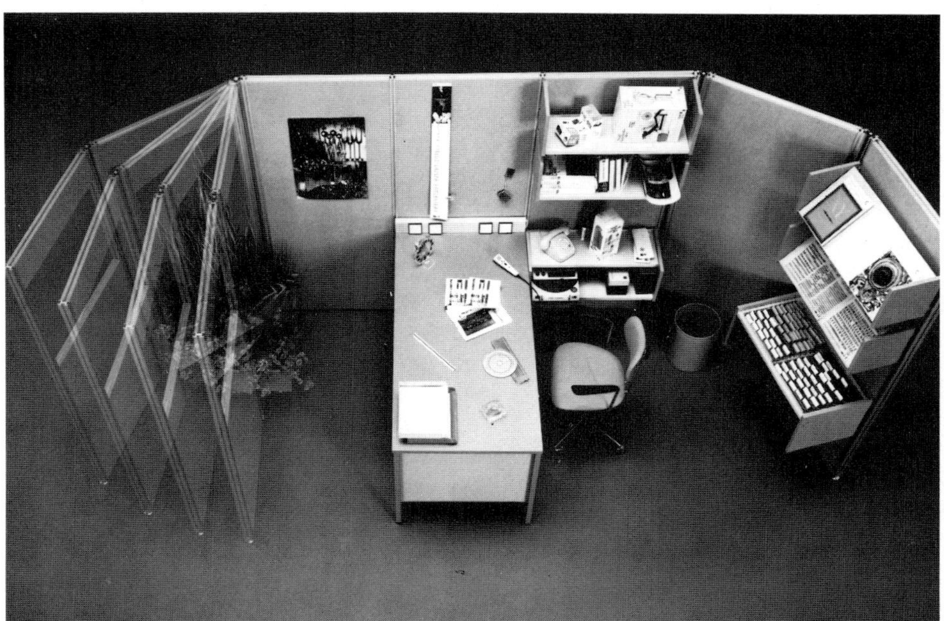

776–778 **Ettore Sottsass jr.** 1970/71 Italy

Office furniture series "Synthesis 45" consisting of two chair models (see ill. 277), desks with legs and stiffeners of light grey enameled sheet metal and tops of plastic laminate which can be combined in numerous ways, drawer pedestals and free standing cabinets of dark or light blue lacquer-finished sheet metal with ABS handles, also on casters, various shelving and storage units. Room dividers are assembled of free standing bookshelves and acoustic screens in brown with hinges and adjusting screws of ABS. All elements can be combined in many ways

779 **Hans Gugelot** 1953 Switzerland
Modular group "M 125" consisting of metal rods and panels covered with light grey plastic, afrormosia edging. Components can be assembled as desired

Cabinets and Shelves

It is probably very difficult for us to realize, years later, what kind of innovation Nisse Strinning's shelving system was when it first appeared. "String" became the guiding object for a design freed from unnecessary bulk (ills. 849, 850). The light grille structure was extremely spartan in its use of materials and the pieces that slot into it, most of them simple in design, strengthened the impression that here was a very uncluttered piece of furniture. In addition, "String" hung on the wall and did not touch the floor; it hovered. The whole system may seem rather too fragile and delicate for today's tastes but when it was created (1950) it was revolutionary "String" broke the predominance of free-standing storage furniture and heavy shelving, it lifted the structure off the floor and introduced cheerfulness into a matter that had previously been dealt with much too solemnly. The ladder system may have tempted people to let stuffed animals and wooden monkeys clamber over it but even that was better than the bronze figures and porcelain knick-knacks that used to serve as ornamentation. That sort of thing did not match "String". Liberation really entered people's houses with this system, one could breathe freely, and suddenly had an amazing amount of space. And that was also necessary because the cramped living conditions after the war and the spare dimensions of new flats did not leave much space for larger pieces of furniture. Nevertheless, "String" was more than just a practical and timely solution to the problem of storing books, magazines, glasses, plates and cutlery. It represented in fact an idea, and it possessed a convincing affinity to the ideas that were influencing architecture at that time. The material economy that the war had previously enforced was transposed here into a statement advocating conscious renunciation. The recent increased demand for "String" proves that the basic thought behind it is still operative.

It should not come as much of a surprise that none of the subsequent systems was equally satisfactory. Modifications, often involving replacing the ladders with vertical rods jammed between ceiling and floor, appeared heavier and therefore more complicated than the original.

In this, they violated the principles behind the whole concept.

The simple fact that a room seems much smaller when a piece of furniture stands higher than table-top height explains why the low sideboard was so popular in the modest flats of the postwar era. Just as "String" replaced the terrible old bookcase, the sideboard did the same for the "buffet" which used to dominate the dining-room. At the very beginning of this development there was an almost classic model by Florence Knoll, where best fabric replaced the usual showy veneer (ill. 791). A large amount of Japanese influence was evident in this piece of furniture, which also had sliding doors.

Among the compact systems, Hans Gugelot's was both one of the first and has remained one of the best (ill. 779). Newer developments dispensed with the combination of individual side, top and connecting elements, which often only appeared to be cheap. They functioned according to the principle of units that could be arranged in any order. Old ship's dressers served as a model for them (ill. 873). In another case of constructive reminiscence, the former wardrobe-trunk celebrated a fine comeback (ills. 937-940).

785 **Taichiro Nakai** c. 1954 Japan
Demountable wardrobe and sideboard of molded plywood

786+787 **Robin Day, Clive Latimer** c. 1950 Great Britain
Cabinets of molded plywood with legs of metal

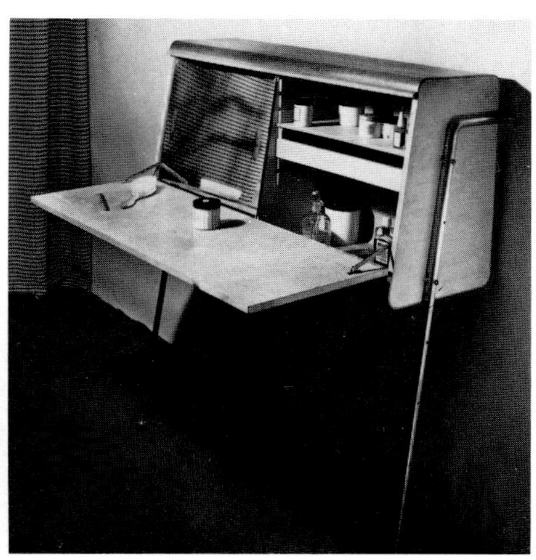

780		781
782	783	784
785		
786		787

◁ 780 **A. Patijn** c. 1951 Netherlands
Sideboard of wood with folding doors

◁ 781–784 **Cees Braakman** c. 1951 Netherlands
Cabinet series of wood comprising sideboards, bookshelves with writing desks, cupboards, and chests; legs of molded wood

788+789 **Hans J. Wegner** c. 1952 Denmark
Chest in oak with doors in teak, also with additional bookshelves for use as writing desk

790 **Franz Füeg** 1950 Switzerland
Series of storage furniture of wood, comprising sideboard, chest of drawers, and wardrobe of wood

791 **Florence Knoll** 1950 USA

Sideboard with bast-covered sliding doors

792 **Nardin & Radoczy** c. 1951 USA

Wall cabinet of wood with lacquered drawers and door, sliding doors of glass, adjustable shelves

793 **Robin Day** c. 1953 Great Britain

Sideboard of wood with lacquered sliding doors and legs of metal

794 **Charles Eames** c. 1950 USA
Storage units with steel construction and plastic-laminated plywood shelves and drawers

795 **Alfred Altherr** c. 1953 Switzerland
Sideboard composed of chest and storage units with bench base and metal legs

796 **George Nelson** c. 1950 USA
Sideboard with sliding doors and legs of chrome-plated tubular steel

797 **George Nelson** c. 1952 USA
Chest of drawers in oak, legs and pulls of lacquered steel tubes

798 **George Nelson** 1952 USA
Chest of drawers in rosewood and natural cane bench

801 **Charles Eames** c. 1950 USA ▷
Chest of drawers "ESU 275", part of "Eames Storage Units" series, with frames of chrome-plated steel, drawer fronts in birch, tops in walnut or birch; side panels in various colors

802 **George Nelson** c. 1953 USA ▷▷
"Steelframe Series" of storage units with frames of black or white painted steel, drawers and shelves in various colors and tops of glass or black or white plastic

799+800 **George Nelson** c. 1951 USA

Sideboard and miniature chest in teak with pulls of white porcelain and legs of turned brass

803 **Florence Knoll** c. 1953 USA
Chests of drawers "135/136/137" with white or black fronts and metal legs

804 **Jens Risom** c. 1953 USA
Chest of drawers composed of wooden units

805 **Paul McCobb** 1954 USA
Drawer chest with rectangular brass legs

806 **William Pahlmann** c. 1952 USA
Series of chests of drawers in wood

807 **Edward J. Wormley** c. 1950 USA
Series of chests of drawers with legs of molded wood

808 **Edward J. Wormley** c. 1950 USA
Wardrobe cabinet with hinged doors and drawers of different heights

809+810 **Hans J. Wegner** c. 1957 Denmark

Teak cabinets with wood or tubular steel legs

▽ 811–813 **Cees Braakman** c. 1957 Netherlands

Modular teak or walnut group with detachable legs of square tubular steel and black plastic pulls. Top cabinets with white flap doors are removable

816 **Alain Richard** 1957 France ▷▽

Dining room furniture group, all parts collapsible. Exteriors in wood or plastic laminate, interiors in mahogany, underframes of chrome-plated steel

814 **Herbert Hirche** 1959 Germany

"LIF" modular group of collapsible elements in walnut, white maple interior, fixtures and underframe of chrome-plated square tubular steel

815 **Herbert Hirche** 1957 Germany

Rosewood sideboard of the "DHS-40" furniture series. White maple interior, underframe of lacquered square tubular steel

817+818 **Reni Trüdinger** c. 1957 Switzerland

Modular bookshelves consisting of lacquered wooden shelves with grooves for sliding doors, black brackets and base parts

819–821 **Works Design** 1955 USA

Chests with metal drawer slides, fronts of natural or white lacquered wood, tops of wood or in white plastic laminate, backs white plastic laminate

822+823 **Dieter Waeckerlin** 1963 Switzerland

Storage units "Serie III (H 110)" with frames of Japanese elm or Brazilian rosewood and white plastic surfaces. Three basic units of different lengths with doors or drawers and with a wide variety of interior equipment may be combined to meet individual needs. Also with doors on both sides for use as room-divider

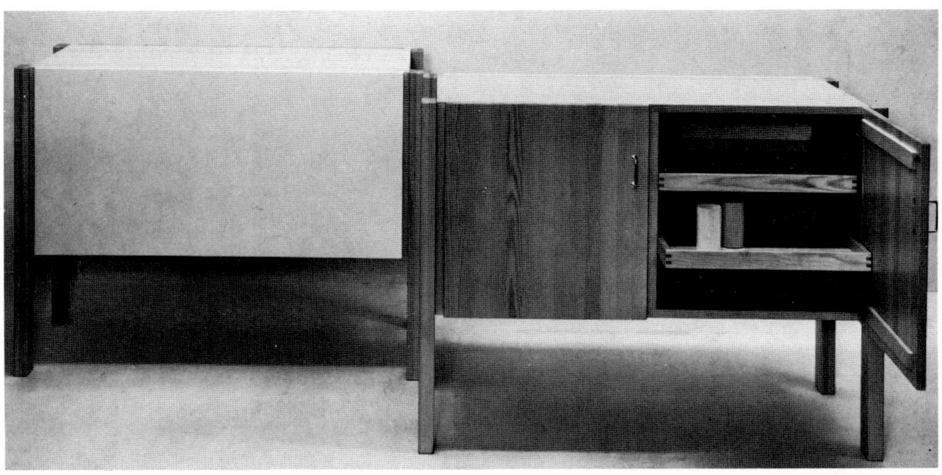

824 **Pirkko Stenros** 1959 Finland

Cabinet units of pine, partly laminated in white plastic

825 **Arne Karlsen** 1960 Denmark

Sideboard "ak-26" consisting of two units in oak

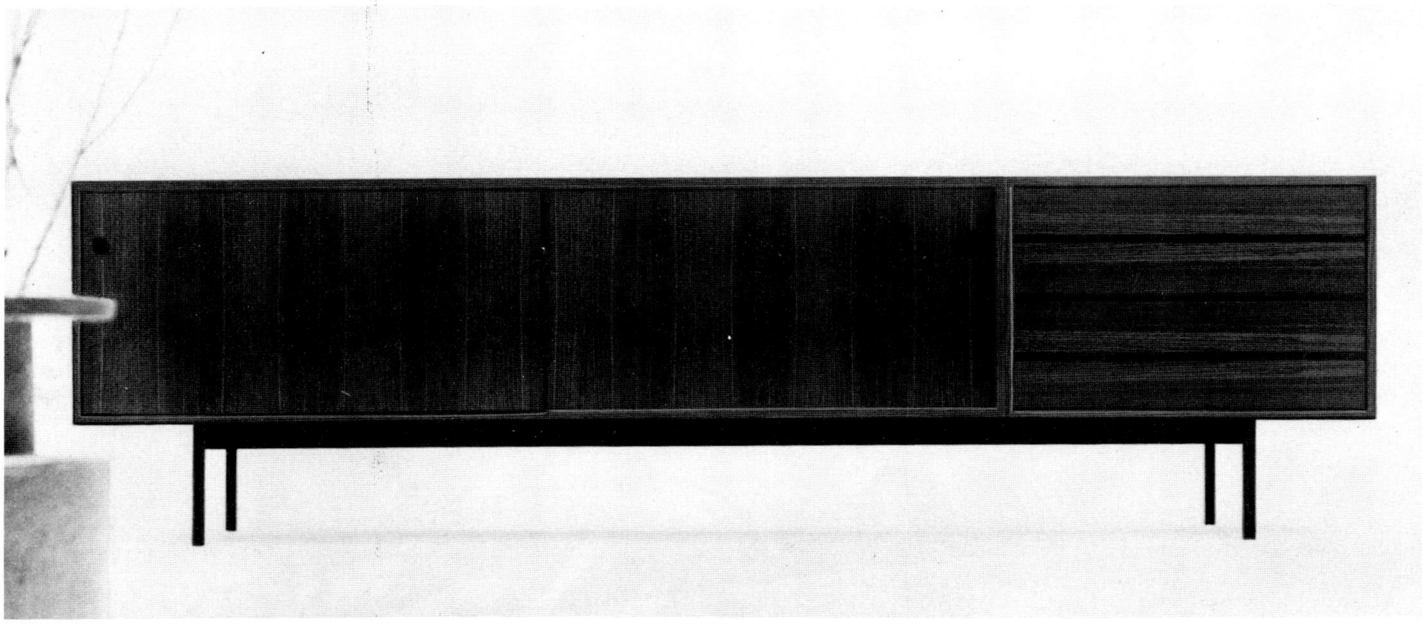

◁ 826 **Gianfranco Frattini** 1960 Italy

Sideboards "502" and "503" with drawers and tambour doors of jacaranda or teak. Units are supported by benchlike frames and may be stacked

◁ 827 **Walter Wirz** 1960 Switzerland

Sideboard in rosewood or teak, underframe of lacquered metal

◁ 828 **Dieter Waeckerlin** 1959 Switzerland

Sideboard "B 40", part of the extensive furniture series "behr waeckerlin-massmöbel", in teak with black lacquered metal underframe

829 **Walter Wirz** 1960 Switzerland

White lacquered bookshelves "190" and "191" and sideboard "192" in rosewood or wengé with white lacquered sliding doors and metal underframe

830 **Hugh Acton** 1960 USA

Modular group in wood with adjustable metal frames. Components are adaptable for living room, bedroom, and studio use, and can be assembled in various combinations as chests, cabinets, sideboards, shelves, and room dividers

831 + 832 **Florence Knoll** 1961 USA

Sideboard "119 H" with four doors of natural-finished walnut with maple interiors, or with doors covered in white plastic laminate. Underframe of solid walnut or of chrome-plated steel

833 **Helmut Fuchs** 1961 Germany

Sideboard "A 240/4-105" of rosewood with white plastic fronts and macoré interior; nickel-plated legs

834 **Frank Bolliger** 1960/61 Switzerland

Sideboard in larch, plastic-faced sliding doors, legs of chrome-plated tubular steel

835 **Helmut Magg** 1964 Germany

Sideboard of Brazilian rosewood with plastic edges and wooden or marble top

836 **Etienne Fermigier** 1961 France

Sideboard "D. 183" of rosewood with three doors and one drop-flap, top in white marble or travertine, anodized aluminum base. Matching low collapsible table with flat profile aluminum legs and rosewood top

837 **Ib Kofod-Larsen** 1962 Denmark

Sideboards "K 6024" and "K 6025" of rosewood or teak with mat finished chrome-plated steel frames and fittings; maple interiors

838 + 839 **Works Design** 1969 Netherlands

Modular wall unit "AK" with supporting side panels of two heights in natural wood or white lacquer finish; cabinet elements and shelves finished in white lacquer

840 **Mogens Koch** 1932/1948 Denmark

Modular storage and bookshelving unit

841 + 842 **Hans J. Wegner** c. 1952 Denmark

Series of chests, cabinets and shelves in oak and teak which can be assembled to larger storage units

843+844 **Hans Bellmann** c. 1950 Switzerland
Adjustable bookshelves of wood

845	846
847	848

845 **Hendrik van Keppel, Taylor Green** c. 1954 USA ▷
Bookshelves with folding metal frame and marble shelves

846 **Bruno Mathsson** c. 1950 Sweden ▷
Bookshelves with L-shaped shelves of molded plywood

847 **Olof Pira** 1956 Sweden ▷
Shelving system with pressure-fitted frame of perforated square steel tubing, spring steel brackets and adjustable shelves of wood

848 **Terence Conran** 1962 Great Britain ▷
"Summa" storage unit of pine, ash, or teak to be put against wall or used as a room divider

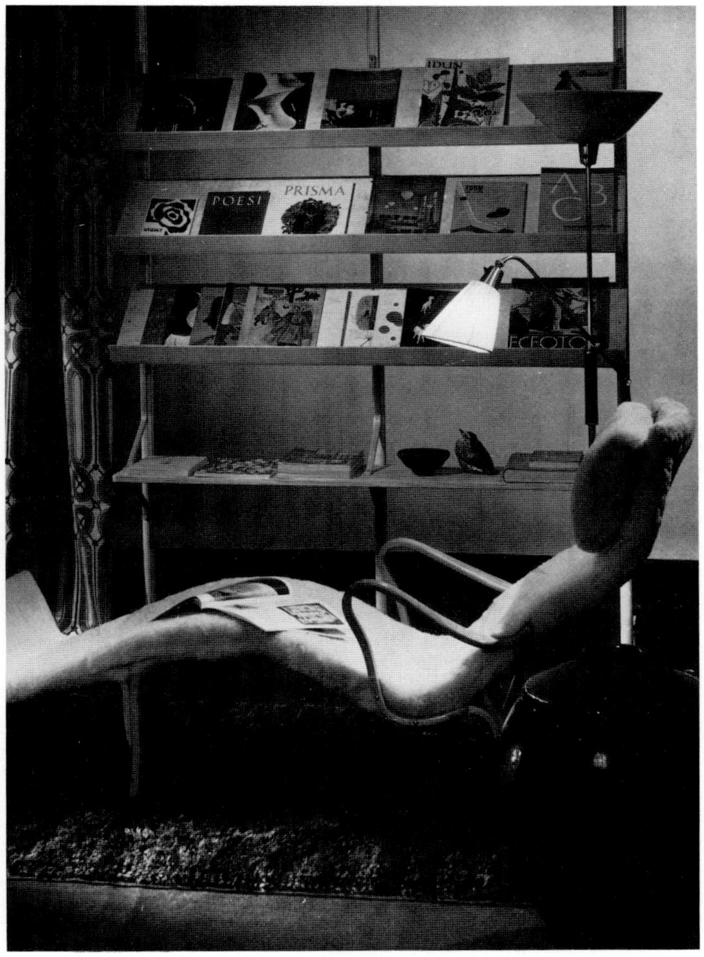
IDUN
POESI
PRISMA

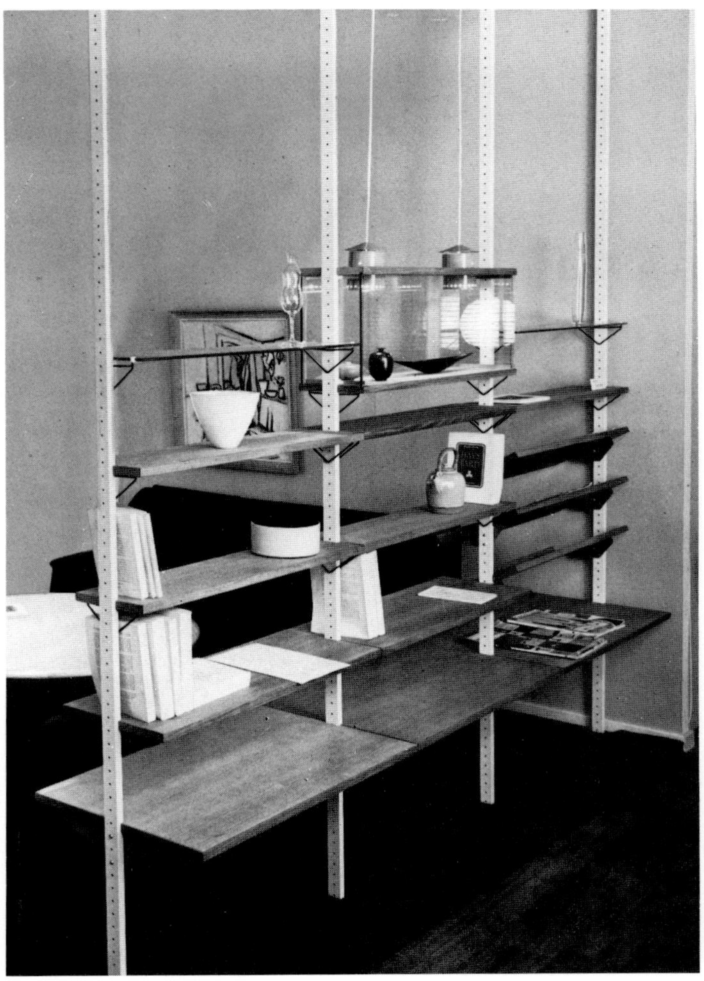

849+850 **Karin and Nisse Strinning** c. 1950 Sweden

Bookshelves with plastic-covered iron rod construction, adjustable shelves and writing desk

851 **Egon Eiermann** c. 1950 Germany

Bookshelves of wood with supports of perforated tubular steel

852 **Angelo Mangiarotti** c. 1950 Italy

Adjustable bookshelves of molded plywood, mounted on black-lacquered steel tubes

854 **Luisa Castiglioni, Margherita Mori** c. 1951 ▷ Italy

Bookshelving system for free standing use with frame of wood and adjustable shelves and cabinets

855 **Jaap Penraat** c. 1951 Netherlands ▷▷

Adjustable bookshelves with lacquered shelves and cabinets, frame of metal

853 **Herbert Hirche** 1955 Germany

Bookshelving system with chests in teak, maple interiors, black lacquered back panels for stiffening purposes. White lacquered steel tube ladders

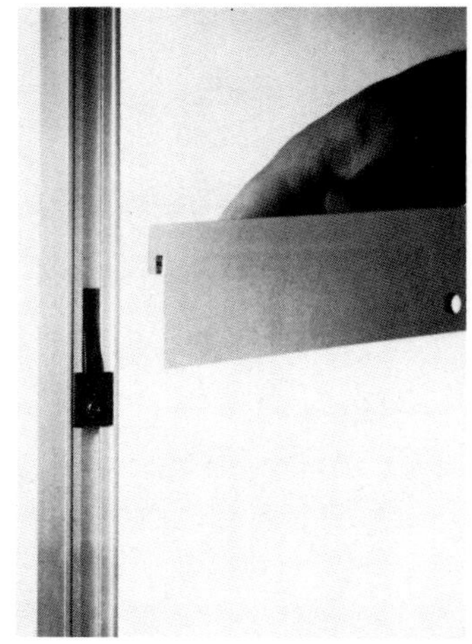

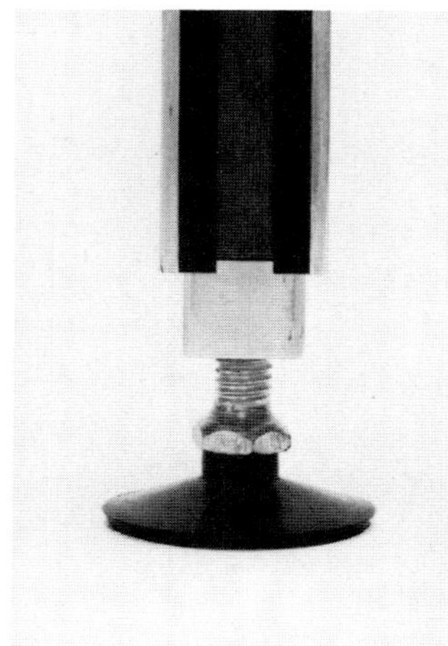

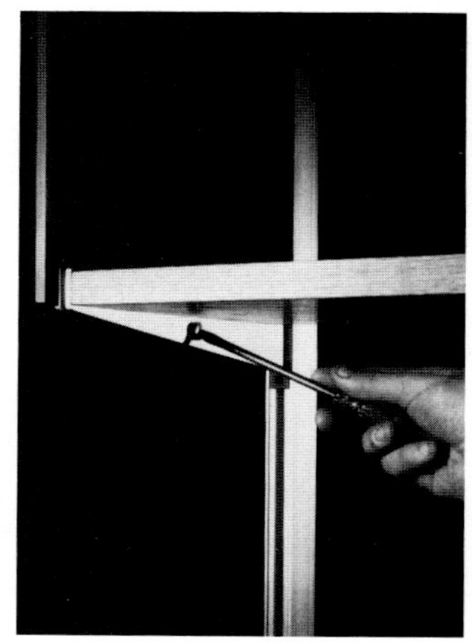

856–864 **George Nelson** 1958 USA

Flexible, assembled "Comprehensive Storage System" which may be used against a wall or as floor-to-ceiling room divider. Numerous basic components including shelves, drop-front desks, cabinets with sliding doors or drawers. Units are suspended on brackets at any desired height between adjustable aluminum poles pressure-fitted between floor and ceiling

865 **Alfred Altherr** c. 1957 Switzerland

"Team" bookshelves combined with cabinet and drawer units, supported by pressure-fitted metal poles

866 **Pierre Guariche** 1958 France

Shelving system with ladder frames of chrome-plated steel tubing; cabinet units of elm, fronts of units for stereo equipment in white plastic laminate

867 **Ico Parisi** 1958 Italy

"Urio" wall unit with interchangeable shelves and cabinets, open and closed compartments, supported by metal poles and brackets

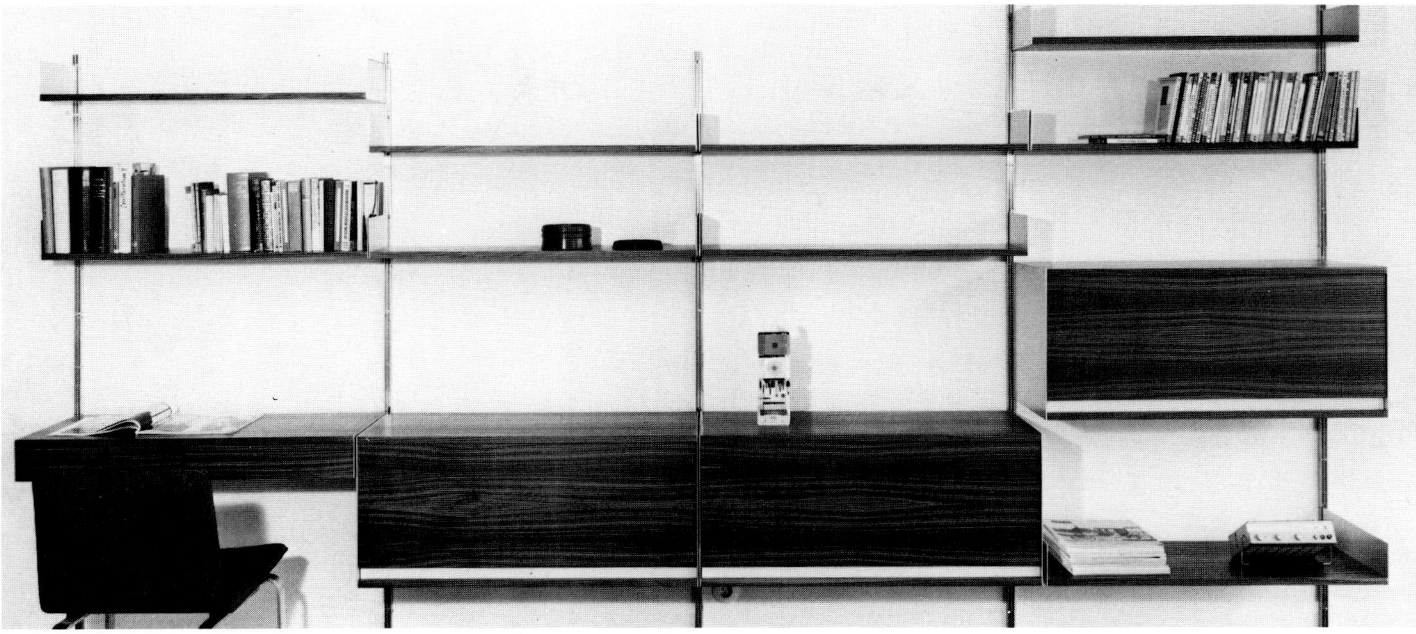

868 **Dieter Rams** 1960 Germany

Wall unit "RZ 60"; shelves and cabinets in beech or walnut veneer or with light grey plastic laminate. Framework of anodized profile aluminum

869 **Jürg Bally** 1961 Switzerland

Wall unit "WK 299" with shelves and cabinets of natural-finished walnut or white plastic laminate, suspended between aluminum poles which are pressure-fitted between floor and ceiling. Units may also be fixed to wall by means of wall panels

870 **Rudolf Lübben** 1963 Germany

Wall storage units "WA" of rosewood or oak with aluminum ladders

871 + 872 **Hans Gugelot** c. 1953 Switzerland

Modular storage and shelving system in maple with lacquered sliding doors and tubular steel supports

873 **Peter Biedermann** 1972 Germany

Range of containers "addition", fitted with doors, drawers, flaps, of black-stained ash with red-brown mahogany frames. The underside of each unit is fitted with adhesive discs; twenty different units may be assembled to a variety of combinations

874 **Joe Colombo** 1968 Italy

Range of containers "Square Plastic System" comprising six units and a number of plastic parts; units may be mounted on wall, stacked, linked, or placed back-to-back to form a variety of combinations such as wall units, partitions, or separate pieces of furniture; available also with casters and in three different colors

875 **Horst Brüning** 1969 Germany

Modular range of furniture that can be mounted on a wall or stand free; may be combined individually as desired. Cabinet or shelf units are suspended between side panels. Doors and drawer fronts in natural or white lacquered wood or in anodized aluminum

876 **Dieter Rams** 1957 Germany
Wall unit "RZ57" with cabinet doors and back panels in light grey plastic laminate, shelves and side panels with beech veneer. Supporting construction of anodized aluminum

877 **Helmut Magg** 1964 Germany
Storage units "DeWe500" with matching table and chairs. All frames and edges of solid oak, drawer and door fronts and back panels white plastic. Seat and back of chairs covered with black leather, table top of plywood with grey plastic laminate

880+881 **Enrico Somaini** 1968 Switzerland ▷
Furniture group "Squadra" consisting of five basic elements (open-frame base, two cabinet units, U-shaped combination pieces of book height, and shelf) of white laminated plastic; can be combined horizontally and vertically as desired. Smaller arrangements may be mounted on casters

878 **Jürgen Lange** 1970/71 Germany

"behr 1600 paneel" series consisting of wall panels of various heights and widths with aluminum edges, fixed on rails of anodized aluminum; joints between panels are covered with plastic extrusions, hiding the wall fastening. Shelves, storage elements, mirrors, lighting fixtures, hooks and tables can be hung into the joints at any desired position

879 **Team Form AG** 1969 Switzerland

Living room and bedroom complex "Umgebung 121" with a wide range of modular elements finished in grey white lacquer creating individual environments. Complex includes beds of various sizes, seats, shelves, chests of drawers, cupboards, numerous table combinations, and a variety of interior storage facilities

882 **Eduard Ludwig** c. 1950 Germany
Demountable sideboard of wood with colored sliding doors

883 **Fred Hochstrasser** 1956 Germany
Bookshelves in birch or teak with black lacquered supports of various heights

884–886 **Jaap Penraat** 1956 Netherlands
Bookshelves consisting of interlocking plywood panels which can be assembled as desired

887–889 **Angelo Mangiarotti, Bruno Morassutti** 1955 Italy ▷
Bookshelves composed of wood elements stacked on each other

890–892 **Angelo Mangiarotti, Bruno Morassutti** 1957 Italy ▷
"Multi-Use" collapsible bookshelves of wood or plastic. Two vertical boards support a series of horizontal and vertical partitions joined by fillets, without screws or any other metal components. The fillets also provide grooves for sliding doors

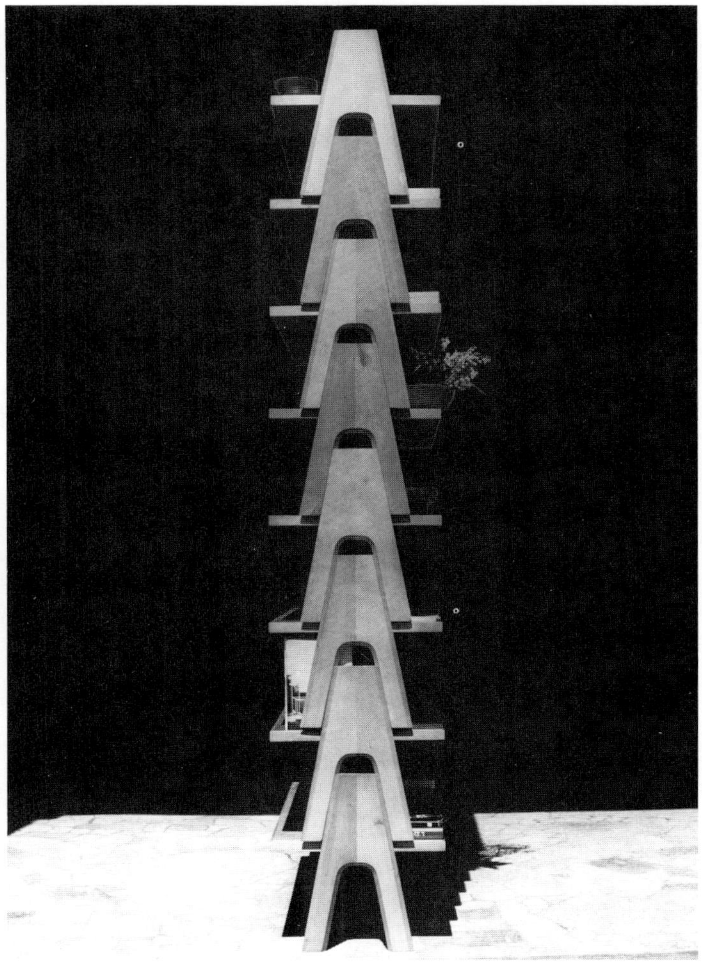

887 | 889
888 |
890 | 891
 | 892

893 **Ueli Berger** 1961 Switzerland

Multi-purpose units "UBE 61" of fir or beech in natural or lacquer finish. Single elements are joined by means of nylon linking devices. Units may be combined with drawers of plastic, glass tops, seat cushions and filing equipment

894 **Emanuele Ponzio** 1960 Italy

Bookshelves "LB-4" of walnut or rosewood; shelves are inserted into notches in side panels. Cabinet units can be added at various heights

895–897 **Gianfranco Frattini** 1960 Italy

Bookshelves "540" of jacaranda or teak. Side panels equipped with guide-rails, into the grooves of which shelves are inserted

898 + 899 **Mario Ravegnani Morosini** 1954 Italy ▷

Modular bookshelves of wood with fronts in plywood and metal fittings

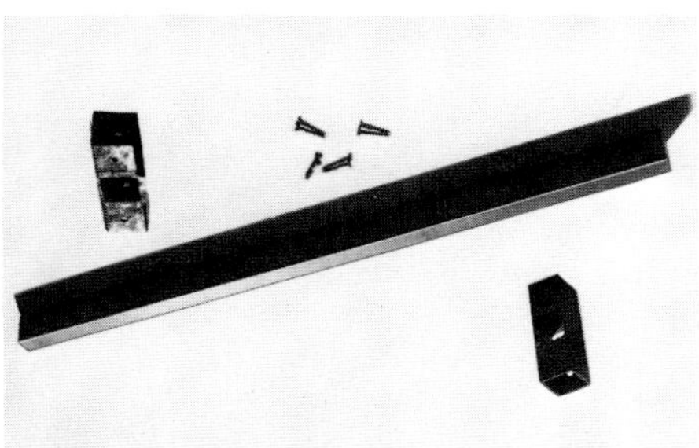

900 **Hans Ebbe Nielsen** 1975 Denmark

Modular bookshelf system "Cubex" of light pinewood with acid-fast varnish or white lacquer finish; bases and panels in different lengths can be assembled by connectors of black plastic without tools. Units may be supplemented with sliding doors, table tops, or back panels

898	900
899	
901	902

901 + 902 **Heinz Witthoeft** 1964 Germany

Furniture system "Tail 12", assembled from modular basic elements of beech, punctured at regular intervals; steel fittings. Accessoires are chipboard panels finished in plastic laminate and seat slings of leather or canvas

903 **Christoph-Albrecht Kühn zu Reineck** 1968 Germany

Shelf complex "C3" of chipboard may be used for circular shelving. Shelf units are assembled from four paired, interlocking boards that are connected with each other by turning them at a 90 degree angle

905 **Hans Staeger, Manfred Malzacher** 1964 ▷ Germany

Room divider and shelving complex "raum technik system rts" can be set up in many combinations including separate pieces of furniture. Panels of glass or white laminated plastic, also veneered panels, are assembled by grey or clear plastic or chromed corner caps. Accessoires include panels with built-in lighting fixtures, slide-projector boxes, mirrors, drawers, hinged or sliding doors

904 **Enzo Mari** 1969 Italy

Shelf complex with side panels of corrugated cardboard and shelves of transparent plastic

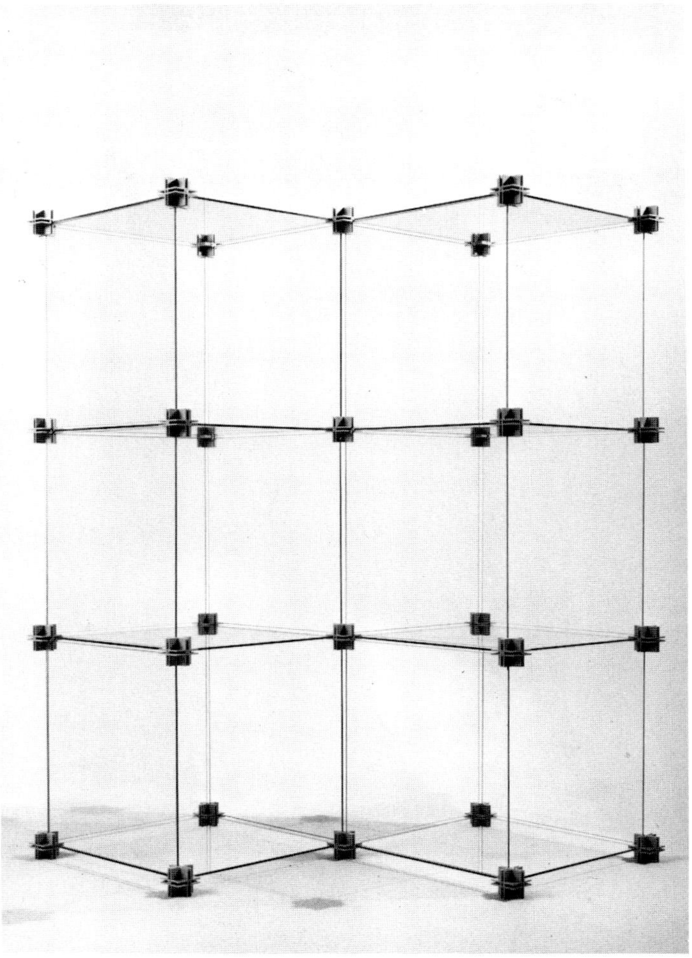

906 **Dieter Schempp** 1967 Germany

Shelving system "easy" of colored or white plastic panels, assembled by connectors of black plastic

907 **OMK Design Ltd.** 1971 Great Britain

"T" shelving system in two heights, assembled of chrome-plated steel tubes and knuckle joints. Shelves of glass

908 **Corrado Cocconi, Fabio Lenci** 1970 Italy

Shelf system of cubes in clear or smoked Plexiglas. Fittings and linking devices of chrome-plated metal, bases of polished aluminum and black Plexiglas

911+912 **Jonathan De Pas, Donato D'Urbino, Paolo Lomazzi** 1971
Italy

Shelf system "Jeep" of injection-molded ABS. End panels with slide connections and bolted with plastic stoppers. Shelves with wide edges for stiffening purposes fixed to the end panels

▷ 913 **Ernesto Gismondi** 1971 Italy

Shelf system "Dodona 300" of ABS resin. Hidden connection of side panels and shelves with angular linking devices, pushed from above into the slots of side panels and fitting into the ends of the shelves

◁◁ 909 **Rolf Heide** 1969 Germany

"Montageregal", shelf system of lacquer-finished sheet steel in three heights and two depths. Shelves, punched frame posts and stiffening elements screwed. Writing top can be mounted in horizontal or slanting position. Base edges protected with black rubber blocks

◁ 910 **Sergio Mazza** 1969 Italy

Book shelf "Sergesto" of ABS resin. Side panels assembled of single elements to desired height. Shelves pushed into built-in tracks of side panels

914 **H. Maier-Aichen** 1968 Germany

Open cubes of molded wood finished in lacquer; elements in three sizes may be combined to shelving units

915 **Olaf von Bohr** 1969 Italy

Shelf complex of injection-molded plastic; four vertical and three horizontal units may be interlocked as desired. Maximum stability and load-bearing capacity is achieved without any fittings

916 **Works Design** c. 1958 Netherlands

"Stabilux" sheet steel wall unit for residental and office interiors, with detachable shelves, drawer inserts, open and closed compartments, sliding writing top, and back panels

917 **The Conran Design Group** 1967 Great Britain

Storage system "Stowaway", built up from five units. Boxes are stained dark brown, with backs, shelves, doors and drawers in natural beech. Units are located on pins

918 **Gino Marotta** 1967/68 Italy

Furniture system "Koan Bonde" of lacquer finished wood. All elements including matching beds are demountable and can be combined as desired

919+920 **Joe Colombo** 1967 Italy

"Triangular System" with units which can be combined as desired. Basic elements in three heights, of white plastic-laminated panels with black edges, are mounted on casters; interior storage facilities include various kinds of shelves and drawers

921+922 **Jonathan De Pas, Donato D'Urbino, Paolo Lomazzi** 1970 Italy

Furniture system "Dado & Vite" with panels in different sizes of natural or white lacquer-finished plywood which can be joined by bolts and nuts of plastic to individual pieces of furniture in a great variety. Several additions like drawers, round table tops and cushions

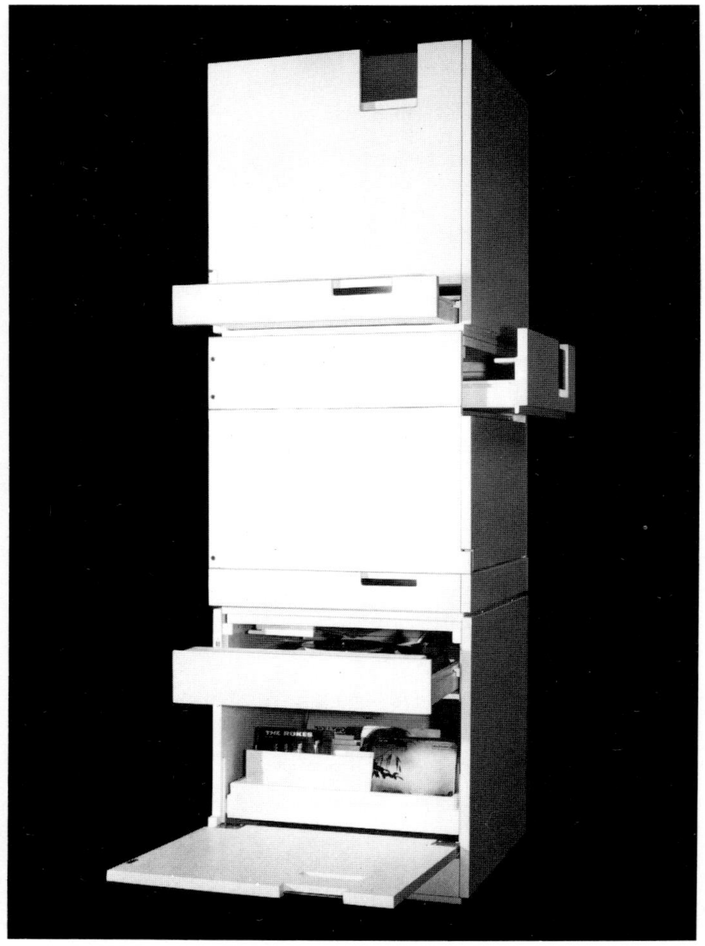

923 **Claudio Salocchi** 1967 Italy
Free-standing revolving bookcase "Centro HiFi"; the lower element can be equipped with a complete hi-fi-set. Wooden parts of rosewood or in lacquer finish, plastic-laminated door fronts, central support of stove-enameled metal

924 **Carlo Viganò** 1968 Italy
Modular container series "Euro 2" of wood in lacquer finish. Units with a great variety of interior equipment are composed of six elements which can be combined horizontally and vertically as desired

925 **Gerhard Schneider** 1970 Germany
Open cubes "WR390/391" with or without casters; may be used individually as side table or tea trolley, or, combined horizontally or vertically, as storage units; wood, lacquer finished

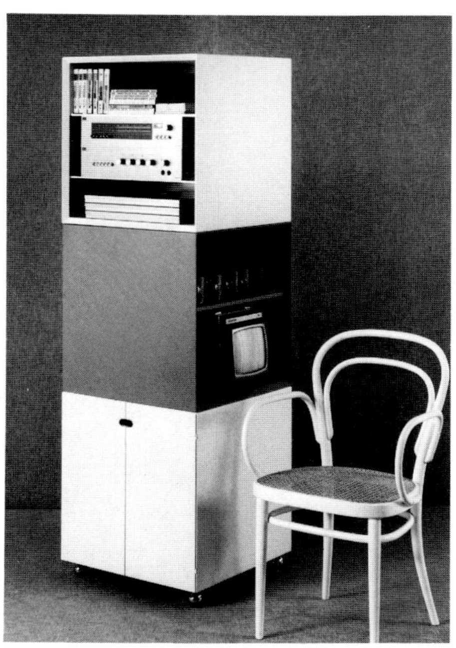

923 | 924
925 | 926

927 **Joe Colombo** 1969 Italy

Range of containers "Square Plastic System", comprising six units and a number of plastic connecting parts. Units may be mounted on a wall, stacked, linked, or placed back-to-back to form a variety of combinations such as wall units, partitions, or separate pieces of furniture

928 **Works Design** 1971 Italy

Stackable shelf cubes "Questo" of plastic-laminated chipboard panels, open or with drawers

929 **Ristomatti Ratia** 1970 Finland

"Palaset", range of cubic elements with various interior compartments manufactured in one piece of injection-molded polystyrol, lacquer finished. Can be assembled as desired for various purposes. Additional drawers, doors and base frames can be added

◁ 926 **Cini Boeri** 1968 Italy

Chest of drawers, movable on casters, made of wood and finished in plastic laminate

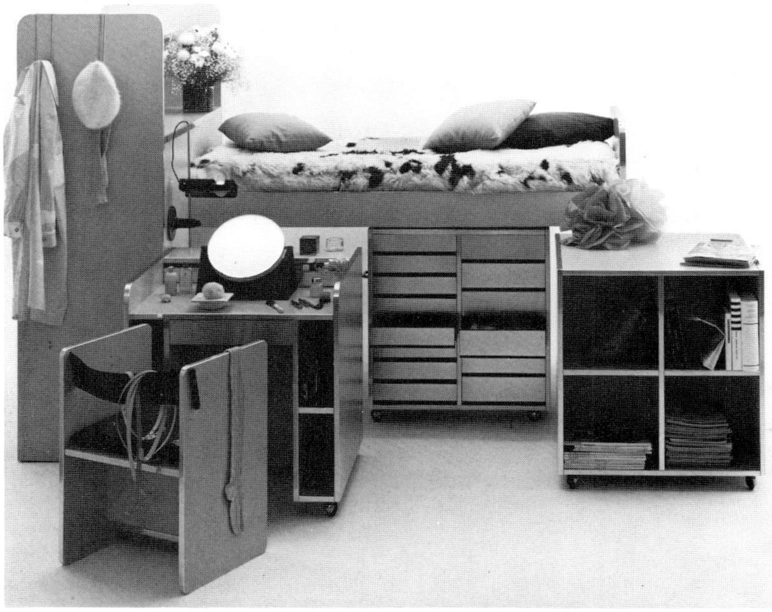

930–932 **Joe Colombo** 1967/68 Italy

"Box 1", a monoblock comprising all furniture one person needs for sleeping, dressing, reading, playing and so on: bed, bedside, table, closet, drawers, bookcase, desk/dressing table, and a chair that can be used as steps, all fitting together to form a space-saving block. Units are made of wood panels with plastic laminate, and trimmed in metallized plastics

933 **Jonathan De Pas, Donato D'Urbino, Paolo Lomazzi** 1970 Italy

Furniture system "Dado & Vite" with panels in different sizes of natural or white lacquer-finished plywood which can be joined by bolts and nuts to individual pieces of furniture in a great variety. Several additions like drawers, round table tops and cushions available

934–936 **Roberto Pamio, Renato Toso, Noti Massari** 1969 Italy

Modular wall unit "Carioca" with elements (plywood supports, plywood frames veneered in ash, side and back panels of plywood covered in plastic) which are set up by a special pressure-fitting method and can be combined vertically and horizontally as desired. Equipment for the storage units includes shelves, hinged doors laminated in plastic, translucent, screened glass doors, drawers of beech with laminated plastic fronts, and also a folding table and a bed. Nickel-plated metal fittings

937–940 **Joe Colombo** 1964/65 Italy

Series of foldable containers, equipped for a variety of purposes. Shown here are: Closed and locked container in walnut, with metal fittings (938), container for men (937), container for ladies (939), container for living room (940)

937	938
939	940

941+942 **Joe Colombo** 1966/67 Italy

Flexible furniture program, designed for production on an industrial scale and for distribution by department stores. The system comprises seating and lighting elements, beds, and a variety of cabinet units, all of which can be arranged and rearranged according to individual needs. Cabinet units, which are joined magnetically, are finished in plastic laminate; upholstered seating elements and beds are supported by L-shaped metal parts

943+944 **Rolf Heide** 1971 Germany

Container units "Rollschränke" with side and back panels of sheet steel; doors, shelves, foot and head parts of wood, stained or lacquered. The units are mounted on casters and can be linked with metal coupling devices

945 **Willy Guhl** c. 1950 Switzerland
Demountable wardrobe cabinet

946 **Works Design** c. 1958 Germany
Beech wardrobe "2702" with square tubular steel legs, plastic-laminated doors, adjustable shelves and drawers

947+948 **Angelo Mangiarotti** c. 1950 Italy ▷
Wall storage unit, composed of four basic elements. Frame of wood, front and side panels lacquered white, fittings of chrome-plated steel

949+950 **Viljo Rewell, Antti Nurmesniemi** ▷
c. 1954 Finland
Collapsible wardrobe with front and side panels in white and frame of wood

947 | 948
949 | 950

951 **Osvaldo Borsani** 1957 Italy

Collapsible wardrobe "A57" consisting of interchangeable closed compartments, drawers, and shelves. Mahogany interior, lacquered doors and side panels

952+953 **Silvio Coppola** 1970 Italy

Wardrobe of polyurethane, assembled of U-formed wall elements, similar foot and head pieces; doors with built-in partitions

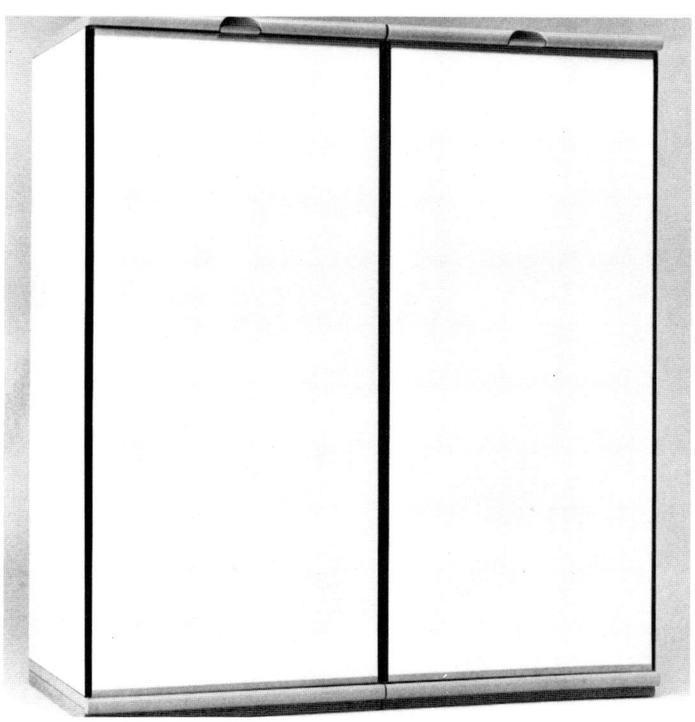

954–956 **Pierluigi Molinari** 1970 Italy

"Box-System", storage units with tambour doors of plastic in various colors and two heights which can be assembled to large combinations. Many varieties for interior partitions: drawers, wardrobe installations and folding tables etc. possible. Table tops can be hung between the storage units with metal supports

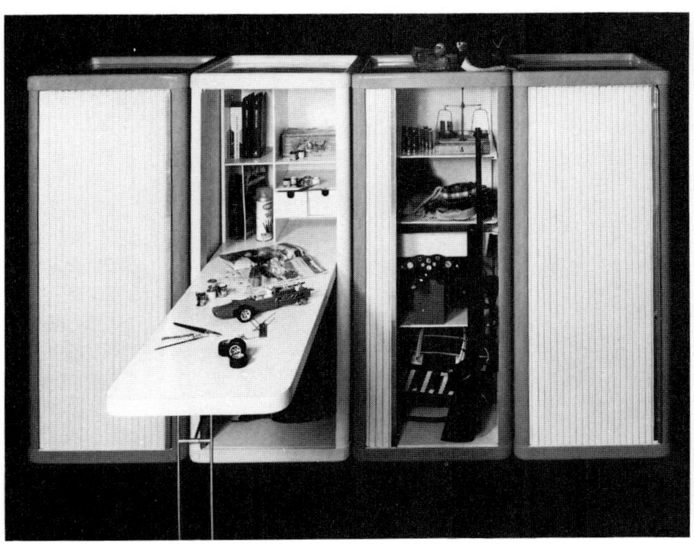

958 + 959 **Cees Braakman** 1961 Netherlands

Modular range of wardrobes of Oregon pine, fronts of sliding doors in white lacquer finish with recessed wooden handles; drawers of molded mahogany. Interior equipment can be arranged as desired

◁ 957 **Grethe Meyer, Børge Mogensen** 1957
Denmark

"Boligens Byggeskabe" versatile storage units which can be arranged to accommodate all space and storage requirements. Fiberboard sides, bottoms, and backs; Oregon pine front frames with visible brass screws; teak veneered doors. Lacquered interiors; drawers in three sizes have grooves for loose partitions. Hinged and sliding doors of top cabinets lacquered. Brass hardware

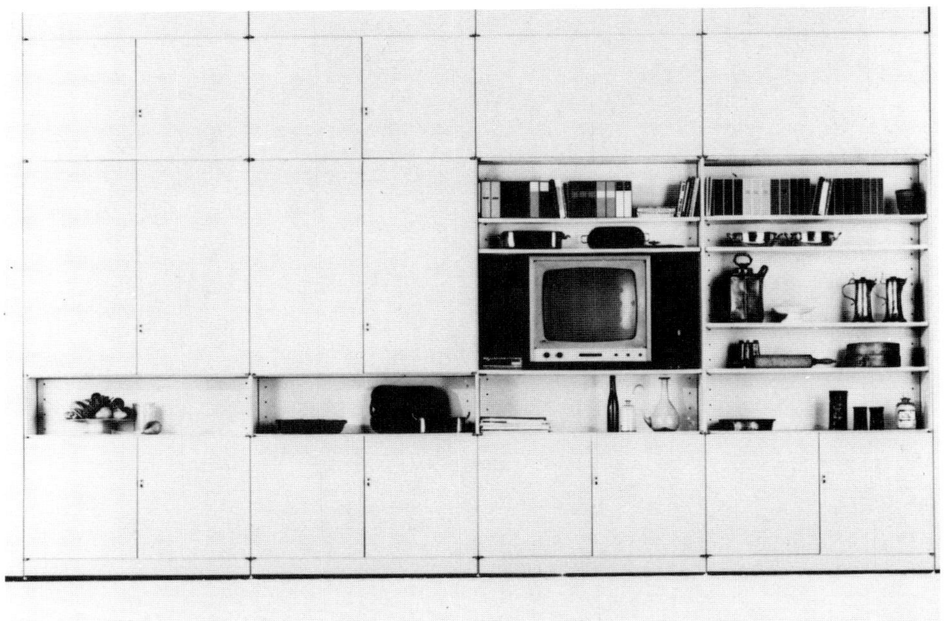

960–962 **Atelier Herbert Hirche** 1959–62
Germany

Demountable wall unit and room dividing system "INwand" of combinable, prefabricated elements. For room dividing, units are available with built-in doors and windows and with cabinets accessible from one or both sides; elements may also be assembled to form built-in cabinets attached to solid walls. Elements are constructed on a module of 12.5 cm in length and 7.5 cm in height

965+966 **Arno Votteler** 1964 Germany

Modular wall storage system in knock-down construction with a wide variety of combinations. Supports of U-shaped profile aluminum poles which are connected at both ends by wooden rails. Side and back panels in light grey plastic laminate, visible wooden parts of teak, ash, walnut, rosewood, or with plastic laminate. Adjustable interior equipment may be installed to meet any individual needs

◁ 963+964 **Charles Eames** 1961 USA

"Eames Contract Storage", a flexible system of storage, study, and sleeping units with minimum space requirements, including two different hanging units, one dressing unit, one folding bed unit, and a study unit with desk and bookshelves, all mounted free from floor and ceiling and hung from standard unstrut section secured to wall. Fronts of birch plywood, side and back panels of plywood with black resin coating

967+968 **Hans Gugelot** 1964 Switzerland

Modular wardrobe units with space-saving folding doors, which may be pressure-fitted between floor and ceiling or used free-standing. Any number of units with a variety of adjustable interior equipment may be joined

969+970 **Works Design** 1963 Germany

Modular wall storage system; basic elements can be assembled to any desired length. Great variety of interior equipment. Door fronts of walnut or larch, also in lacquer finish

971 **Nanna Ditzel** 1962 Denmark

Stools and tables of different heights and diameters in Oregon pine

Nursery and School Furniture

Of necessity, children's furniture looks the way adults think children imagine it should look. The consumers' judgement is irrelevant because it is partly influenced by that of others. The fact is that children do not possess the necessary experience really to be able to know what they like. So they have to put up with what others have chosen for them with a greater or lesser amount of care and understanding.

It is generally believed that children prefer simple things which allow their fantasy plenty of scope. This means things that do not proclaim loudly what they are for, but whose possibilities can be gradually discovered. In this respect, the round stools by Nanna Ditzel (ill. 971) are very successful examples because their form is beautiful, clear and stimulating. They can be used to sit on or as tables, and if they are put on their side, they can be rolled. Children can use them to discover what an axle and two wheels are, and-as the picture shows-how to make a tower. In addition, the stools are sturdy, robust and not dangerous.

The wooden boxes that Hans Gugelot designed as play furniture (ills. 977, 978) are similarly sensible. It appears that their educational value was so great that they later moved into adults' rooms in a modified form. The simple idea of stacking up cube-shaped containers and filling them as required is really so obvious one wonders why it is not more common. The traditional attitude was that a piece of furniture must always be a complete object which, although it may be taken apart, cannot be assembled in various ways. This was so widespread that it appeared that a different concept had hardly any chance of gaining acceptance. It took children's furniture to teach us the error of our ways.

And so the position is now exactly the opposite of what it used to be. Whereas children's furniture was often a smaller-scale version of things adults used, the furniture we adults have now seems to be a continuation of what we grew up with. Children's furniture tended to act as preparation for adulthood and contained in its supposed childishness a clearly domesticating style. Today one could often think that furniture allows adults to carry on their childhood games. This is true above all for "do-it-yourself" furniture in kit form. It is based on the experience gathered with children's furniture. This observation reminds us of the influence a toy-Frobel's building set-had on modern architecture (the American architect Frank Lloyd Wright freely admitted the important stimuli he obtained from this quarter). At the root of it all lies the rediscovery of primary needs and the attempt to face up to them instead of artificially suppressing them.

So the nursery has been regarded for some time as a place for experimenting and making observations. Accordingly, education is seen these days as training in essential experiences, and not so much as the anticipation of adulthood.

972 **Marcel Breuer** c. 1950 USA

Nursery furniture

973 **Jaap Penraat** c. 1952 Netherlands

Nursery furniture

974 **Eduard Ludwig** c. 1950 Germany

Nursery, table and stools with demountable legs

975 **Herbert Hirche** 1954 Germany ▷

Shelf for toys with steel tube frame and detachable wooden cases

976 **Nisse Strinning** 1955 Sweden ▷▷

Nursery furniture

977+978 **Hans Gugelot** 1953/1964 Germany ▷

Nursery and play furniture of four basic units: long bridge, short bridge, lacquered panel (to be used as blackboard), open box. All elements of pine with hardboard edging, panels with red, yellow, green, and blue lacquer finish. Unites may be used for various purposes and combined in any desired way

979+980 **Nanna Ditzel** 1963 Denmark ▷

Range of nursery furniture, comprising a variety of single units: wardrobes, open and closed cabinets of different sizes with drawers and shelves, tables for play and hoolwork. Wooden parts of Oregon pine, back panels in colored plastic laminate. Units may be used for adults

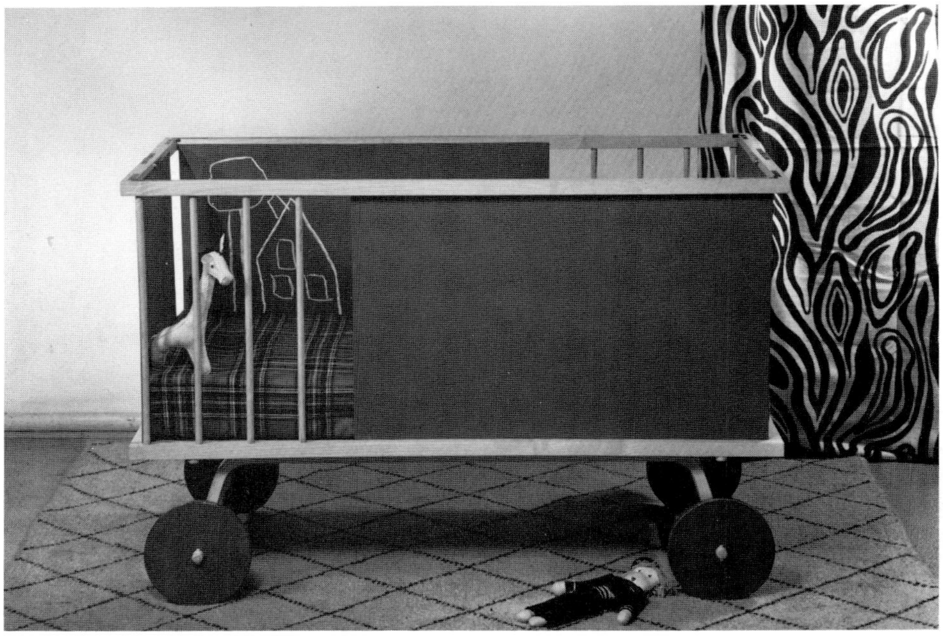

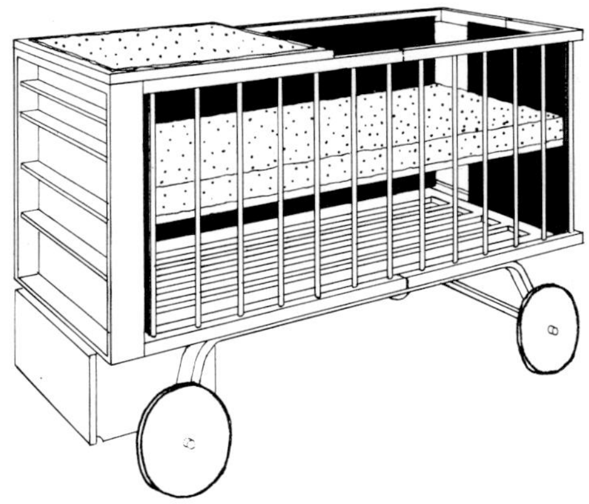

△ 981–983 **Franz Füeg** c. 1953 Switzerland
Demountable cot

◁ 984 **Vera Catz** c. 1952 Netherlands
Cot

▽ 985–987 **Emil Guhl** c. 1956 Switzerland
Adjustable cot with removable wood pen and chest

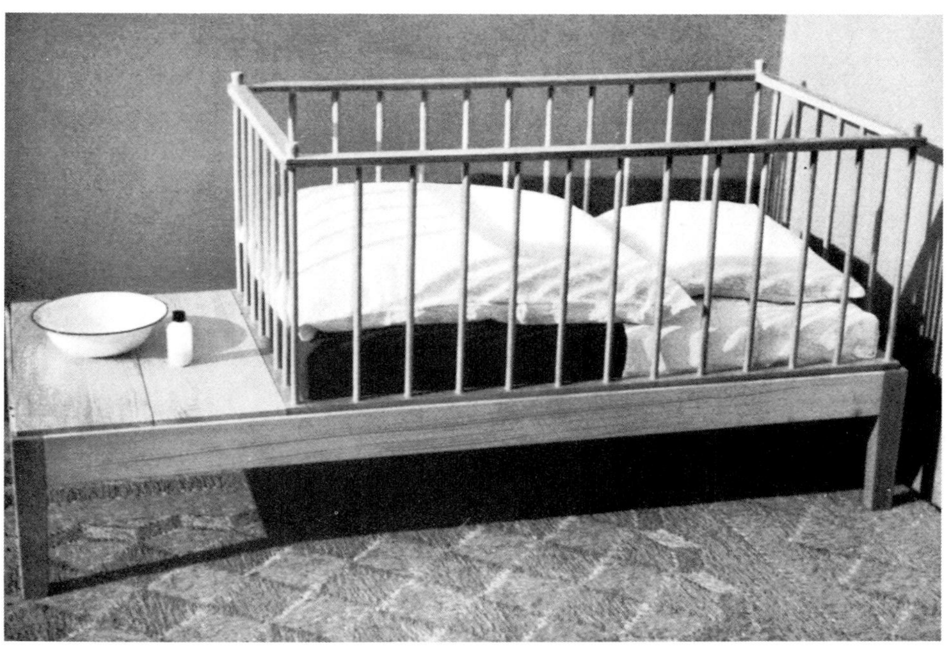

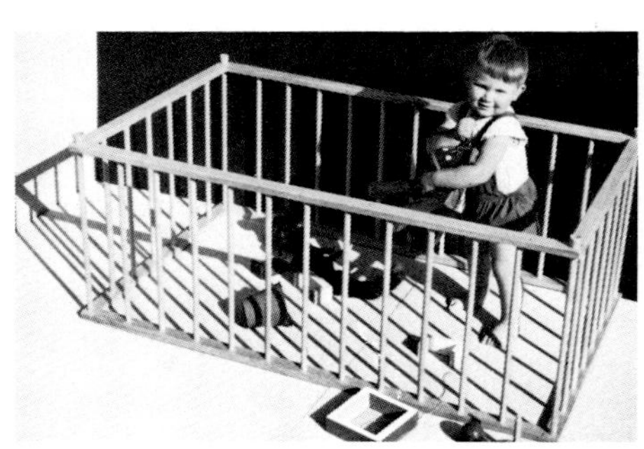

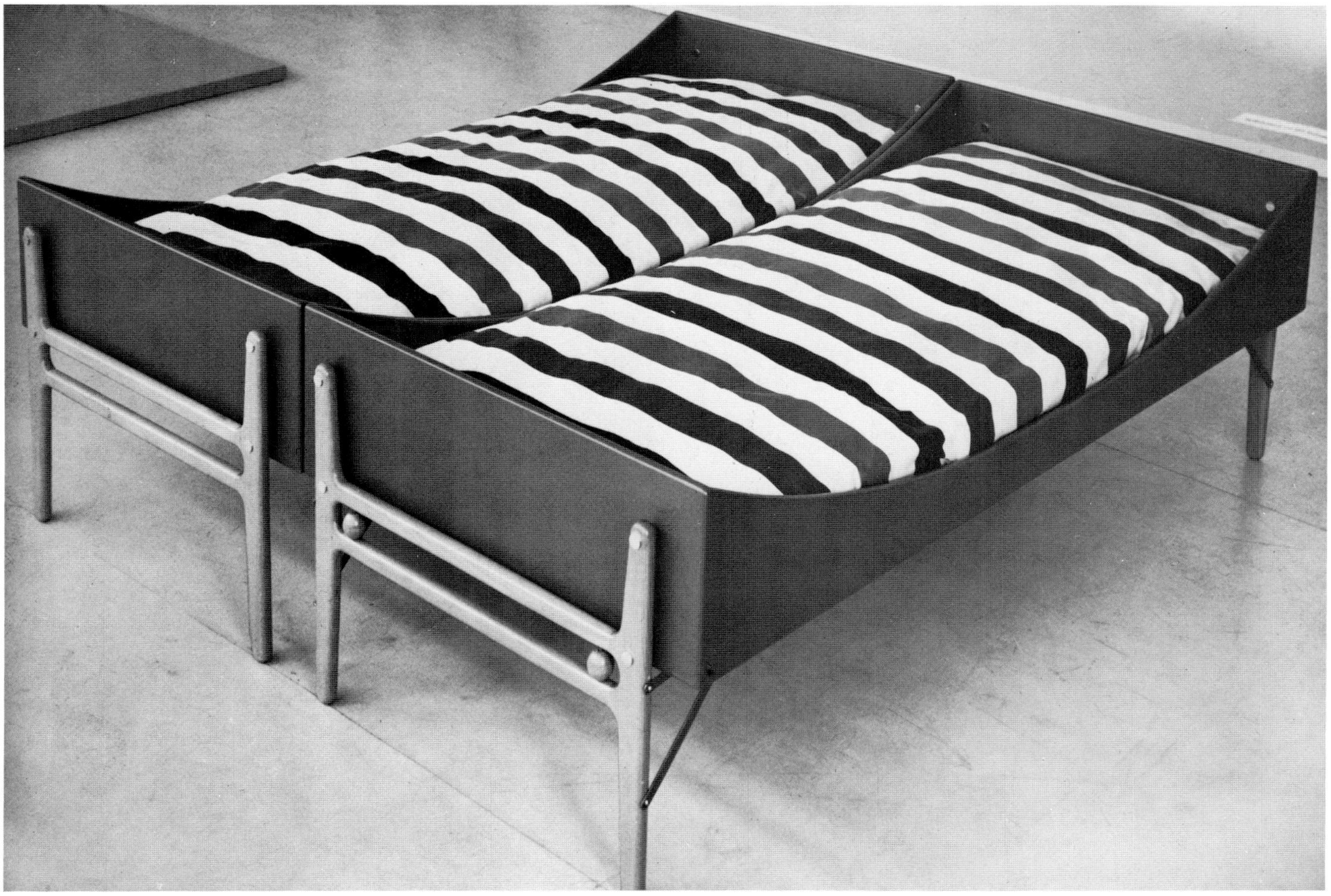

△ 988+989 **Thea Leonhard** c. 1950 Sweden
Cots with polished wooden frame and lacquered wooden beds; can be pushed one under the other

▽ 990–992 **Nanna Ditzel** 1964 Denmark
Demountable children's bed of Oregon pine with adjustable railing; without rails to be used as sofa

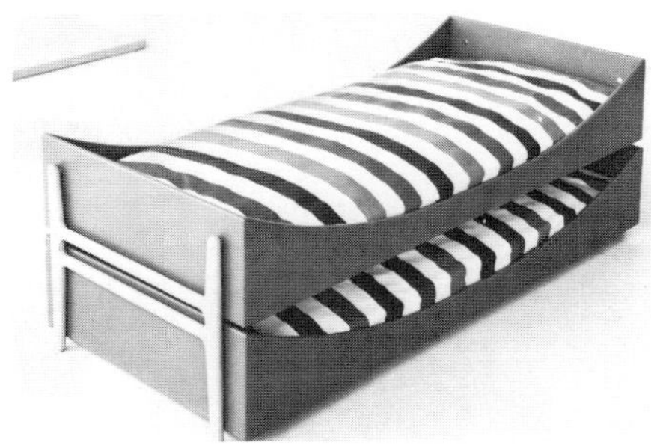

993 **Eva and Nils Koppel** 1952 Denmark
Children's beds to be placed one upon the other

994 **René Jean Caillette** 1964 France
Nursery furniture of Formica; bed and cabinet unit in front of window red, play box black, stool white

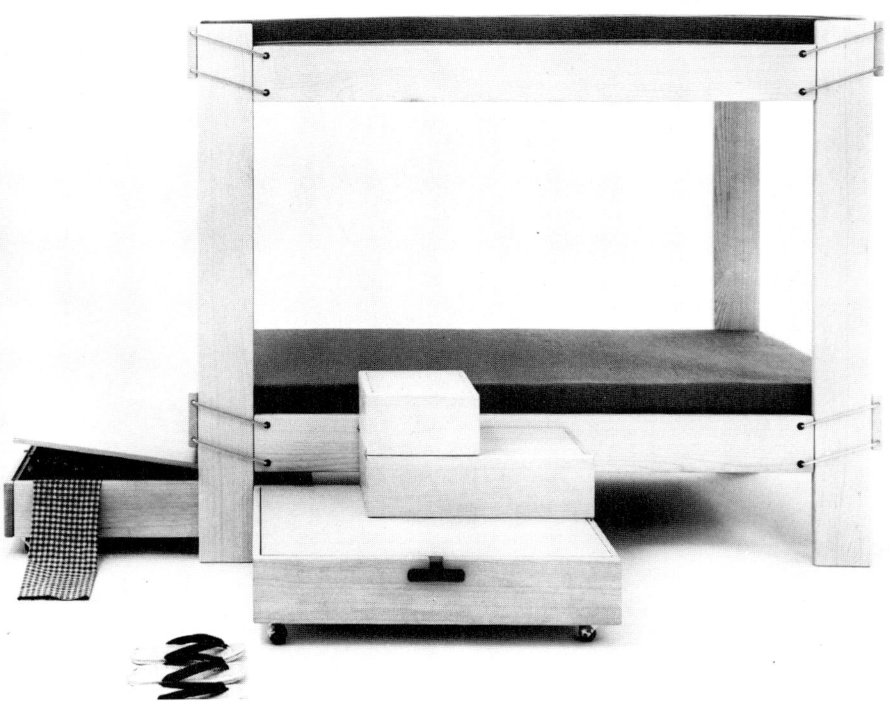

995 **Gigi Sabadin** 1971 Italy
Bunk bed "Bibo" of natural ash. Beds can be hung at any height, joints with metal pegs which fit into borings of the posts. Pedestal drawers on casters in two widths

998 **Roberto Pamio, Renato Toso, Noti Massari** 1969 Italy ▷
Children's desk "Grillo" with wooden top and folding frame in blue, red or white

999 **Giancarlo Piretti** 1972 Italy ▷▷
Folding table "Platone" with frame of chrome-plated steel tube and plastic top in various colors with molded tray

996+997 **Marc Berthier** 1972 France
Children's furniture range "Twentytube" of lacquer-finished steel tube in yellow, red or green. Canvas slings, shelves and table tops with white plastic laminate. The range consists of single and double beds, wardrobes and shelves, tables and desks with matching chairs

1000+1001 **Angelo Mangiarotti, Bruno Morassutti** 1955 Italy

Collapsible nursery school tables composed of beech elements

1002 **Wilhelm Kienzle** c. 1952 Switzerland

Kindergarten tables in manifold combinations

1005–1007 **Kristian Vedel** 1956/57 Denmark ▷

Children's furniture with molded plywood backs, adjustable seats and boards. Various possibilities of use as chair, playtable and swing

1003 **Alain Richard** c. 1953 France
Toy cases

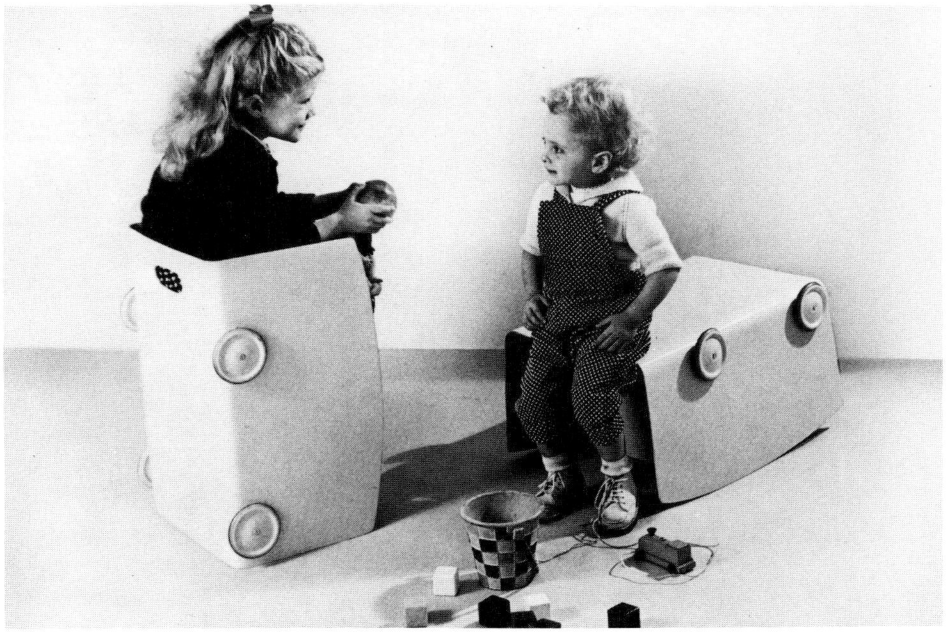

1004 **Kristian Vedel** 1956/57 Denmark ▷
Play-table composed of one table and four chairs

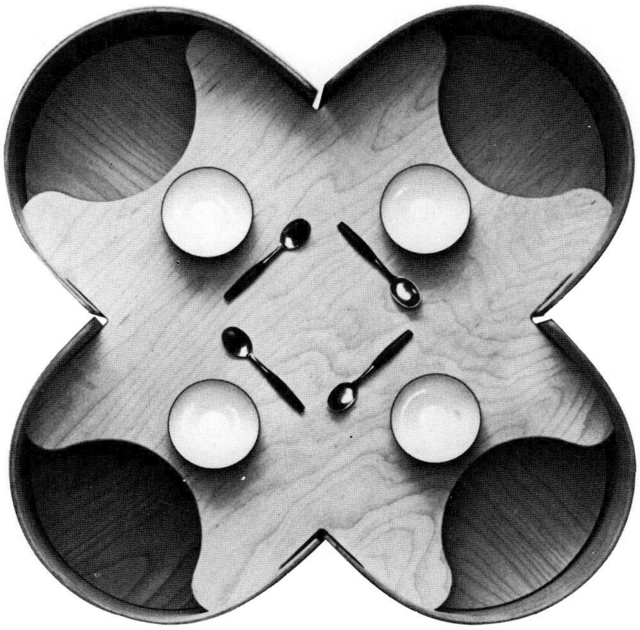

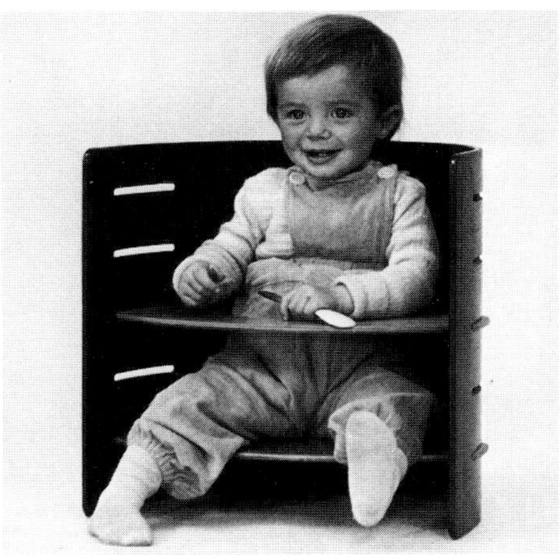

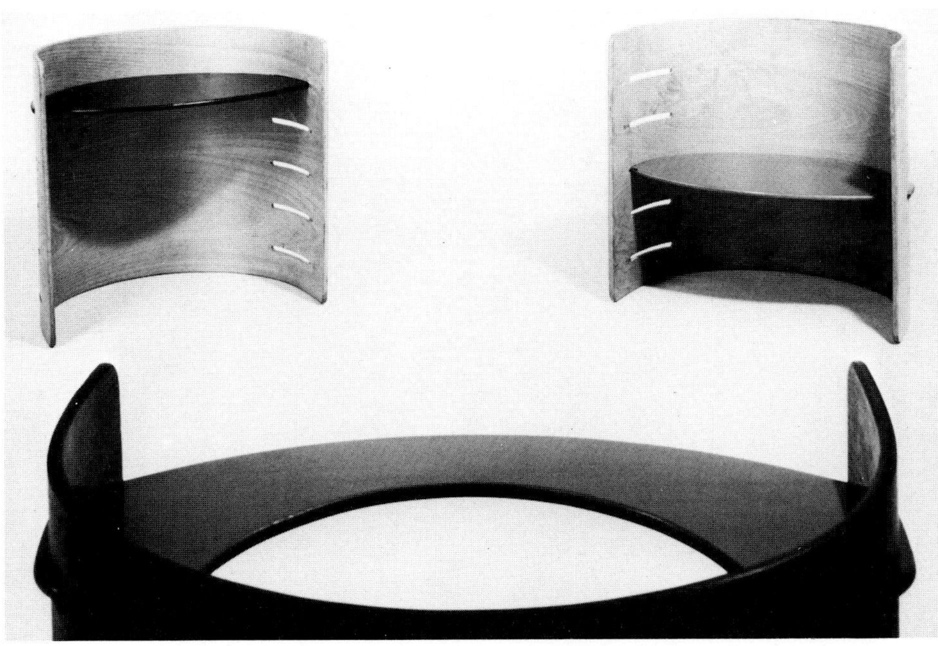

1008–1012 **Works Design** 1969 Germany

"Die Baukiste", a range of children's play furniture, consisting of ten items of strong corrugated board in three shapes (triangle, square, circle); may be combined to form a variety of furniture and playthings; units are laminated in plastic in various colors on one side, the other side is left untreated to be painted or decorated by the children; parts are combined by means of easy-to-handle big, plastic screws with rounded corners

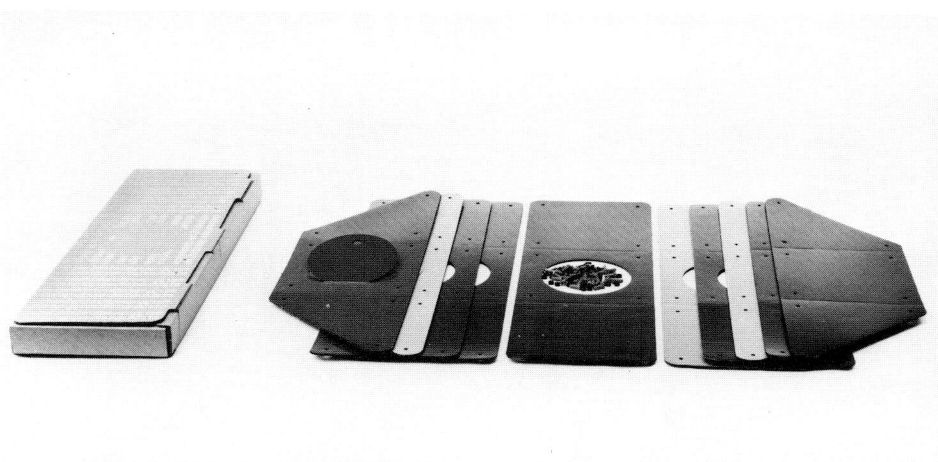

1013+1014 **Jonathan De Pas, Donato D'Urbino, Paolo Lomazzi** 1973 Italy

Children's chair "Chica" of injection die-casted ABS resin in yellow or red, consisting of four parts which can be put together as desired

1015+1016 **Marco Zanuso, Richard Sapper** 1964 Italy/Germany

Children's chair "K 1340" of injection molded low density polyethylene, available in white, yellow, blue, or red, consisting of three elements which are joined under pressure (seat, legs, gliders). Developed for nursery and small school children, chairs may be used as building units

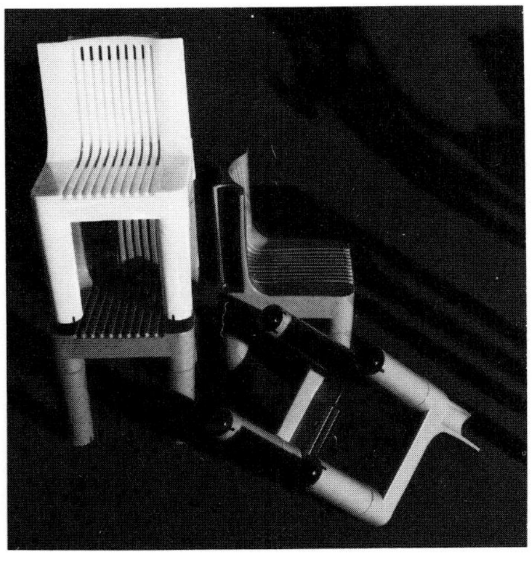

1017–1019 **Peter Raake** 1968 Germany

Folding furniture of specially stabilized, corrugated cardboard with kraftliner covering, unfinished or with plastic laminate

1020 **Works Design** 1973 Germany

Multi-purpose cube "Papperlapapp" of strong cardboard with plastic laminate in various colors. Available in three sizes

1021–1024 **Richard Thern** 1969/1974 Germany
Playing units of hard surfaced, foamed polyurethane, white or colored; can be used in a multiplicity of ways

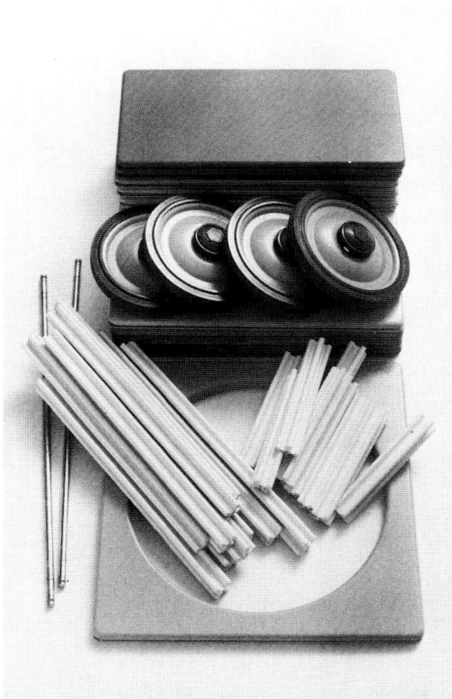

1025–1030 **Works Design** 1971–74 Germany

"Mobilix" children's playing and constructing system. Solid colored plastic panels with notches may be combined with cross slats of extruded plastic to form a variety of playthings and furniture. Supplement elements are panels with round cutout, table tops, drawers, casters, bed mattresses, wheels and chrome-plated steel axles

1031 + 1032 **Stanley Selengut** 1970 USA

Children's environmental system. Grill structure consisting of solid maple or birch dowels with threaded ends and cubic wooden joints. Can be extended with bed boards, side and end panels, ladders, swings and other play equipment. Basic system can also be combined to form tables and shelves

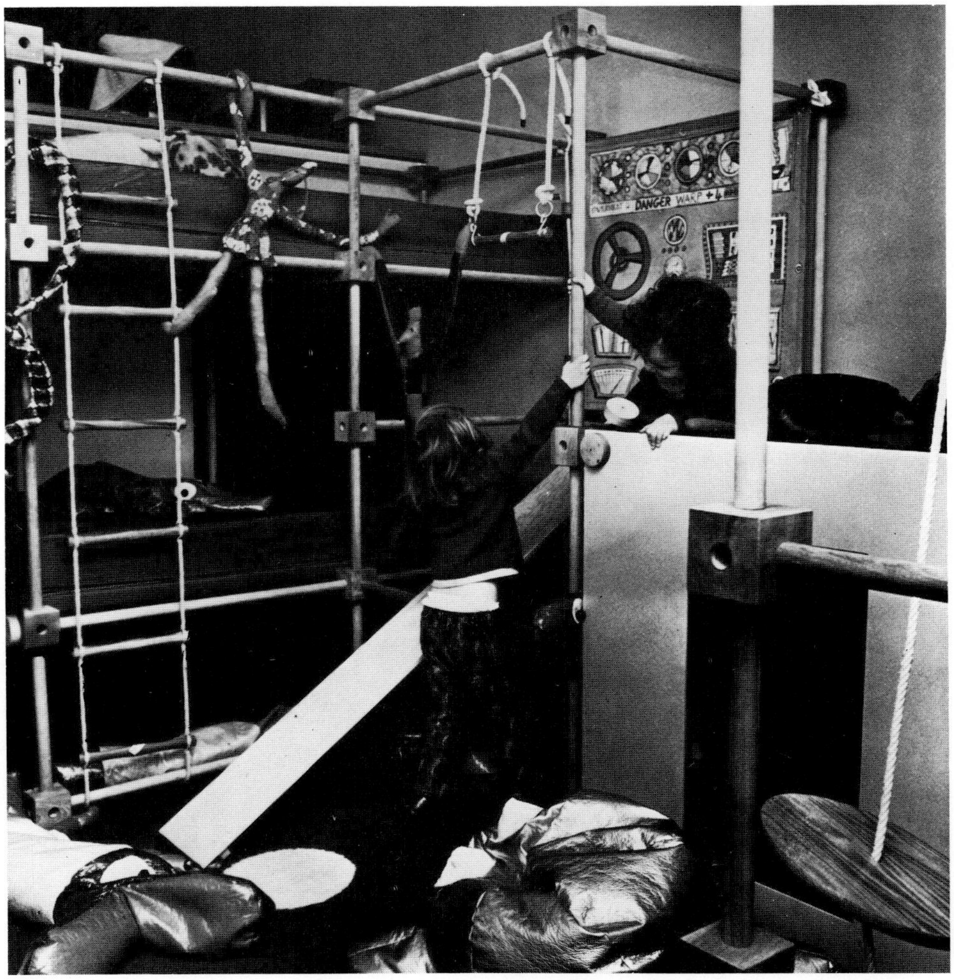

1033 **Günter Renkel** 1976 Germany

"Robinson" children's environmental system of solid pine. The basic element is the wide ladders, on the range of which beds, bookshelves, desks, and drawers are suspended

Index of Manufacturers

Manufacturers

Index of Designers

Index of Photographers

Photographers

Value Guide

This value guide is based upon auction and retail prices of similar pieces. It is presumed that the item is in excellent condition, even if the example shown is either better or worse.

As with all value guides this one should be used in an intelligent way, to establish an approximate and relative worth of piece. Use this and other books to become thoroughly familiar with the furniture and its current market prices. Most importantly, get out in the field, visiting reputable dealers and auction houses. The best of them are usually happy and even anxious to provide you with all the information you may want.

Pg.	Pos.	Value
10	BR	$1,000-1,500
11	TL	$2,000-3,000
	BR	$2,000-3,000
12	T	$30,000-50,000+
	BL	$15,000-20,000+
		$15,000-20,000+
13	TL	$6,000-8,000
	TC	$4,000-6,000
	TR	$1,000-1,500
	B	$20,000-30,000+
14	TL	$15,000-20,000+
	B	$20,000-30,000
15	TR	$1,000-1,500 each
	B	$2,000-3,000 each
16	T	$10,000-15,000+
	C	$10,000-15,000+
	BL	$15,000-2,000
	BR	$6,000-8,000+
17	T	$10,000-15,000+
	BL	$8,000-10,000
18	TL	$2,000-3,000
	TR	$2,000-3,000
	BL	$1,000-1,500
19	T	$4,000-6,000
	CL	$3,000-5,000
	CR	$10,000-15,000
	BL	$10,000-15,000
	BR	$10,000-15,000
20	TL	$15,000-20,000
	TR	$3,000-5,000
	CL	$3,000-5,000
	CR	$3,000-5,000
	BR	$4,000-6,000
21	TL	$2,000-3,000
	TC	$4,000-6,000
	TR	$10,000-12,000
	BL	$6,000-8,000
	BR	$10,000-15,000
22	T	$15,000-20,000
	C	$2,000-3,000 each
	B	$2,000-3,000 each
23	T	$600-800 each
	CL	$1,500-2,000
	C	$2,000-3,000
	CR	$2,000-3,000
24		$1,500-2,000
26		$1,000-1,500
28	TL	$200-400
	TC	$300-500
	TR	$200-300
29	TL	$600-800
	TR	$600-800

Pg.	Pos.	Value
29	BR	$600-800
30	TR	$600-800
	BC	$800-1,200
	BR	$600-800
31	TL	$400-600
	TR	$400-600
	B	$800-1,200
32	TL	$600-800
	BL	$1,000-1,500
	BC	$1,000-1,500
	BR	$1,000-1,500
33	TR	$300-500
	BL	$2,000-3,000
	BR	$600-800
34	All	$800-1,200 each
35		$1,000-1,500 each
36	All	$800-1,200
37	All	$800-1,200 each
38	T	$1,000-1,500 each
	C	$800-1,200 each
	B	$600-800 each
39	T	$1,500-2,000
	B	$75-150
40	T	$1,000-1,500
41	T	$800-1,200
	B	$600-800
42	T	$1,500-2,000
	B	$1,200-1,500
43	T	$600-800
	B	$300-500
44	TL	$400-600
	TR	$100-150
	BL	$100-150
	BC	$200-300
	BR	$200-300
45	T	$300-500
	C	$300-500
	B	$400-600
46	T	$2,000-3,000
	BR	$100-150
47	T	$200-300
	C	$1,200-1,500
	B	$600-800
48	T	$1,200-1,500
	CR	$1,200-1,500
	B	$600-800
49	TL	$600-800
	TR	$1,200-1,500
	C	$1,200-1,500
	B	$600-800
50	T	$300-500 each
	C	$300-500

Pg.	Pos.	Value
51	TL	$300-500
	B	$300-500
52	TR	$2,000-3,000
	B	$1,500-2,000
53	TR	$2,000-3,000
	CL	$2,000-3,000
	BL	$1,000-1,500
	BR	$600-800
54	TL	$600-800
	TR	$600-1,000
	CL	$1,000-1,500 each
	CR	$600-800
	BR	$1,000-1,500
55	TR	$1,000-1,500
	BL	$600-800
	BR	$1,000-1,500
56	T	$1,200-1,500
	BL	$1,000-1,500
	BR	$1,000-1,500
57	T	$300-500
	B	$400-600
58	T	$50-100
	B	$100-150
59	T	$50-100
	BL	$50-100
	BC	$50-100
	BR	$50-100
60	T	$50-100
	B	$50-100
61	T	$100-150
	BL	$50-100
	BC	$50-100
	BR	$50-100
62	All	$50-100
63	TL	$50-100
	TC	$50-100
	TR	$50-100
	C	$100-200
	BL	$100-200
	BR	$50-100
Pg.	Pos.	Value
64	T	$600-800
	BL	$50-100
	BR	$100-200
65	All	$50-100
66	TL	$50-100
	BR	$50-100
67	TL	$200-300
	TR	$200-300
	B	$50-100
68	TL	$300-500
	CR	$200-300

Pg.	Pos.	Value
68	BL	$1,000-1,500
	BR	$300-500
69	T	$1,000-1,500
	C	$600-800
	B	$1,000-1,500
70	TL	$50-100
	B	$50-100
71	All	$50-100
72	All	$100-150
73	TL	$100-150
	TC	$100-150
	TR	$300-500
	B	$1,000-1,500
74	All	$50-100
75	All	$50-100
76	All	$50-100
77	All	$50-100
78	All	$50-100
79	TR	$200-300
	BL	$400-600
	BC	$100-150
	BR	$100-150
80	TL	$100-150
	CR	$200-300
	BL	$200-300
81	All	$50-100
82	T	$200-300
	B	$300-500
83	TR	$200-300
	CL	$200-300
	BL	$300-500
	BC	$300-500
	BR	$300-500
84	TL	$100-200
	CL	$100-200
	B	$600-800
85	T	$500-700
	BL	$500-700
	BR	$100-200
86	T	$600-800
	BL	$1,000-1,200
	BR	$100-200
87	TL	$1,000-1,500
	TR	$800-1,200
	BL	$1,200-1,500
	BR	$800-1,200
88	TL	$300-500
	TR	$300-500
	BL	$1,000-1,200
	BR	$400-600
89	TR	$500-700
	CL	$500-700
	B	$600-800
90	TL	$300-500
	CR	$600-800
	BL	$400-600
	BR	$300-500
91	T	$500-700
	B	$300-500
92	All	$100-150
	TL	$200-300
	TR	$300-500
	BL	$300-500
93	BR	$100-150
94	TL	$600-800
	TR	$600-800
	BL	$200-300
	BR	$600-800
95	TL	$600-800
	TR	$600-800
	BL	$600-800
	BR	$200-300
96	TL	$200-300
	B	$400-600
97	All	$200-300
98	All	$200-300
99	T	$1,000-1,500 each
	CR	$600-800 each
	B	$1,000-1,500 each
100	T	$600-800 each
	BL	$200-300
	BC	$200-300
	BR	$600-800
101	TR	$300-500
	BL	$400-600
	BR	$200-300
102	TL	$1,000-1,500
	TR	$1,000-1,500
	B	$1,500-2,000
103	T	$2,500-3,500
	B	$1,000-1,500 each
104	TL	$300-500
	BL	$400-600
	BR	$200-300
105	T	$2,000-3,000
	BL	$100-150
	BC	$100-150
	BR	$200-300
106	T	$800-1,000
	CL	$800-1,000
	BL	$400-600
107	All	$400-600
108	T	$400-600
	C	$500-700
	B	$300-500
109	TL	$200-300
	TR	$500-700
	C	$500-700
	BL	$200-300
	BR	$200-300
110	T	$700-900
	B	$300-500
111	T	$1,200-1,500
	BL	$1,200-1,500
	BC	$1,000-1,200
	BR	$700-900
112	TL	$3,000-5,000
	BL	$600-800
	BR	$800-1,200
113	T	$1,000-1,500
	B	$1,500-2,000
114	All	$200-300
115	TL	$200-300
	TR	$100-150
	BR	$100-150
116	All	$50-75 each
117	All	$100-150 each
118	T	$800-1,200 each
	CL	$200-300
	BL	$300
	BR	$600-800
119	TL	$400-600
	TR	$400-600
	C	$100-200
	B	$100-200
120	All	$50-100 each
121	TL	$300-500
	BL	$1,000-1,500
	BR	$200-300
122	All	$600-800
123	All	$1,000-1,500
124	TL	$300-500
	TR	$1,000-1,500
	BL	$3,000-5,000
125	T	$200-300 each
	B	$100-150 each
126		$1,000-1,500
128	TL	$800-1,200
	TR	$1,000-1,500
	C	$1,000-1,500
	B	$1,000-1,500
129	T	$800-1,200
	CL	$1,000-1,200
	C	$500-700
	CR	$600-800
	B	$1,500-2,000
130	TL	$600-800
	CL	$800-1,200
	B	$1,500-2,000
131	T	$1,200-1,500
	C	$1,500-2,000
	B	$600-800
132	T	$2,000-3,000
	C	$1,000-1,500
	B	$1,500-2,000
133	T	$2,000-3,000
	C	$1,500-2,000
	B	$2,000-3,000
134	T	$2,000-3,000
	C	$2,000-3,000
	B	$1,500-2,000
135	T	$1,000-1,500
	C	$800-1,200
	B	$1,500-2,000
136	T	$1,500-2,000
	C	$1,500-2,000
	BL	$1,000-1,500
	BR	$1,000-1,500
137	T	$1,500-2,000
	B	$800-1,200
138	T	$2,000-3,000+
	C	$2,000-3,000+
	BL	$3,000-5,000+
	BR	$3,000-5,000+ each
139	T	$8,000-10,000+
	B	$8,000-10,000+
140	TL	$3,000-5,000
	CL	$600-800 each
	BL	$600-800 each

Pg.	Pos.	Value
141	TL	$1,000-1,500
	TR	$1,000-2,000 each
	CL	$2,000-3,000
	CR	$600-800 each
	BL	$600-800 each
	BR	$600-800 each
142	T	$600-800 each
	C	$1,000-1,500 set
	B	$600-800 each
143	T	$4,000-6,000
	CL	$1,000-1,500
	CR	$600-800 each
	BL	$300-500 each
	BR	$1,000-1,500
144	T	$3,000-5,000
	B	$4,000-6,000 set
145	All	$10,000-15,000+
146	T	$1,000-1,500
	C	$2,500-3,500
	BR	$1,000-1,500
147	T	$2,000-3,000 suite
148	T	$1,000-1,500
	C	$600-800
	B	$1,000-1,500
149	T	$1,500-2,000
	B	$2,000-3,000
150	TL	$600-800
	TR	$600-800
	BL	$600-800
	BR	$1,200-1,500
151	T	$1,200-1,500
	B	$2,000-3,000 set
152	TL	$1,500-2,000
	TR	$1,200-1,500
	BL	$1,500-2,000
153	T	$1,500-2,000
	C	$1,500-2,000
	B	$1,000-1,500
154	T	$3,000-5,000
	C	$1,000-1,500
	BL	$1,000-1,500
	BR	$1,000-1,500
155	T	$800-1,200
	C	$600-800
156	T	$1,500-2,000
	B	$1,500-2,000
157	T	$1,500-2,000
	B	$2,000-3,000
158	T	$1,000-1,500 each
	C	$2,000-3,000
159	T	$2,000-3,000 set
	B	$1,500-2,000
160	T	$800-1,200
	B	$800-1,200
161	T	$1,000-1,500
	C	$1,000-1,500
	B	$1,000-1,500
162		$300-500
164	T	$1,000-1,500 set
	C	$600-800
	B	$800-1,200
	T	$600-800
	C	$800-1,200
165	B	$700-900
166	TL	$2,000-3,000
	TR	$400-600
	CL	$800-1,200
	BL	$2,000-3,000 set
167	T	$400-600
	C	$400-600
	C2	400-600
	B	$800-i,200
168	T	$1,500-2,000 set
	C	$2,000-3,000 set
	B	$1,000-15,000 set
169	TL	$600-800 set
	TR	$600-800 each
	C	$300-500 each
	B	$700-900
170	TL	$400-600
	TR	$1,000-1,500
	B	$1,000-1,500
171	T	$600-800
	C	$1,500-2,000 set
	B	$2,000-3,000+
172	T	$800-1,200
	C	$400-600
	B	$800-1,200 each
173	TL	$300-500
	TR	$300-500
	BL	$600-800
	BR	$300-500
174	T	$100-200
	C	$300-500
	BL	$300-500
	BR	$100-200
175	T	$1,000-1,500
	B	$500-700
176	T	$600-800
	C	$600-800
	BL	$600-800
	BR	$300-500
177	T	$600-800
	C	$300-500
	B	$300-500
178	All	$300-500
179	All	$200-300
180	T	$1,000-1,500
	C	$1,000-1,500
	B	$1,000-1,500
181	T	$1,000-1,500
	C	$2,000-3,000
	B	$1,000-1,500
182	T	$600-800
	C	$2,000-3,000+
	B	$5,000-7,000+
183	T	$5,000-7,000+
	B	$5,000-7,000+
184	T	$2,000-3,000
	BL	$400-600
	BR	$1,000-1,500
185	T	$300-500
	B	$300-500
186	TL	$300-500
	TR	$200-300
	BL	$1,000-1,500
186	BR	$300-500
187	T	$500-1,000 each
	BL	$400-600
	BR	$700-900
188	T	$200-300 each
	C	$200-300 each
	B	$200-300 each
189	T	$300-500
	C	$1,000-1,500
	B	$200-300 each
190	T	$400-600
	C	$1,000-1,500
	B	$600-800
191	T	$300-500 lg. table
	$	$200-500 sm. table
	BL	$600-800
	BR	$200-300
192	TL	$300-500
	TR	$200-300
	B	$1,000-1,500
193	T	$300-500
	C	$100-200 each
	B	$100-200 each
194	TL	$100-200 each
	TR	$100-200
	B	$100-200
195	TR	$100-200
	CL	$200-300
	B	$100-200
196	T	$100-200
	C	$100-200
	BL	$400-600
	BR	$200-300
197	T	$300-500 set
	C	$800-1,200 set
	B	$600-800
198		$1,000-1,500
200	All	$1,000-1,500
201	All	$1,000-1,500
202	TL	$800-1,200
	TR	$1,000-1,500
	C	$500-700
	B	$500-700
203	T	$2,000-3,000
	B	$1,500-2,000
204	T	$1,000-1,500
	C	$600-800
	B	$600-800
205	T	$600-800
	C	$600-800
206	T	$1,000-1,500
	C	$600-800
	B	$1,000-1,500
207	TL	$600-800
	TR	$1,200-1,500
	CR	$1,500-2,000
208	T	$300-500 each
	C	$200-300
	B	$200-300
209	T	$3,000-5,000 set
	BL	$800-1,200
	BR	$800-1,200
210	T	$1,500-2,000

Pg.	Pos.	Value
210	C	$1,000-1,500
	B	$800-1,200
211	C	$300-500
	B	$300-500
212	T	$2,000-3,000
	CL	$2,000-3,000
	CR	$1,000-1,500
	BL	$1,000-1,500
	BR	$1,000-1,500
213	T	$2,000-3,000
	CR	$1,000-1,500
	BL	$600-800
	BR	$600-800
214	BR	$800-1,200
215	T	$2,000-3,000 set
	C	$1,000-1,500
	B	$300-500
216	T	$400-600
	CL	$800-1,200
	CR	$400-600
	B	$300-500
218	C	$2,000-3,000
	BR	$1,000-1,500
219	T	$300-500
	C	$300-500
	BL	$800-1,200
220	T	$1,000-1,500
221	BL	$300-500
223	TL	$300-500
	B	$300-500
224		$1,000-1,500
226	TR	$800-1,200
	CL	$400-600
	C	$500-700
	CR	$800-1,200
	C2	$1,000-1,500
	BR	$600-800
227	TR	$800-1,200
	CL	$300-500
	B	$800-1,200
228	T	$1,000-1,500
	C	$1,000-1,500
	B	$600-800
229	T	$3,000-5,000
	B	$3,000-5,000
230	T	$1,000-1,500
	C	$800-1,200
	B	$1,000-1,500
231	T	$2,000-3,000
	C	$1,000-1,500
	BL	$3,000-5,000
	BR	$2,000-3,000
232	TL	$800-1,200
	TR	$1,200-1,500
	C	$800-1,200
	B	$1,000-1,500
233	T	$600-800 each
	C	$1,000-1,500 each
	B	$2,000-3,000
234	TL	$1,000-1,500
	CL	$600-800
	C	$600-800
	CR	$800-1,200

Pg.	Pos.	Value
234	B	$800-1,200 each
235	T	$600-800 each
	C	$800-1,200
	BL	$1,200-1,500
	BR	$800-1,200
236	TL	$800-1,200
	TR	$800-1,200
	CR	$800-1,200
	BL	$600-800
	BR	$600-800
237	T	$1,200-1,500
	CL	$600-800
	CR	$600-800
	B	$1,200-1,500
238	TL	$1,000-1,500
	TR	$1,000-1,500
	C	$2,000-3,000
	B	$2,000-3,000
239	T	$2,000-3,000
	B	$1,000-1,500
240	T	$1,000-1,500
	C	$1,000-1,500
	B	$1,000-1,500
241	All	$1,000-1,500
242	T	$2,000-3,000
	B	$1,500-2,000 each
243	All	$1,500-2,000 each
244	T	$600-800 each
	B	$600-800 each
245	TL	$1,000-1,500
	TR	$800-1,200
	BL	$2,000-3,000
246	T	$2,000-3,000
	BL	$600-800
	BR	$600-800
247	All	$2,000-3,000 set
248	All	$2,000-3,000
249	All	$2,000-3,000 each
250	All	$3,000-5,000 each
251	All	$3,000-5,000 each
252	TL	$1,000-1,500
	TR	$4,000-6,000
	B	$3,000-5,000
253	T	$4,000-6,000
	B	$1,000-1,500
254	T	$2,000-3,000
255	T	$2,000-3,000
	BL	$800-1,200
256	T	$600-800 each
	B	$300-500 each
257	CL	$600-800
	BL	$1,000-1,500
258	BL	$1,000-1,500 set
259	TL	$1,000-1,500
260	T	$2,000-3,000
	B	$200-300 each
261	All	$100-200 each
262	All	$50-75 each
263	T	$1,000-1,500 set
	BL	$100-200 each
	BR	$100-200 each
264	T	$1,000-1,500 set
	B	$3,000-5,000 set

Pg.	Pos.	Value
265	T	$100-200 each
	B	$1,000-1,500 set
266	TL	$3,000-5,000+ each
	TR	$3,000-5,000+ each
267	T	$3,000-5,000+ set
	BL	$800-1,200 each
	BR	$3,000-5,000+ each
268	T	$2,000-3,000+ set
	B	$1,000-1,500
269	All	$5,000-7,000 set
270	TL	$4,000-6,000 set
	TR	$1,000-1,500
	B	$4,000-6,000 set
271	T	$5,000-7,000 set
	B	$800-1,200 each
272	All	$1,000-1,500 each
273	All	$1,000-1,500 each
274	T	$1,000-1,500
	B	$800-1,200
275	T	$3,000-5,000
	BL	$1,000-1,500 set
	BR	$1,500-2,000 set
276	All	$2,000-3,000 each
277	C	$3,000-5,000
	B	$2,000-3,000
278	T	$5,000-7,000 set
	C	$2,000-3,000
	B	$2,000-3,000
279	C	$1,000-1,500
	B	$1,000-1,500
280		$200-300 each
282	T	$200-300
	C	$200-300
	B	$200-300
283	TL	$60-200
	TR	$100-200 each
	C	$800-1,200
	B	$1,500-2,000 set
284	T	$200-300
	C	$100-150
	B	$100-150
285	T	$800-1,200
	B	$100-200
286	T	$1,000-1,500
	C	$1,000-1,500
	B	$2,000-3,000
287	T	$1,000-1,500 set
	BL	$300-500
	BR	$200-300
288	T	$50-75 each
	B	$50-75 each
289	T	$50-75 each
	B	$300-500
290		$1,200-1,500
291	T	$800-1,200
	B	$75-100 each
292	T	$75-150 each
	B	$25-50 each
293	All	$100-150 each
294	All	$100-150 each
295	T	$800-1,200
	B	$2,000-3,000